Ted Naifeh's

PRINCESS UGG

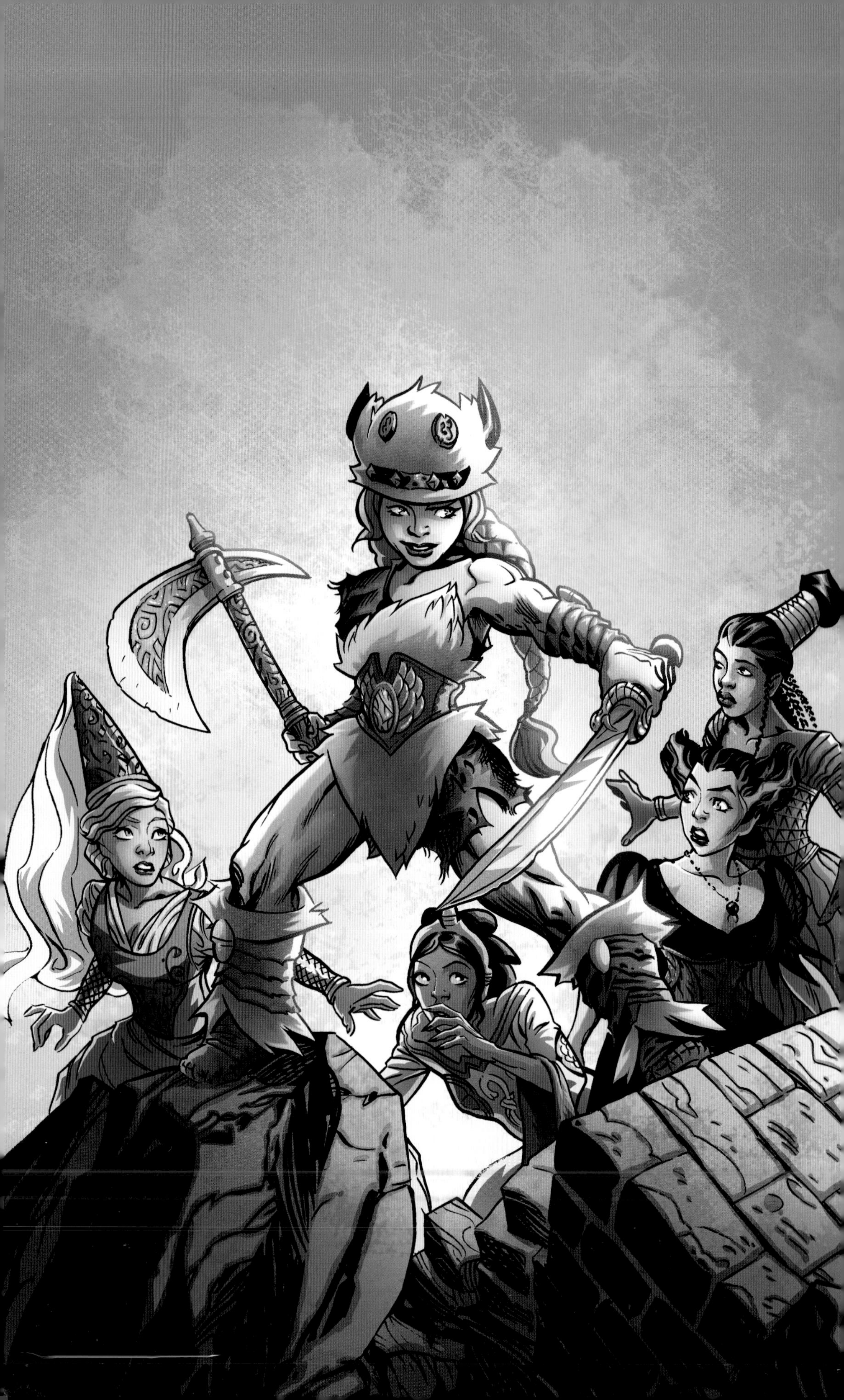

Ted Naifeh's

Written and Illustrated by
ted naifeh

Colored and Lettered by
warren wucinich

Watercolor Sequences by
ted naifeh

‡

Princess Ugg Volume 1 Cover Colored by
warren wucinich

Chapter 4 Flats by
jason fischer

Edited by
robin herrera

Designed by
jason storey

Published by Oni Press, Inc.
Joe Nozemack, publisher
James Lucas Jones, editor in chief
Tim Wiesch, v.p. of business development
Cheyenne Allott, director of sales
John Schork, director of publicity
Charlie Chu, editor
Robin Herrera, associate editor
Troy Look, production manager
Jason Storey, senior designer
Ari Yarwood, administrative assistant
Brad Rooks, inventory coordinator
Jung Lee, office assistant
Jared Jones, production assistant

Originally published as issues 1-4 of the Oni Press comic series *Princess Ugg*.

Oni Press, Inc.
1305 SE Martin Luther King, Jr. Blvd.
Suite A
Portland, OR 97214

www.onipress.com
facebook.com/onipress · twitter.com/onipress · onipress.tumblr.com

tednaifeh.com · warrenwucinich.carbonmade.com

First Edition: November 2014
ISBN 978-1-62010-178-0 · eISBN 978-1-62010-179-7

1 3 5 7 9 10 8 6 4 2

Library of Congress Control Number: 2014936802

Printed in China.

for
JILL

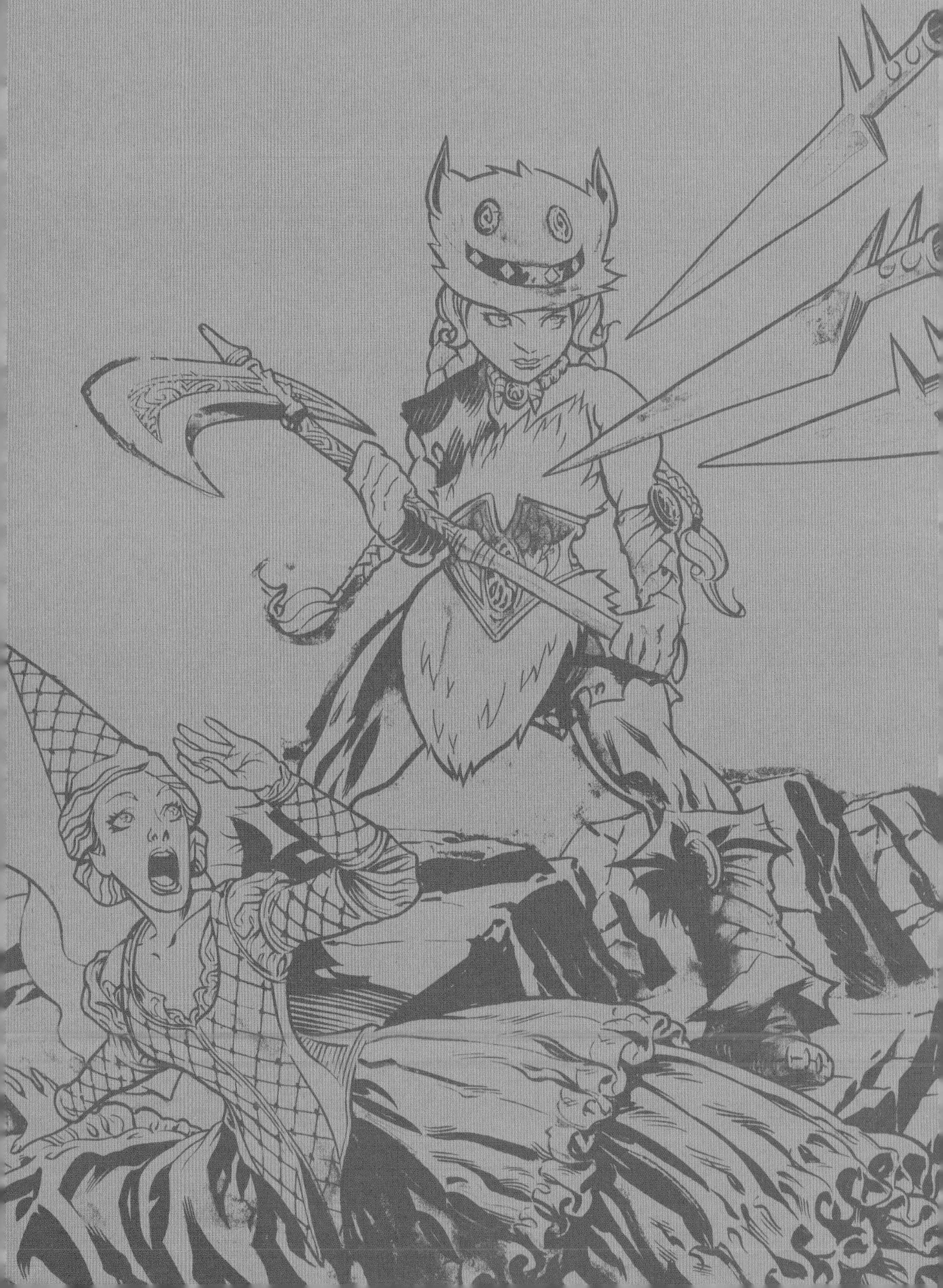

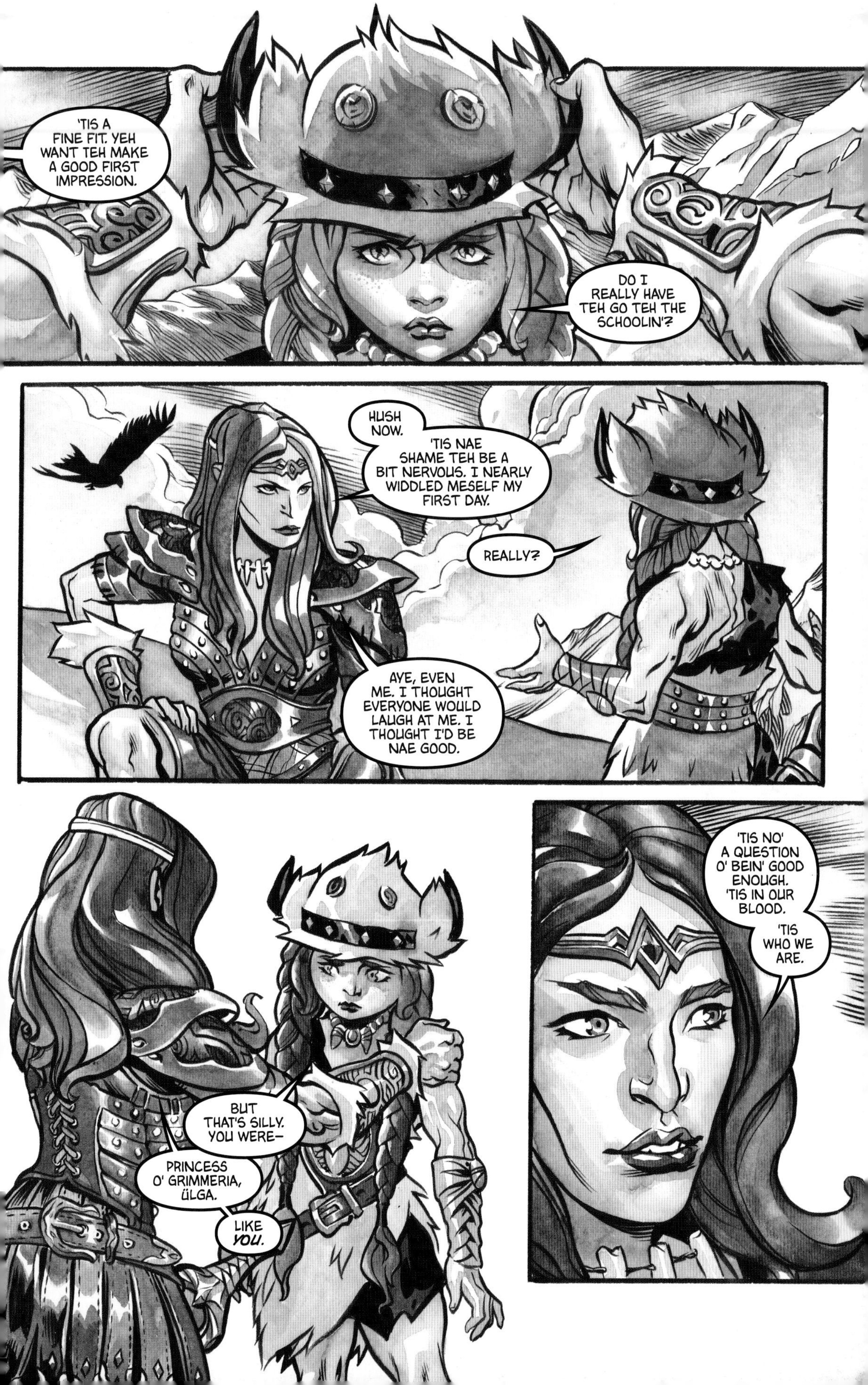

'TIS A FINE FIT. YEH WANT TEH MAKE A GOOD FIRST IMPRESSION.
DO I REALLY HAVE TEH GO TEH THE SCHOOLIN'?
HUSH NOW.
'TIS NAE SHAME TEH BE A BIT NERVOUS. I NEARLY WIDDLED MESELF MY FIRST DAY.
REALLY?
AYE, EVEN ME. I THOUGHT EVERYONE WOULD LAUGH AT ME. I THOUGHT I'D BE NAE GOOD.
BUT THAT'S SILLY. YOU WERE–
PRINCESS O' GRIMMERIA, ÜLGA.
LIKE *YOU*.
'TIS NO' A QUESTION O' BEIN' GOOD ENOUGH. 'TIS IN OUR BLOOD.
'TIS WHO WE ARE.

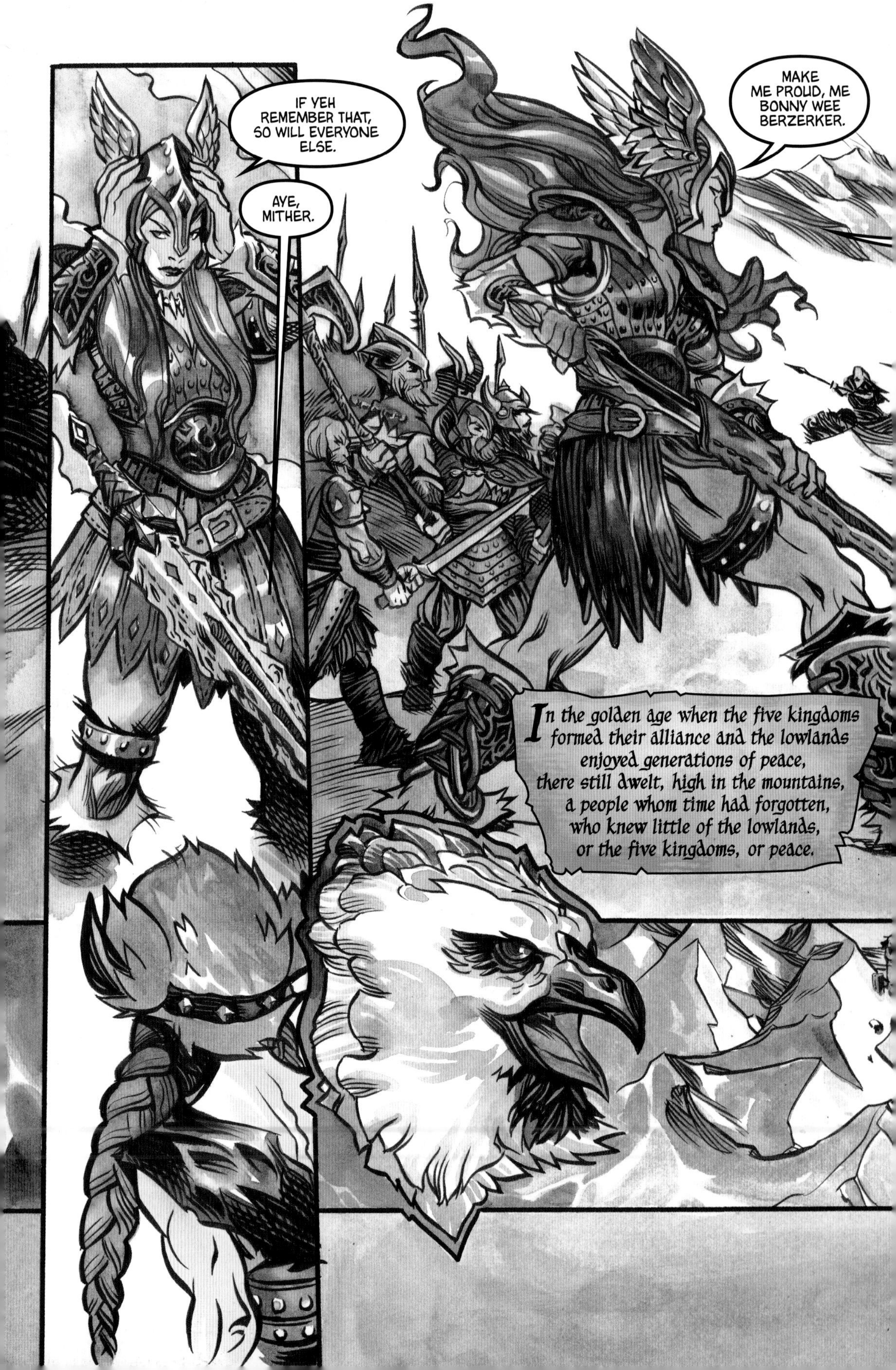
IF YEH REMEMBER THAT, SO WILL EVERYONE ELSE.
AYE, MITHER.
MAKE ME PROUD, ME BONNY WEE BERZERKER.
In the golden age when the five kingdoms formed their alliance and the lowlands enjoyed generations of peace, there still dwelt, high in the mountains, a people whom time had forgotten, who knew little of the lowlands, or the five kingdoms, or peace.

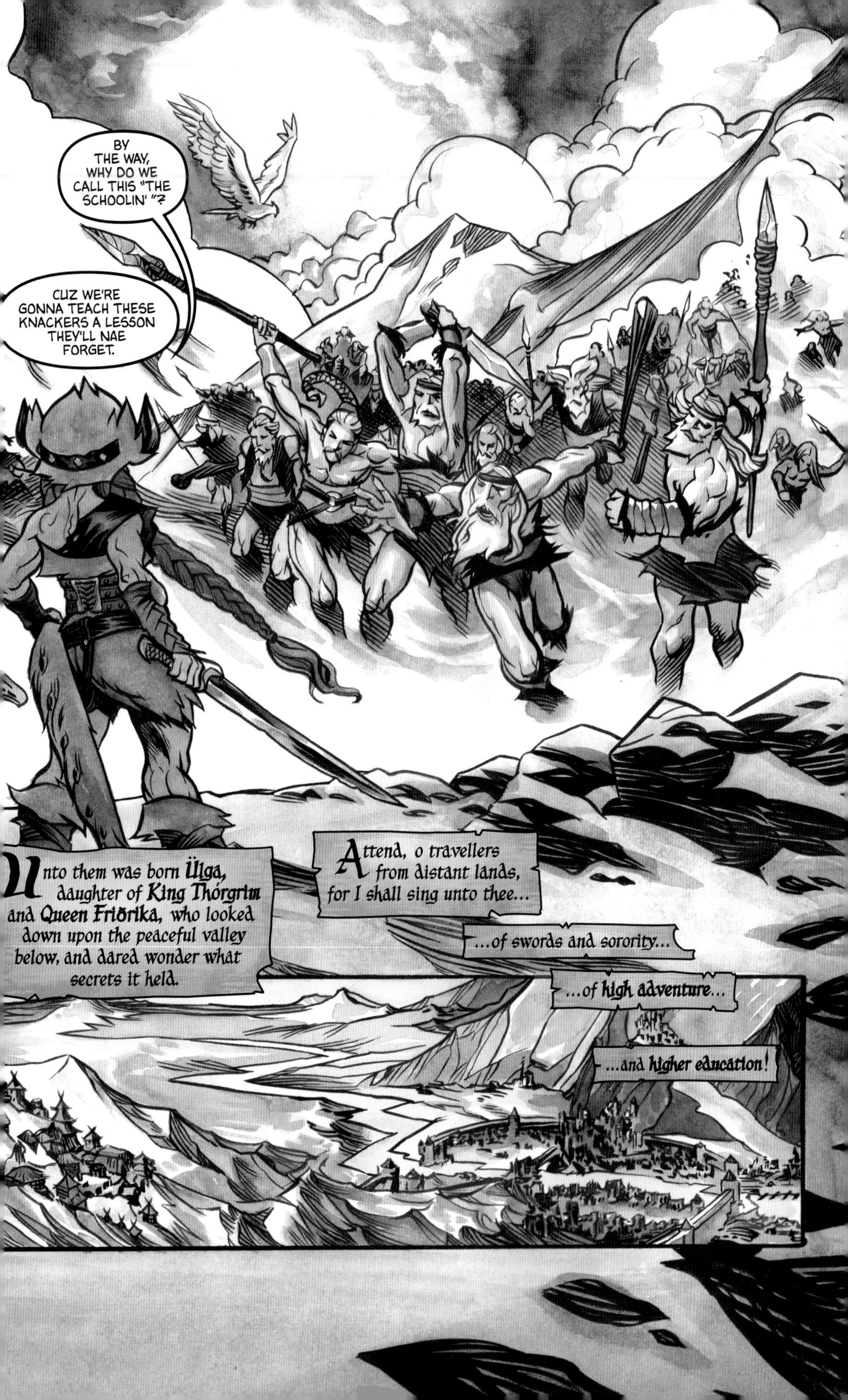
BY THE WAY, WHY DO WE CALL THIS "THE SCHOOLIN' "?
CUZ WE'RE GONNA TEACH THESE KNACKERS A LESSON THEY'LL NAE FORGET.
Unto them was born Ülga, daughter of King Thórgrim and Queen Friðrika, who looked down upon the peaceful valley below, and dared wonder what secrets it held.
Attend, o travellers from distant lands, for I shall sing unto thee...
...of swords and sorority...
...of high adventure...
...and higher education!

Chapter 1

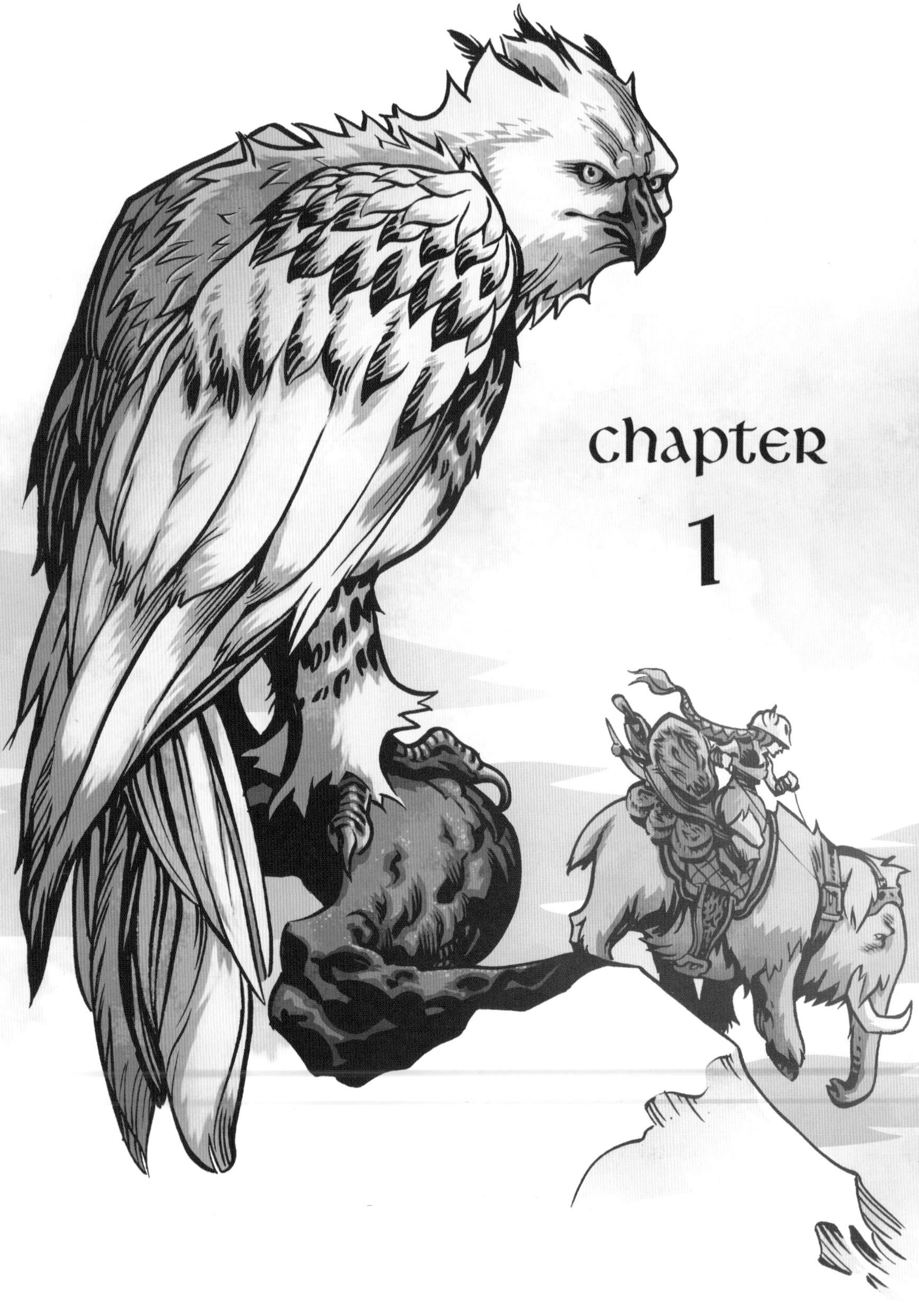

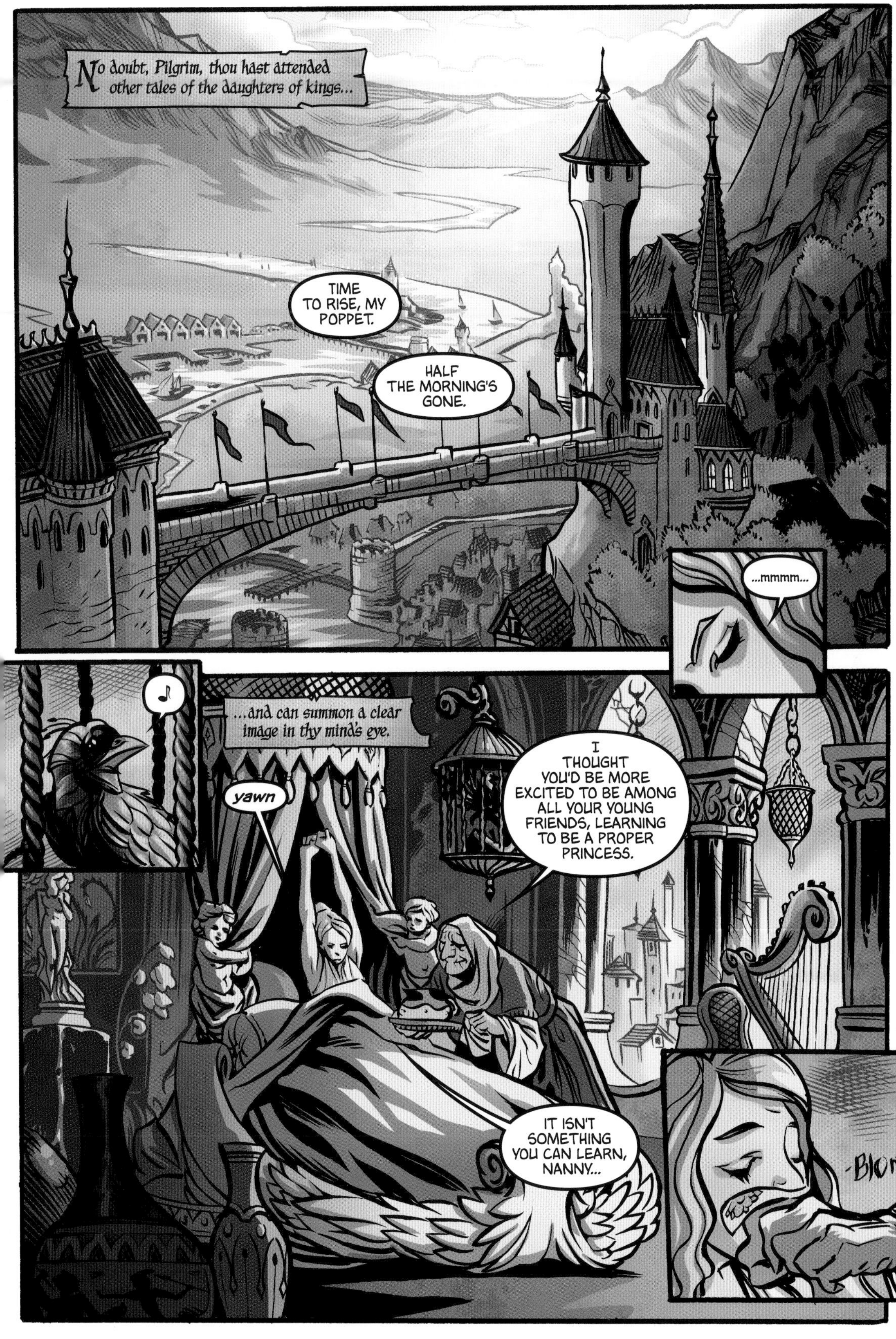
No doubt, Pilgrim, thou hast attended other tales of the daughters of kings...
TIME TO RISE, MY POPPET.
HALF THE MORNING'S GONE.
...mmmm...
♪
...and can summon a clear image in thy mind's eye.
yawn
I THOUGHT YOU'D BE MORE EXCITED TO BE AMONG ALL YOUR YOUNG FRIENDS, LEARNING TO BE A PROPER PRINCESS.
IT ISN'T SOMETHING YOU CAN LEARN, NANNY...
-Blort

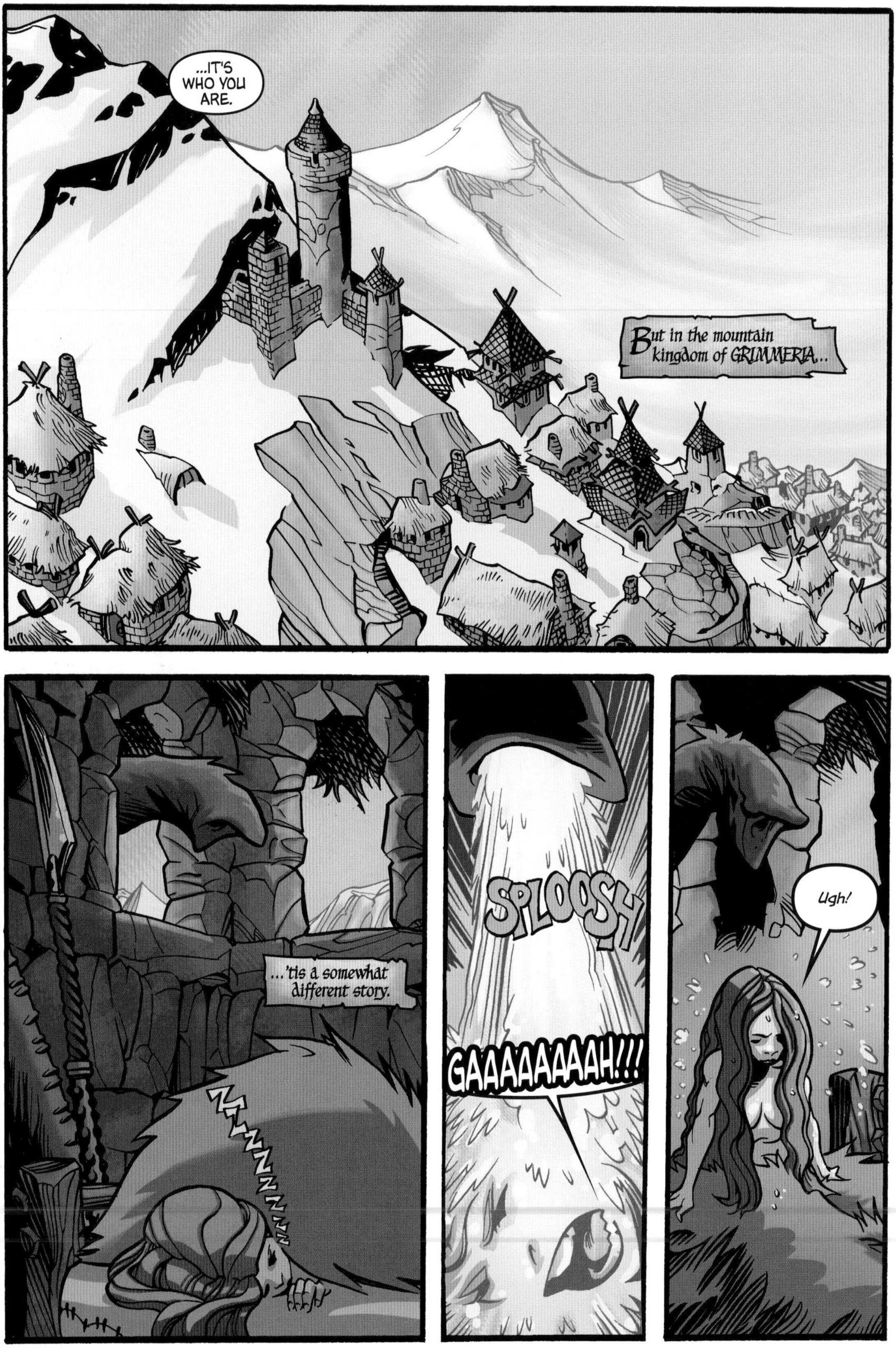
...IT'S WHO YOU ARE.
But in the mountain kingdom of GRIMMERIA...
...'tis a somewhat different story.
ZZZZZZZZ
SPLOOSH
GAAAAAAAH!!!
Ugh!

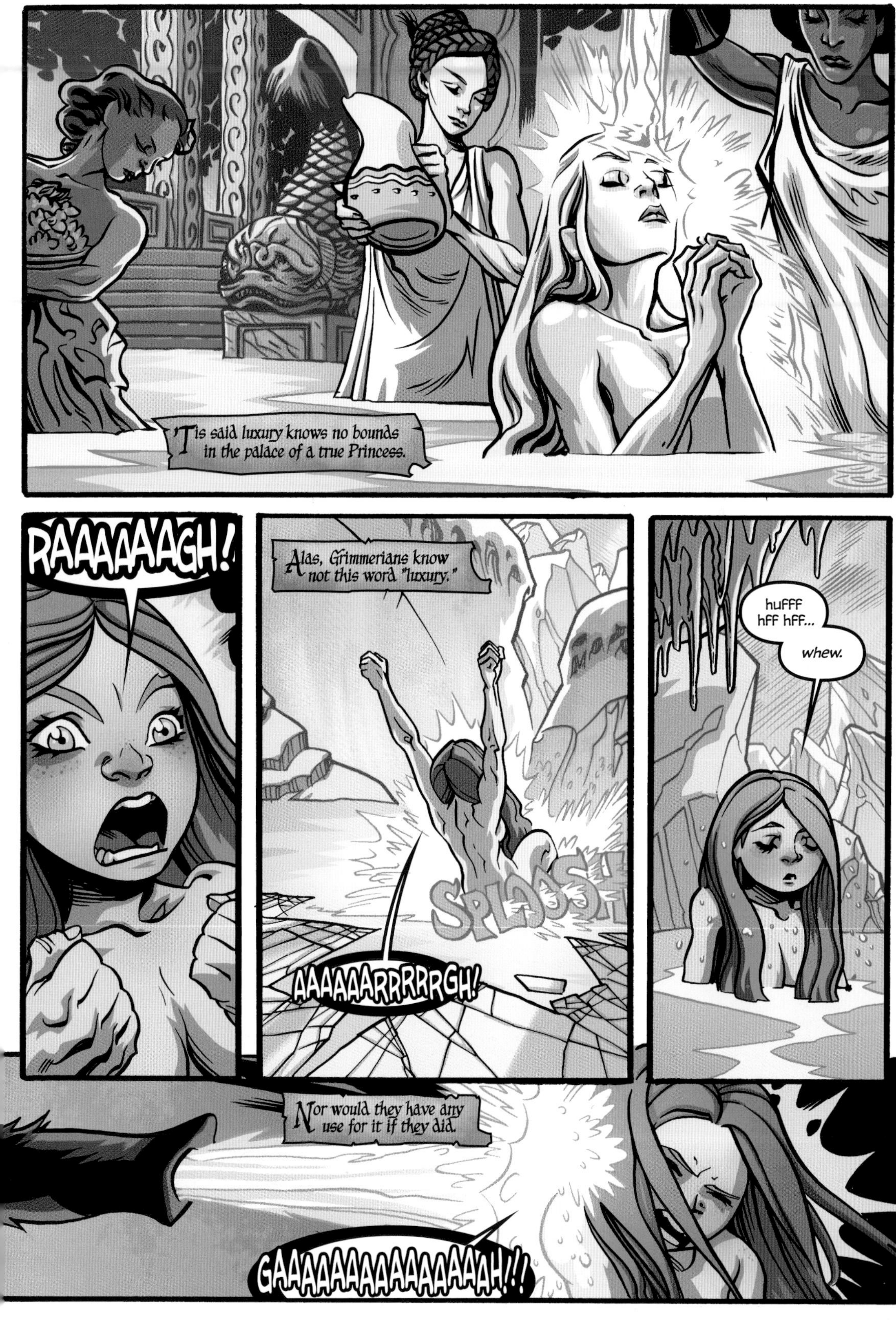
'Tis said luxury knows no bounds in the palace of a true Princess.
RAAAAAAGH!
Alas, Grimmerians know not this word "luxury."
SPLOOSH!
AAAAAARRRRRGH!
huffff hff hff...
whew.
Nor would they have any use for it if they did.
GAAAAAAAAAAAAAAH!!!

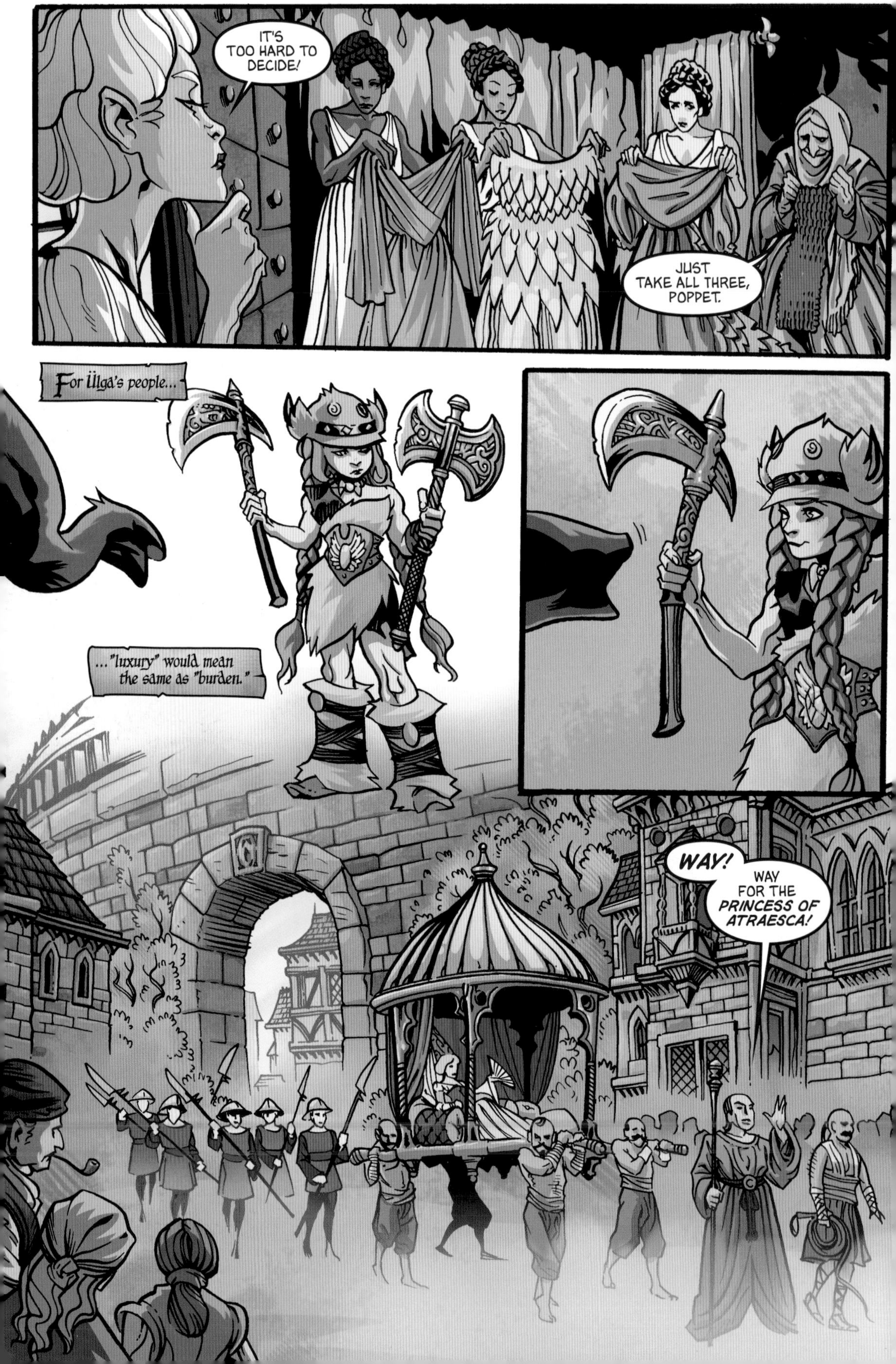
IT'S TOO HARD TO DECIDE!
JUST TAKE ALL THREE, POPPET.
For Ülga's people...
..."luxury" would mean the same as "burden."
WAY!
WAY FOR THE PRINCESS OF ATRAESCA!

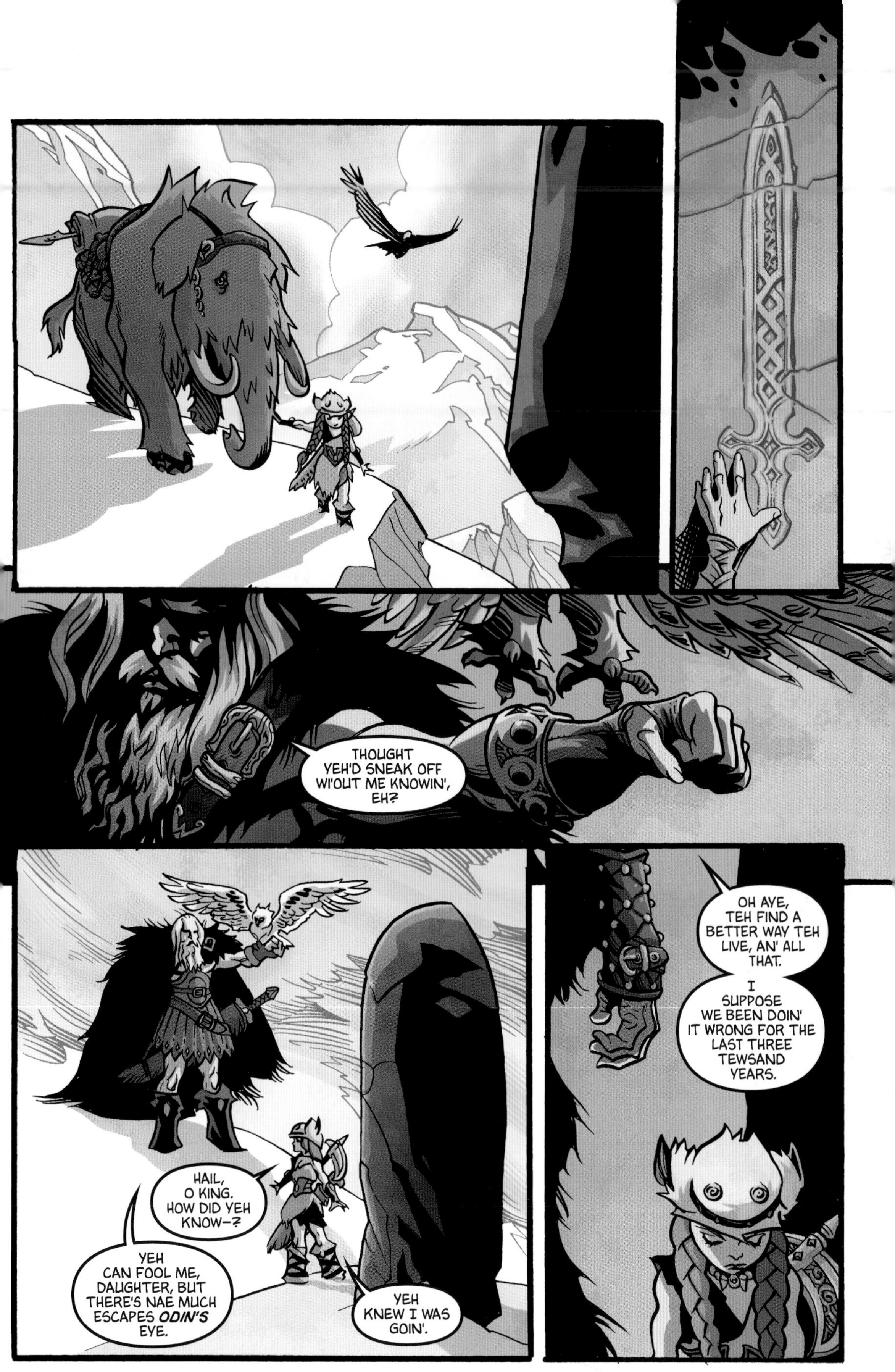
THOUGHT YEH'D SNEAK OFF WI'OUT ME KNOWIN', EH?
HAIL, O KING. HOW DID YEH KNOW–?
YEH CAN FOOL ME, DAUGHTER, BUT THERE'S NAE MUCH ESCAPES ODIN'S EYE.
YEH KNEW I WAS GOIN'.
OH AYE, TEH FIND A BETTER WAY TEH LIVE, AN' ALL THAT.
I SUPPOSE WE BEEN DOIN' IT WRONG FOR THE LAST THREE TEWSAND YEARS.

FIRST YER MITHER AND NOW YOU. I DINNAE KNOW WHAT I DONE TEH BE ABANDONED LIKE THIS.

I GAVE HER ME WORD, FATHER. I CANNAE JUST BREAK IT.

AYE, I KNOW THAT. BUT I DINNAE KNOW WHAT YEH EXPECT TEH FIND AMONG THEM LOWLANDERS.

Many times have I gazed upon the city of Atraesca, O Princess, and seen nought of true worth that cannot be found in the mountains.

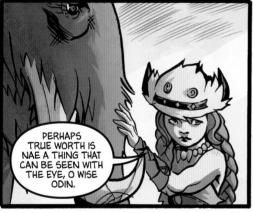

PERHAPS TRUE WORTH IS NAE A THING THAT CAN BE SEEN WITH THE EYE, O WISE ODIN.

EVEN YOUR MARVELOUS EYE.

HAIL AND FAREWELL, FATHER.

FAREWELL, ME BONNY WEE BERZERKER.

16

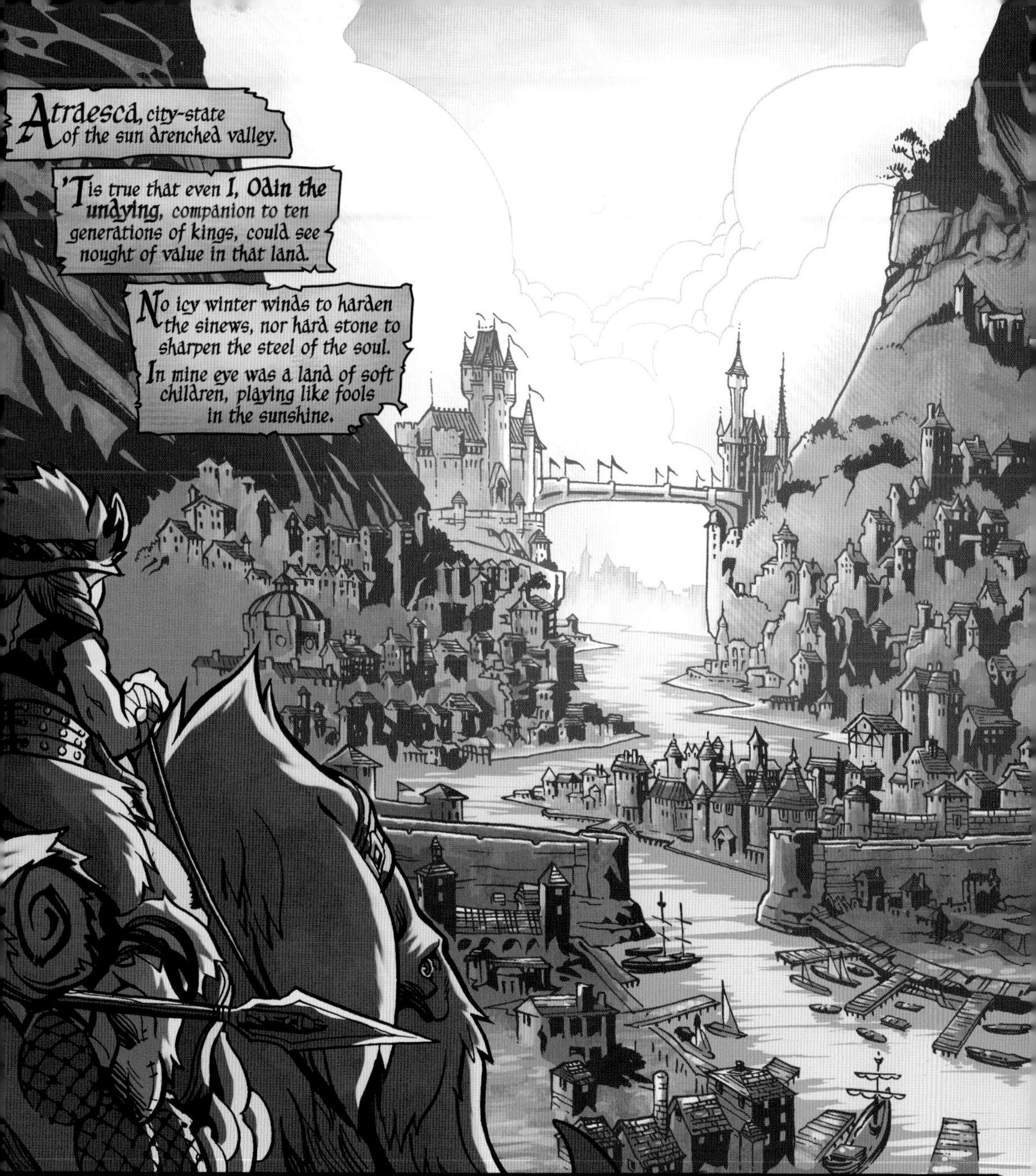
Atraesca, city-state of the sun drenched valley.
'Tis true that even I, Odin the undying, companion to ten generations of kings, could see nought of value in that land.
No icy winter winds to harden the sinews, nor hard stone to sharpen the steel of the soul.
In mine eye was a land of soft children, playing like fools in the sunshine.

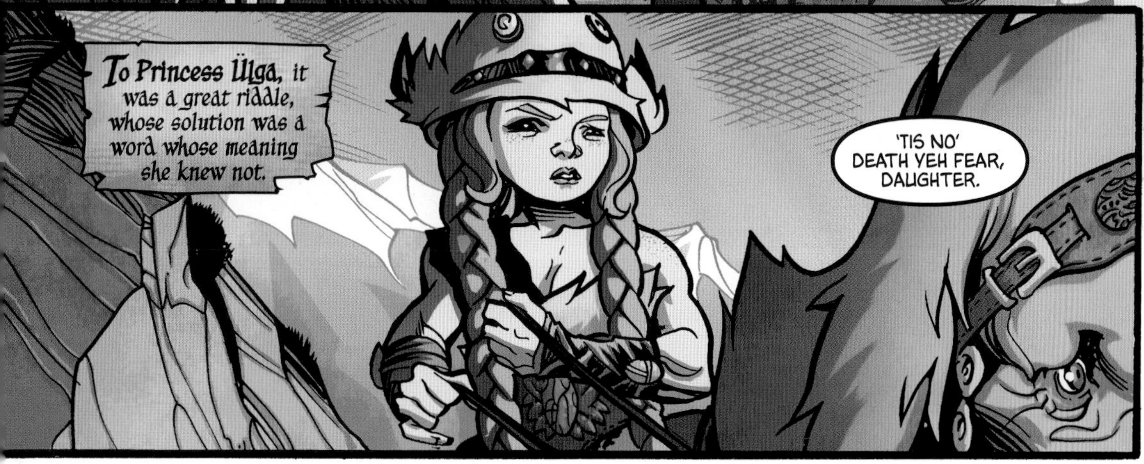
To Princess Ülga, it was a great riddle, whose solution was a word whose meaning she knew not.
'TIS NO' DEATH YEH FEAR, DAUGHTER.

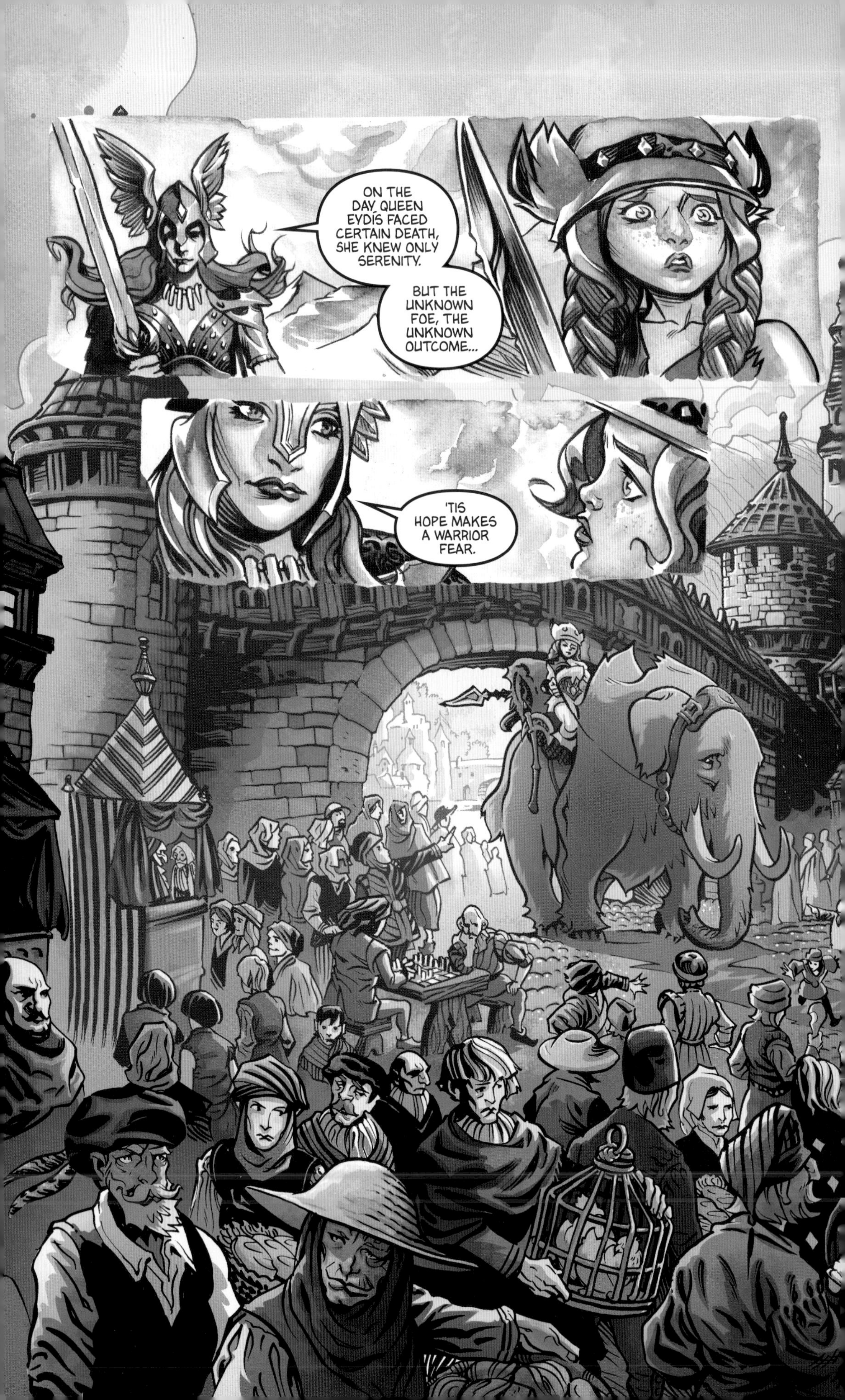
ON THE DAY QUEEN EYDÍS FACED CERTAIN DEATH, SHE KNEW ONLY SERENITY.
BUT THE UNKNOWN FOE, THE UNKNOWN OUTCOME...
'TIS HOPE MAKES A WARRIOR FEAR.

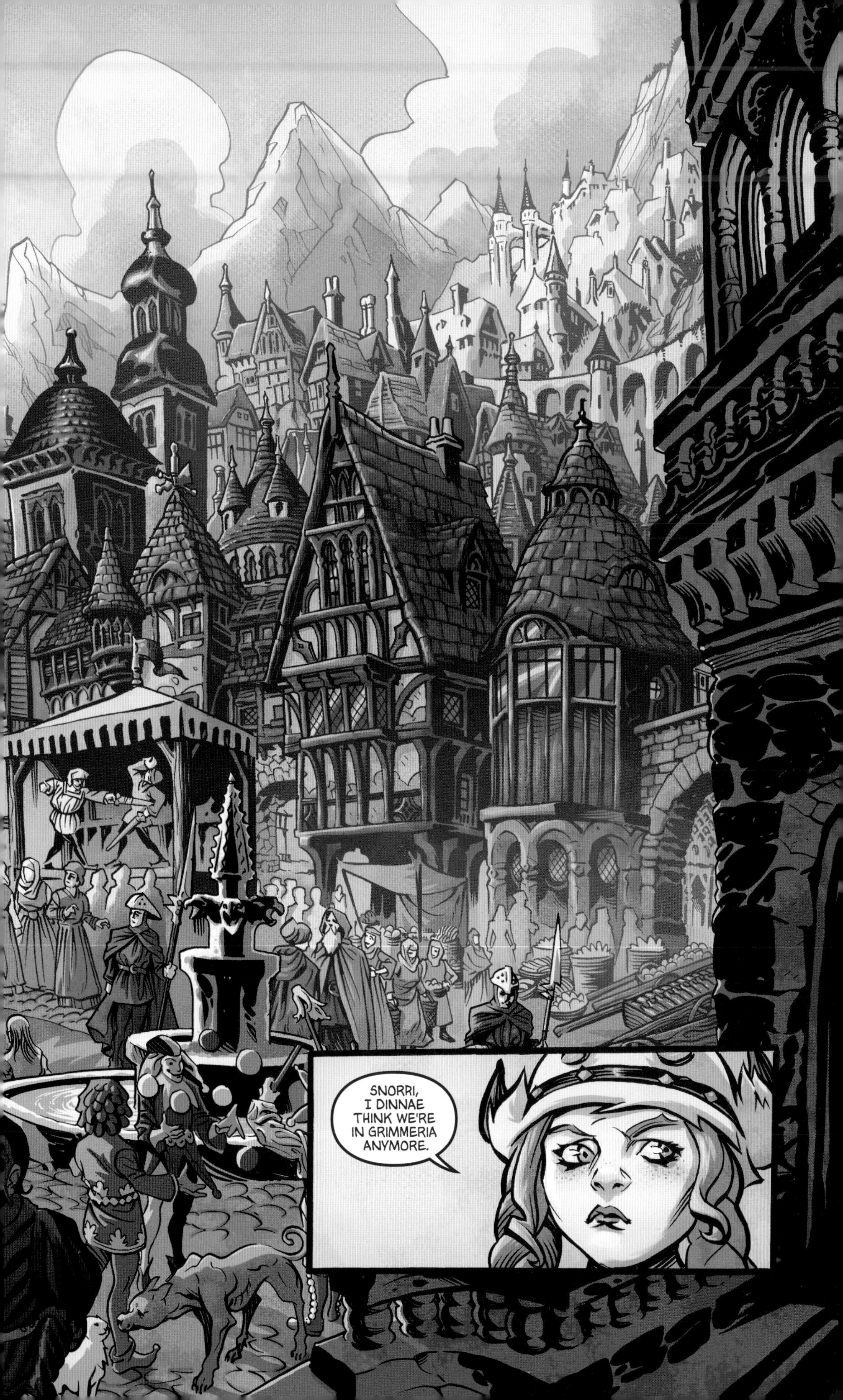
SNORRI, I DINNAE THINK WE'RE IN GRIMMERIA ANYMORE.

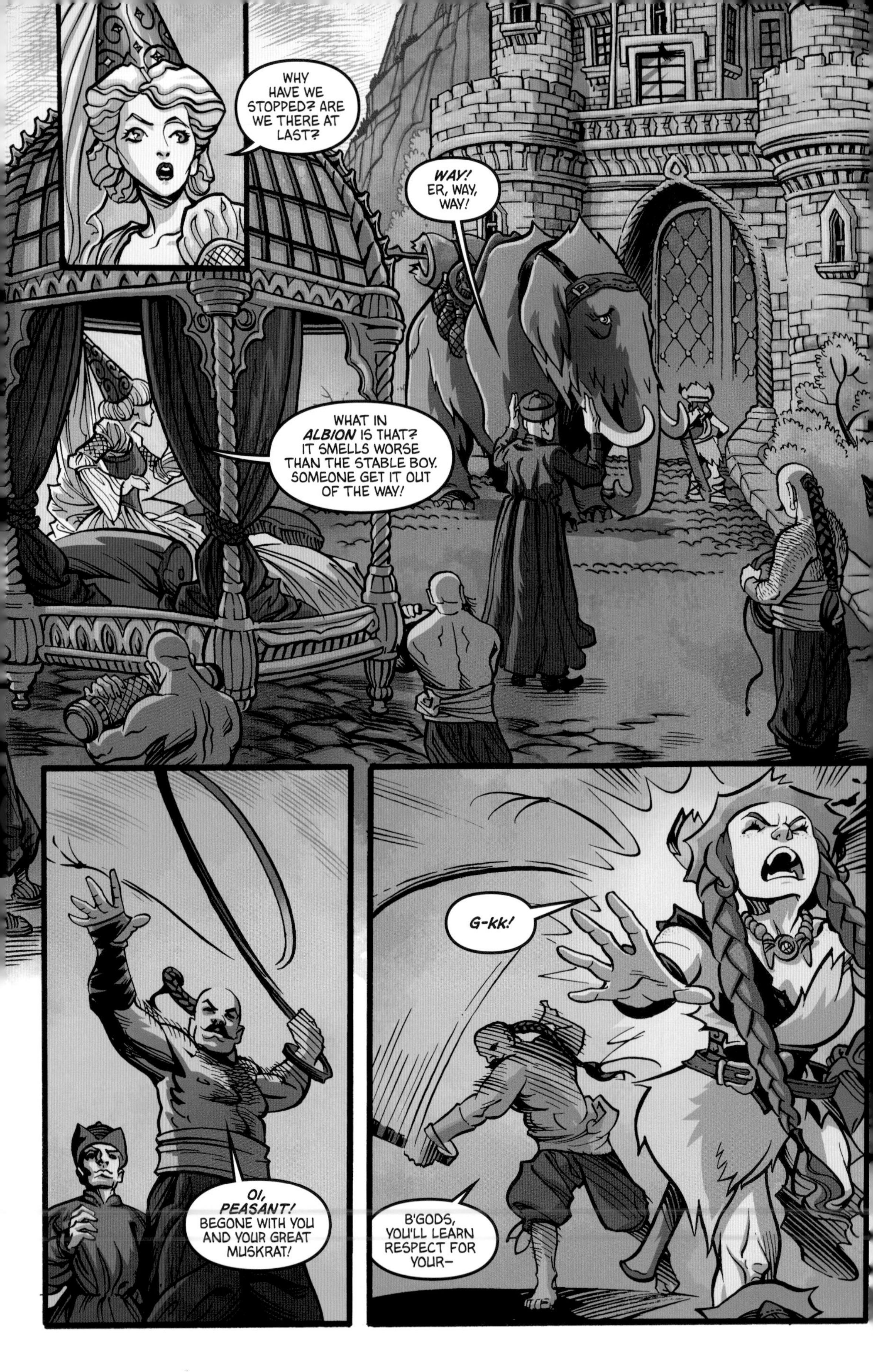
WHY HAVE WE STOPPED? ARE WE THERE AT LAST?
WAY! ER, WAY, WAY!
WHAT IN ALBION IS THAT? IT SMELLS WORSE THAN THE STABLE BOY. SOMEONE GET IT OUT OF THE WAY!
OI, PEASANT! BEGONE WITH YOU AND YOUR GREAT MUSKRAT!
G-KK!
B'GODS, YOU'LL LEARN RESPECT FOR YOUR–

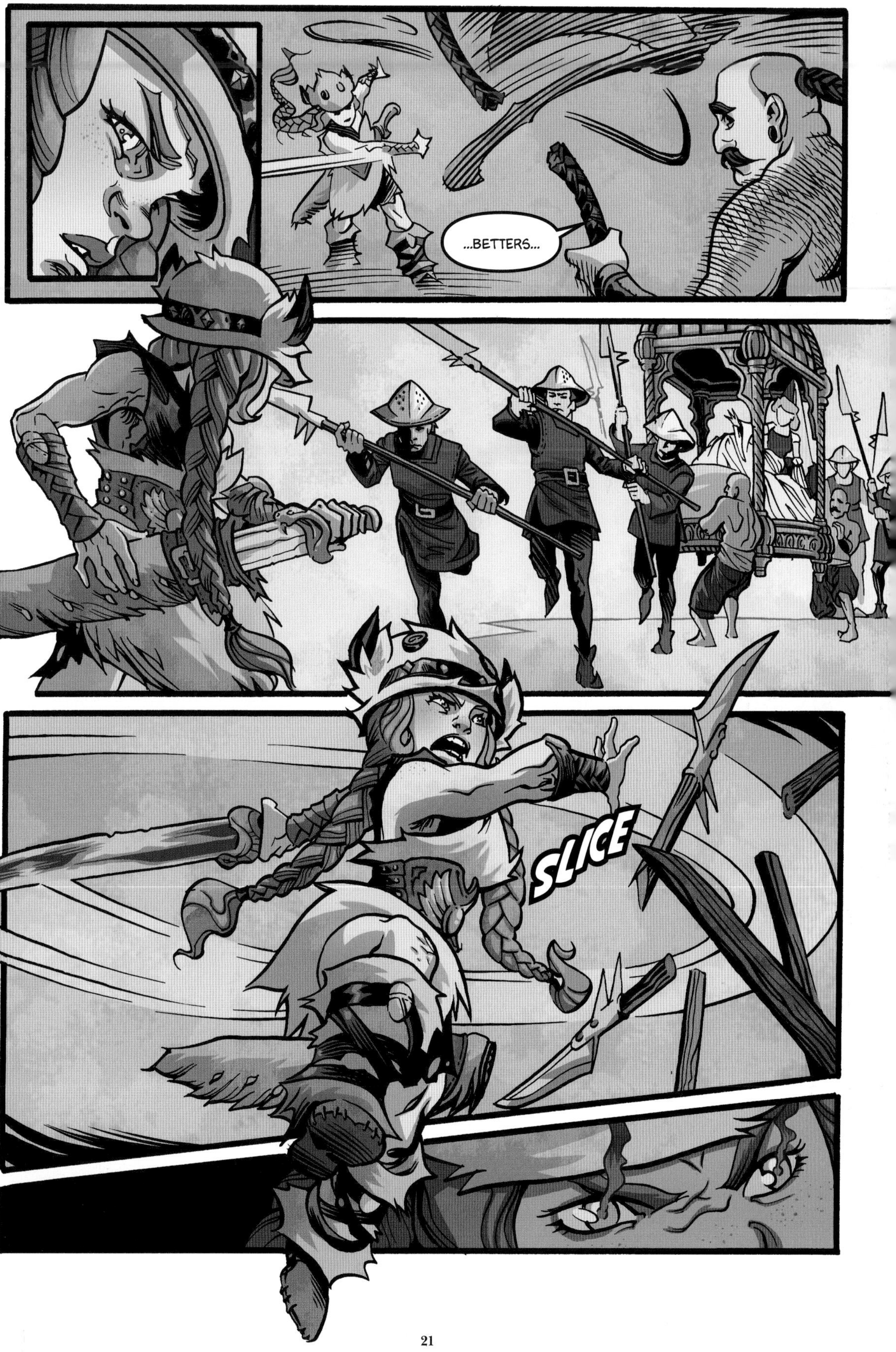
...BETTERS...
SLICE

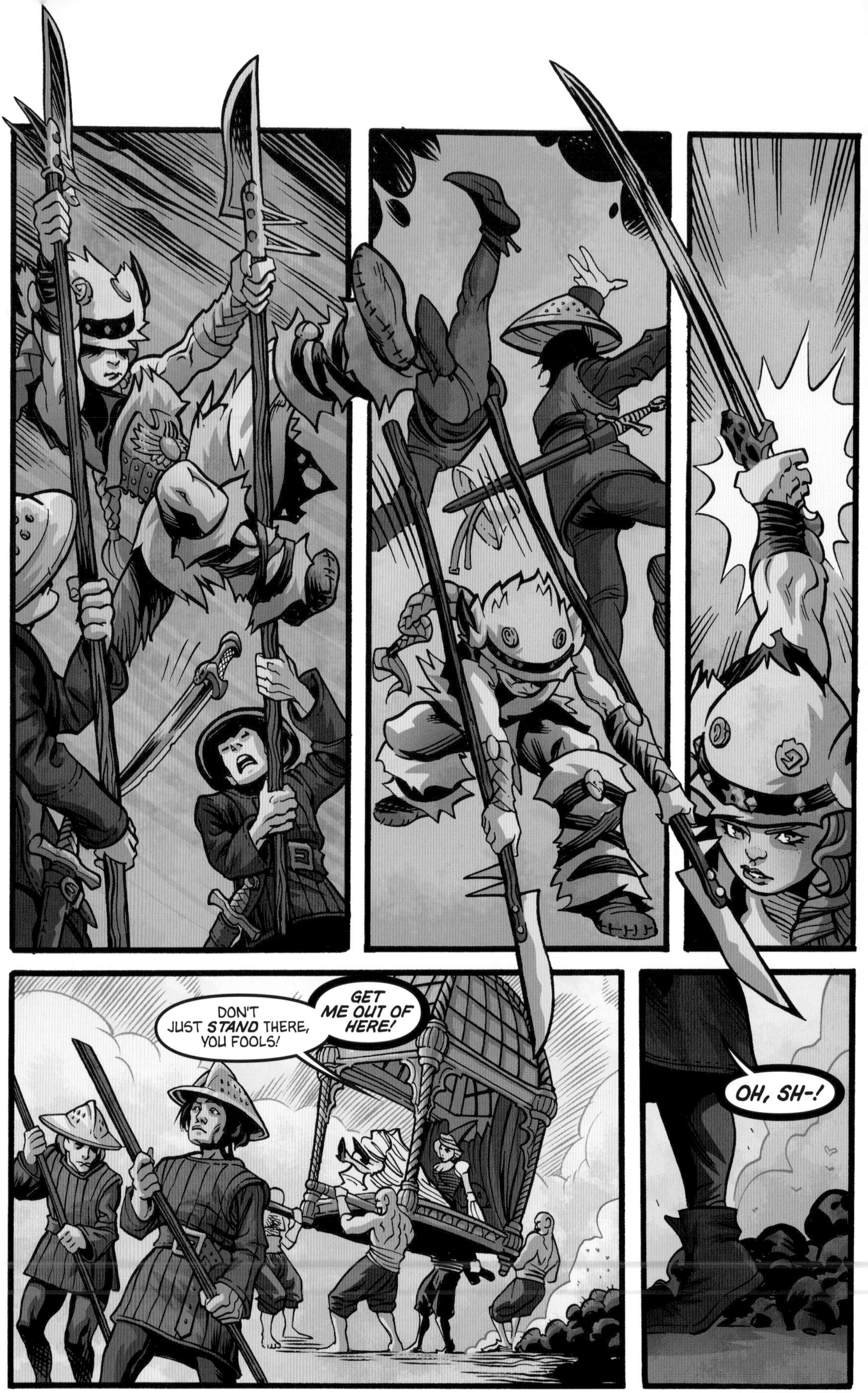
DON'T JUST STAND THERE, YOU FOOLS!
GET ME OUT OF HERE!
OH, SH-!

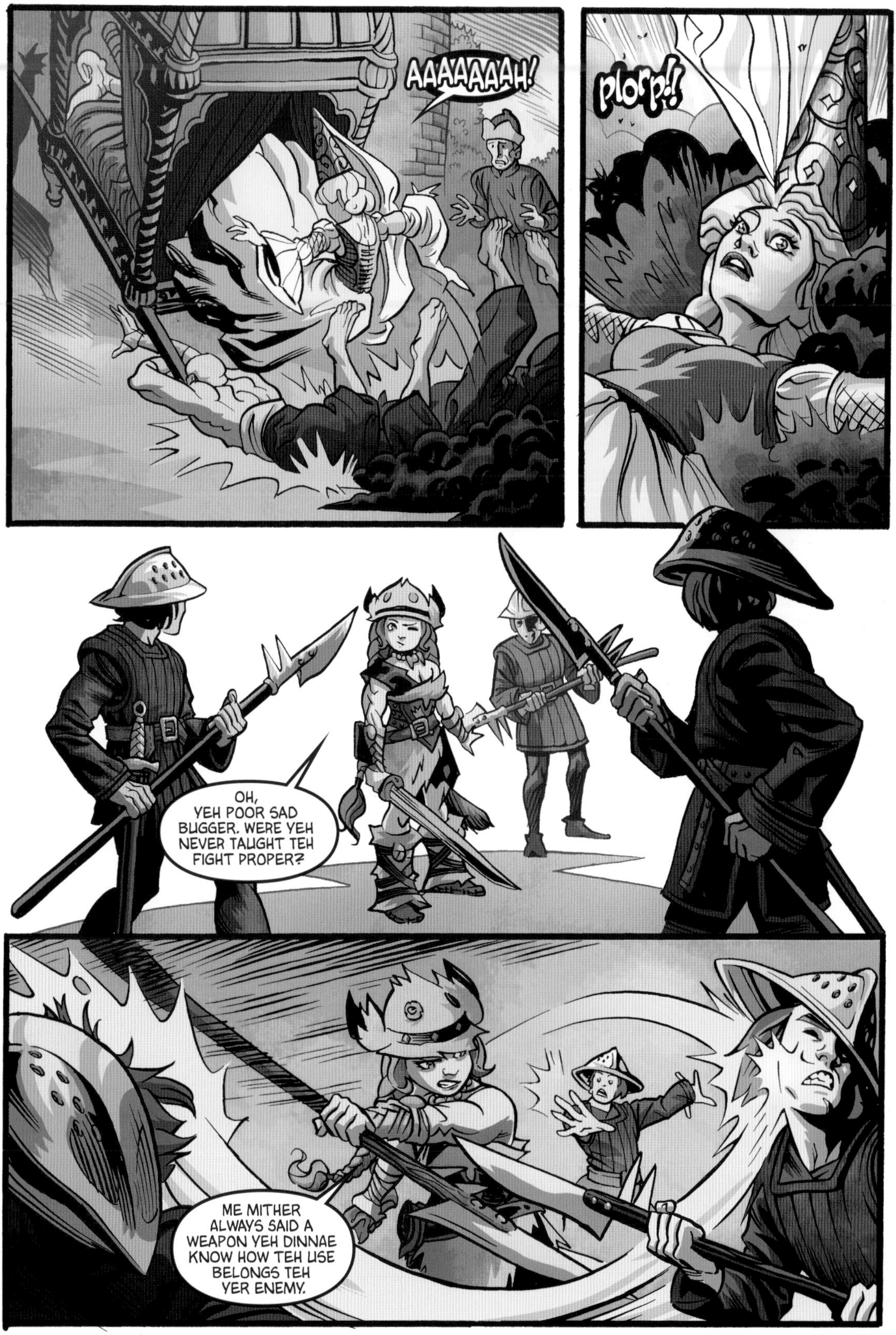
AAAAAAAH!
plorp!!
OH, YEH POOR SAD BUGGER. WERE YEH NEVER TAUGHT TEH FIGHT PROPER?
ME MITHER ALWAYS SAID A WEAPON YEH DINNAE KNOW HOW TEH USE BELONGS TEH YER ENEMY.

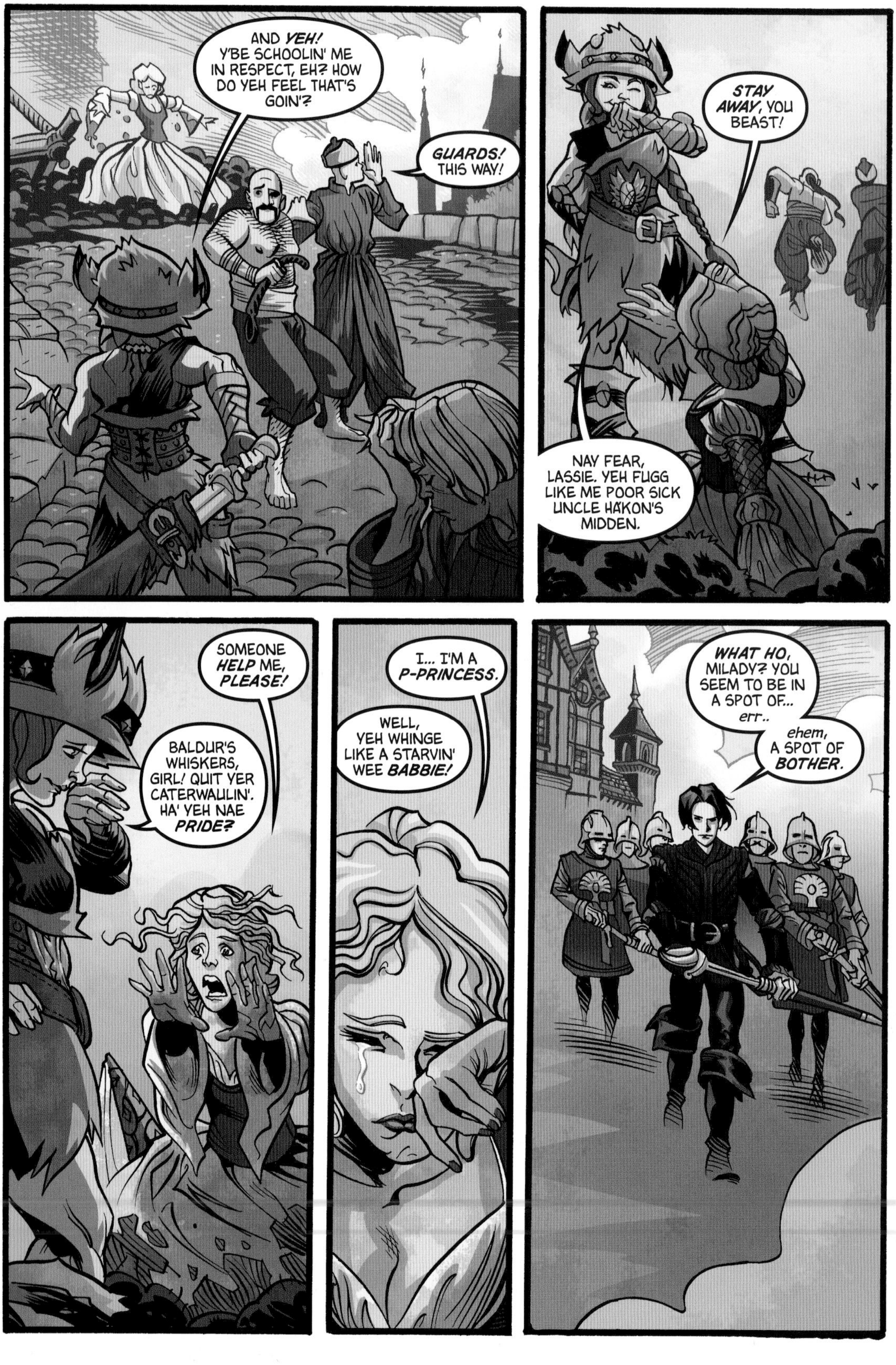
AND YEH! Y'BE SCHOOLIN' ME IN RESPECT, EH? HOW DO YEH FEEL THAT'S GOIN'?
GUARDS! THIS WAY!
STAY AWAY, YOU BEAST!
NAY FEAR, LASSIE. YEH FUGG LIKE ME POOR SICK UNCLE HÅKON'S MIDDEN.
SOMEONE HELP ME, PLEASE!
BALDUR'S WHISKERS, GIRL! QUIT YER CATERWAULIN'. HA' YEH NAE PRIDE?
I... I'M A P-PRINCESS.
WELL, YEH WHINGE LIKE A STARVIN' WEE BABBIE!
WHAT HO, MILADY? YOU SEEM TO BE IN A SPOT OF... err..
ehem, A SPOT OF BOTHER.

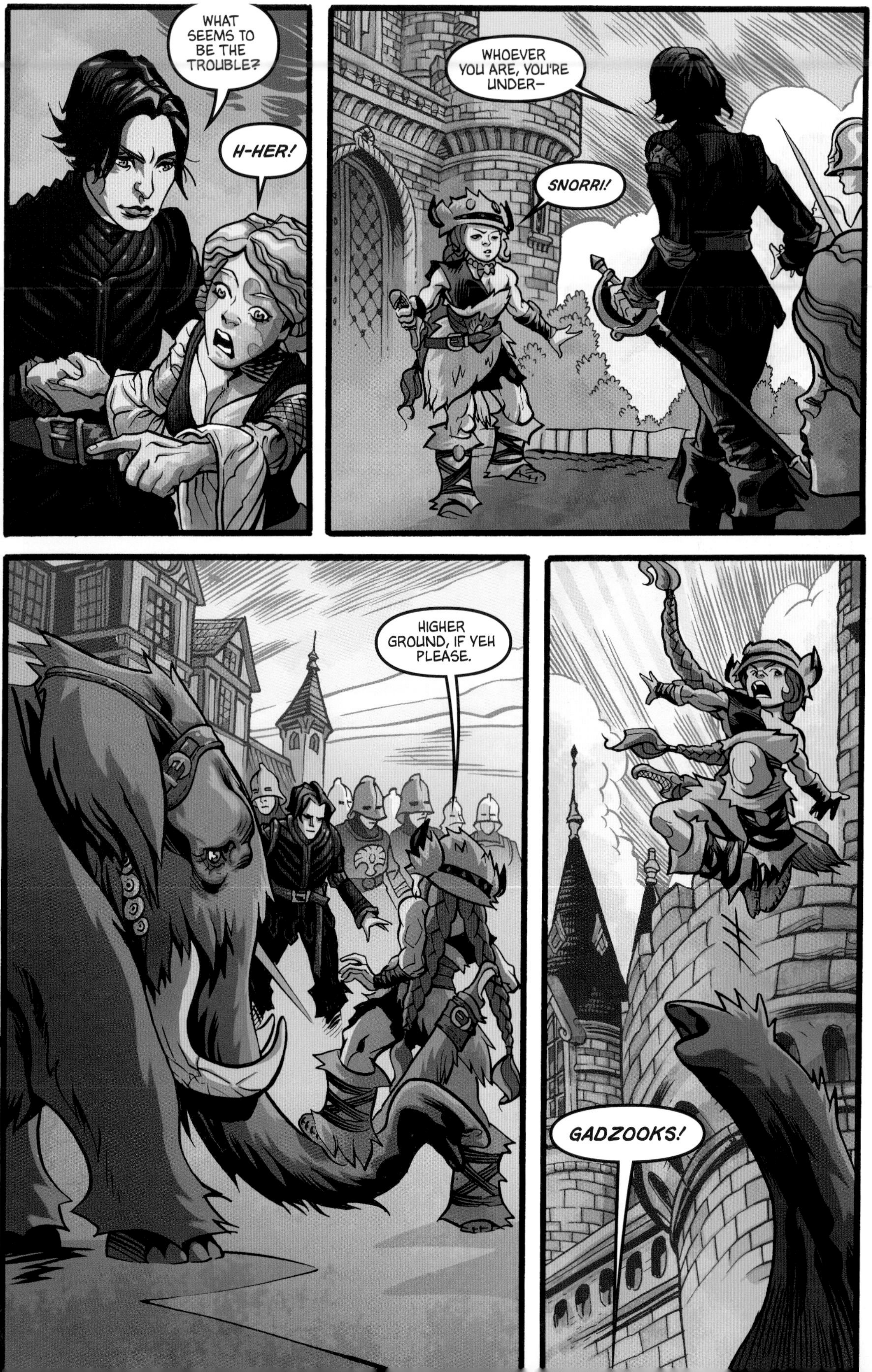
WHAT SEEMS TO BE THE TROUBLE?
H-HER!
WHOEVER YOU ARE, YOU'RE UNDER—
SNORRI!
HIGHER GROUND, IF YEH PLEASE.
GADZOOKS!

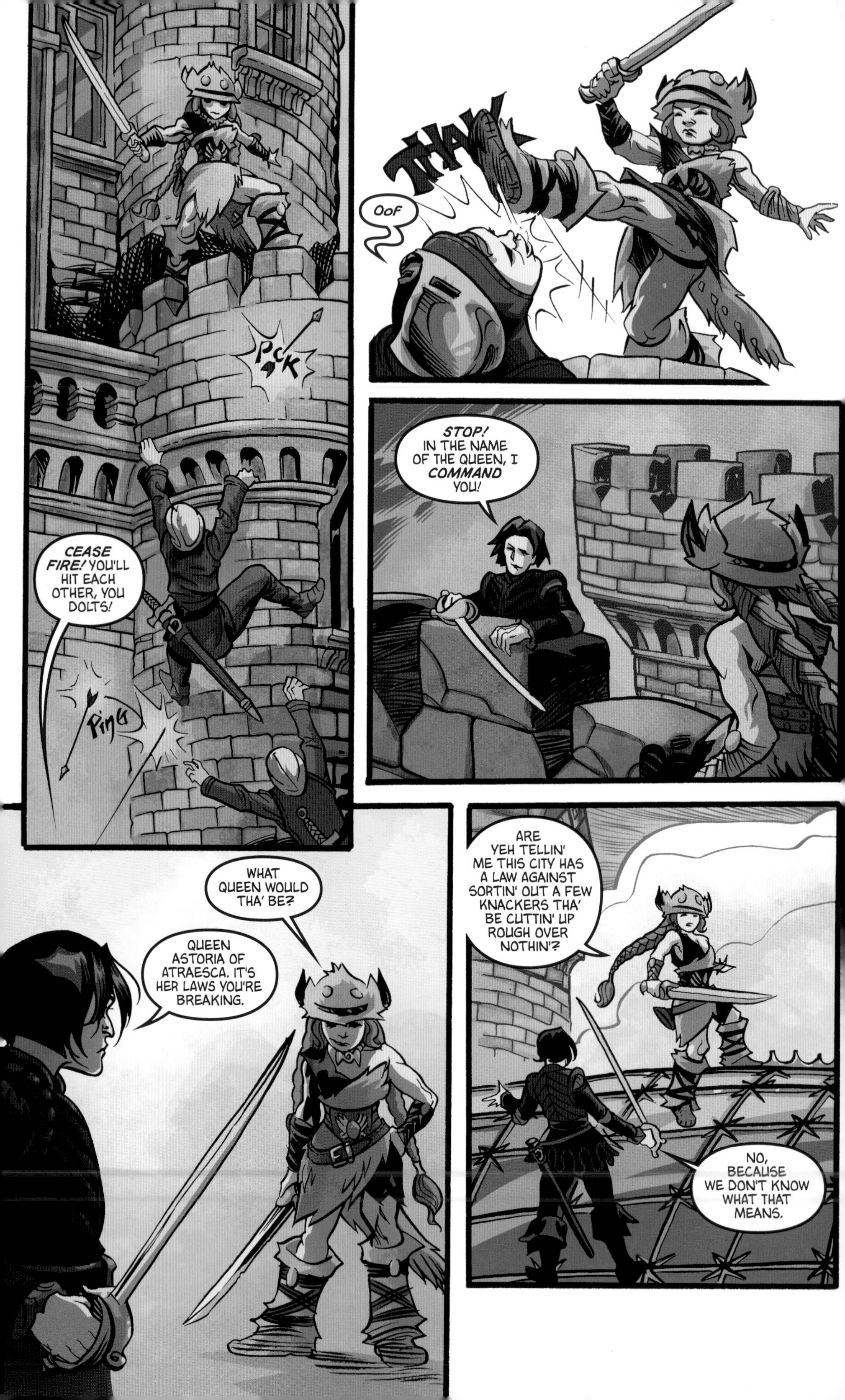
THAK
OOF
PCK
CEASE FIRE! YOU'LL HIT EACH OTHER, YOU DOLTS!
PING
STOP! IN THE NAME OF THE QUEEN, I COMMAND YOU!
WHAT QUEEN WOULD THA' BE?
QUEEN ASTORIA OF ATRAESCA. IT'S HER LAWS YOU'RE BREAKING.
ARE YEH TELLIN' ME THIS CITY HAS A LAW AGAINST SORTIN' OUT A FEW KNACKERS THA' BE CUTTIN' UP ROUGH OVER NOTHIN'?
NO, BECAUSE WE DON'T KNOW WHAT THAT MEANS.

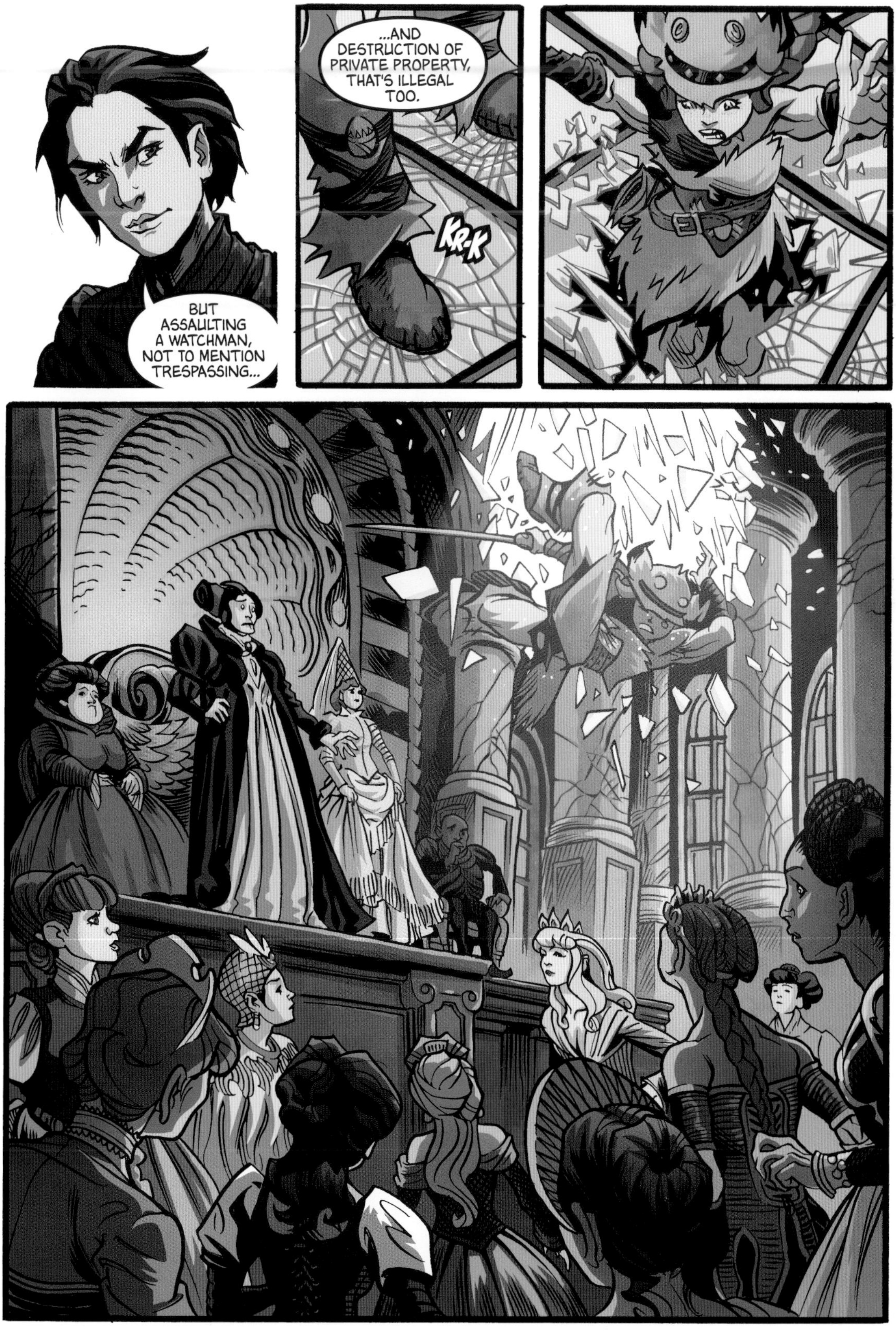
BUT ASSAULTING A WATCHMAN, NOT TO MENTION TRESPASSING...
...AND DESTRUCTION OF PRIVATE PROPERTY, THAT'S ILLEGAL TOO.
KR-K

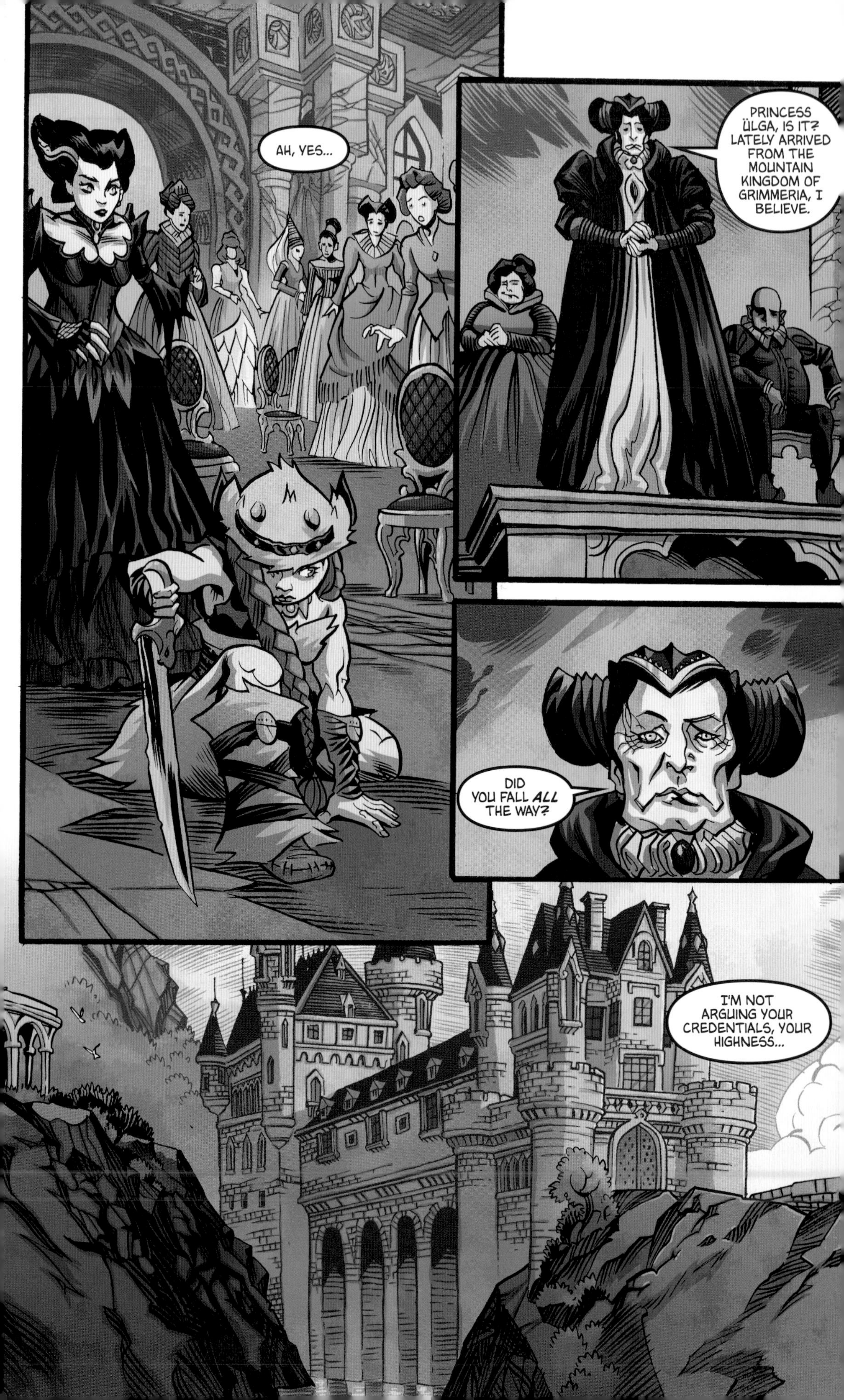
AH, YES...
PRINCESS ÜLGA, IS IT? LATELY ARRIVED FROM THE MOUNTAIN KINGDOM OF GRIMMERIA, I BELIEVE.
DID YOU FALL ALL THE WAY?
I'M NOT ARGUING YOUR CREDENTIALS, YOUR HIGHNESS...

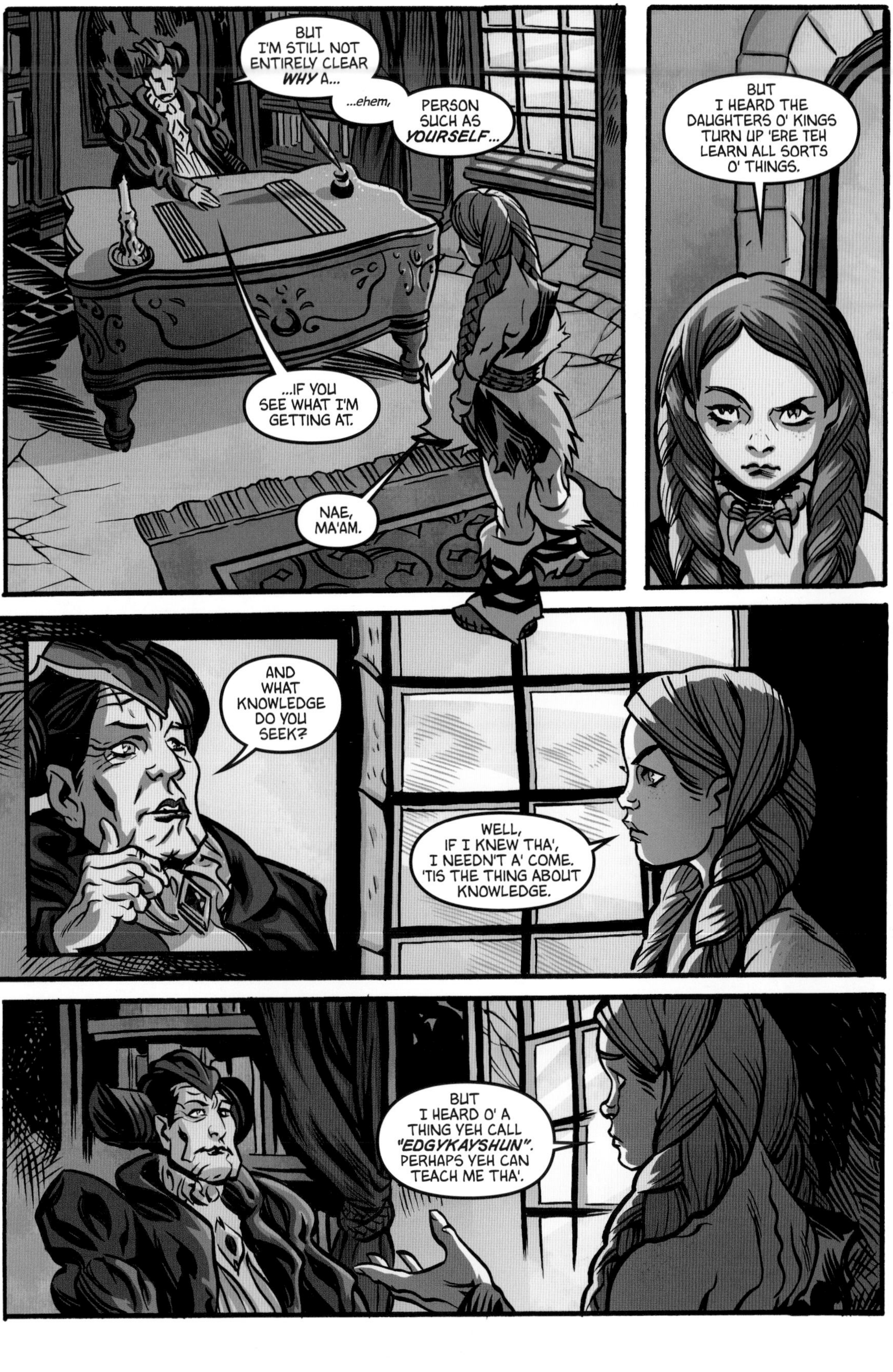
BUT I'M STILL NOT ENTIRELY CLEAR WHY A...
...ehem,
PERSON SUCH AS YOURSELF...
...IF YOU SEE WHAT I'M GETTING AT.
NAE, MA'AM.
BUT I HEARD THE DAUGHTERS O' KINGS TURN UP 'ERE TEH LEARN ALL SORTS O' THINGS.
AND WHAT KNOWLEDGE DO YOU SEEK?
WELL, IF I KNEW THA', I NEEDN'T A' COME. 'TIS THE THING ABOUT KNOWLEDGE.
BUT I HEARD O' A THING YEH CALL "EDGYKAYSHUN". PERHAPS YEH CAN TEACH ME THA'.

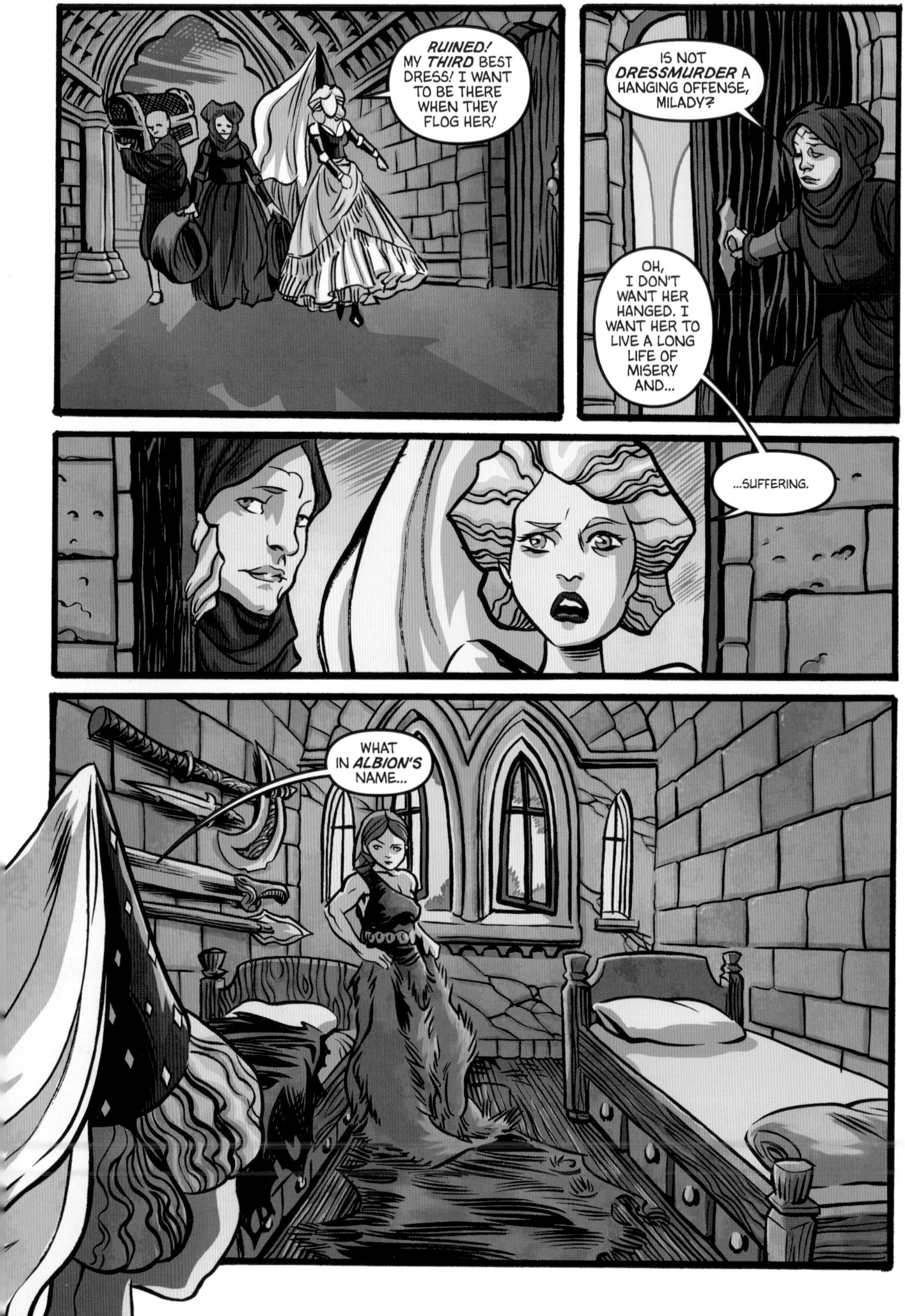

RUINED! MY THIRD BEST DRESS! I WANT TO BE THERE WHEN THEY FLOG HER!
IS NOT DRESSMURDER A HANGING OFFENSE, MILADY?
OH, I DON'T WANT HER HANGED. I WANT HER TO LIVE A LONG LIFE OF MISERY AND...
...SUFFERING.
WHAT IN ALBION'S NAME...

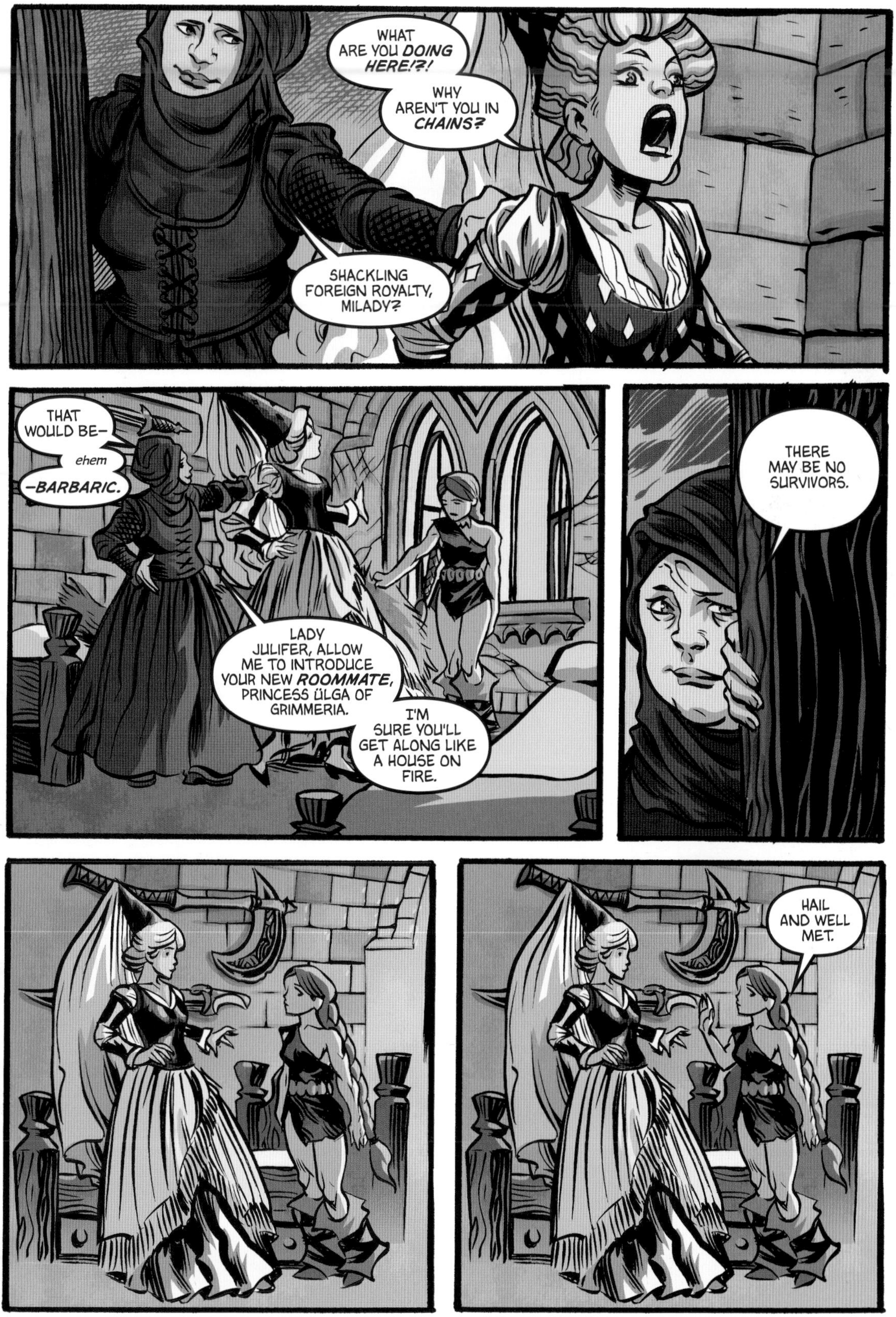
WHAT ARE YOU DOING HERE!?!
WHY AREN'T YOU IN CHAINS?
SHACKLING FOREIGN ROYALTY, MILADY?
THAT WOULD BE—
ehem
—BARBARIC.
LADY JULIFER, ALLOW ME TO INTRODUCE YOUR NEW ROOMMATE, PRINCESS ÜLGA OF GRIMMERIA.
I'M SURE YOU'LL GET ALONG LIKE A HOUSE ON FIRE.
THERE MAY BE NO SURVIVORS.
HAIL AND WELL MET.

chapter 2

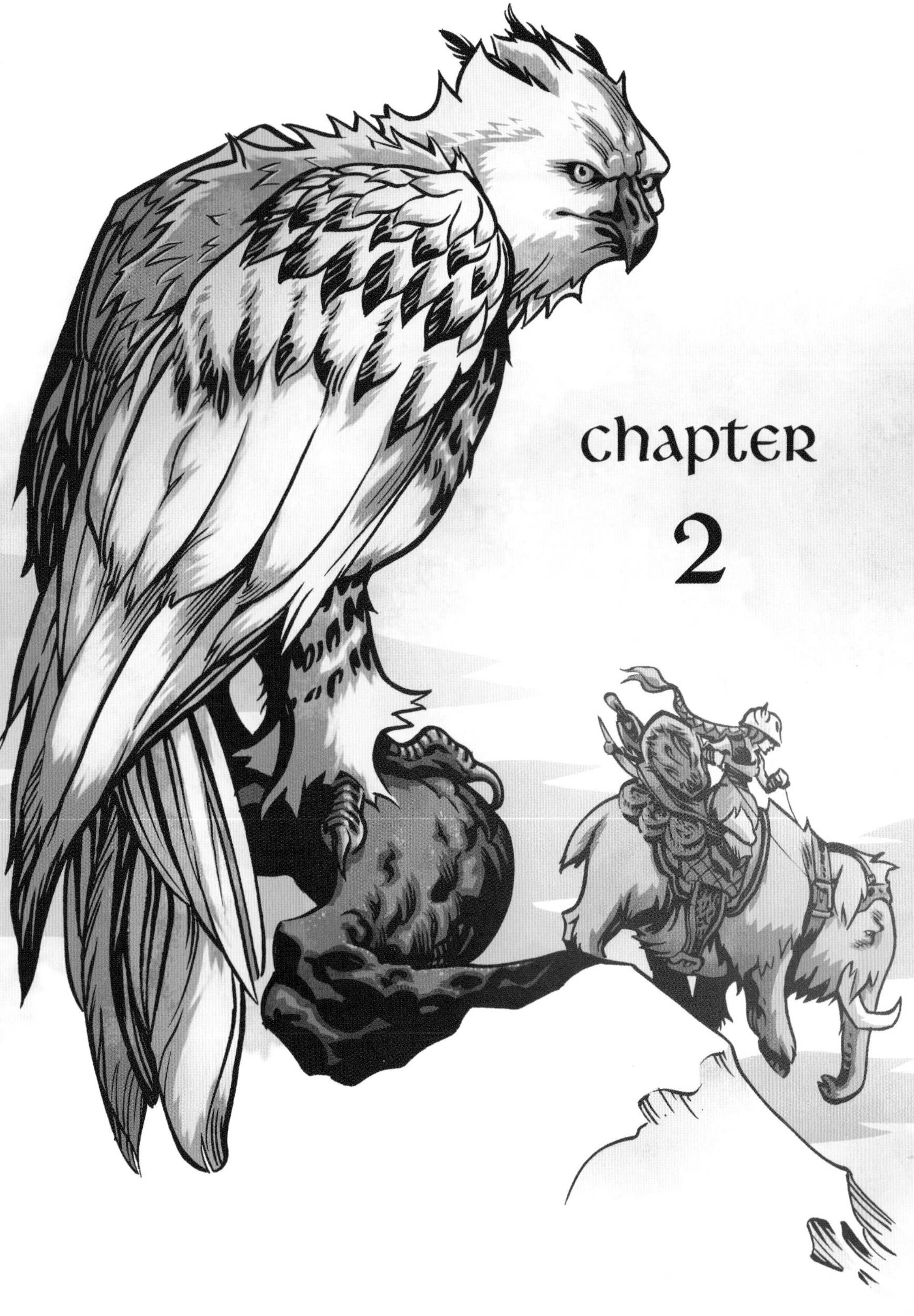

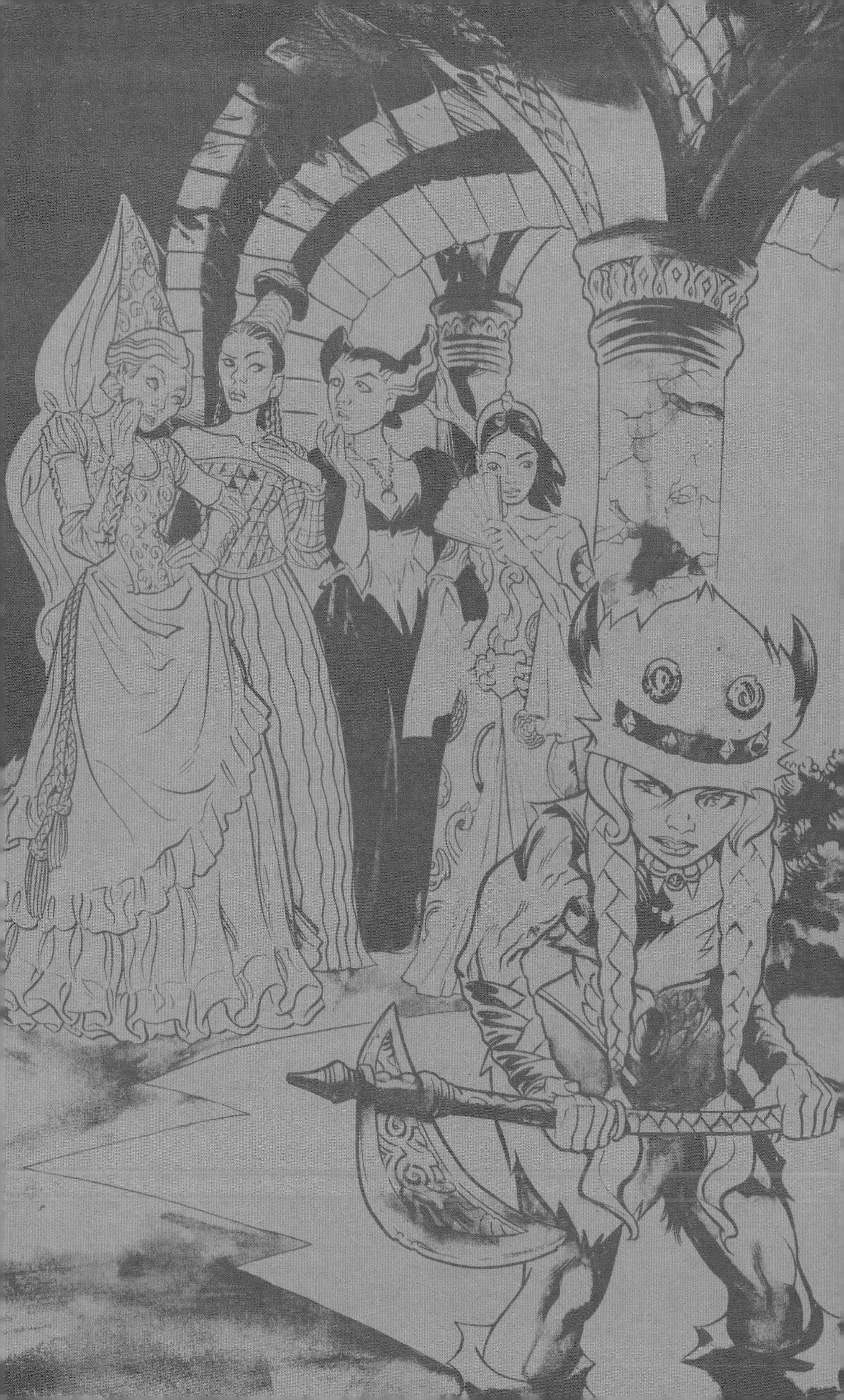

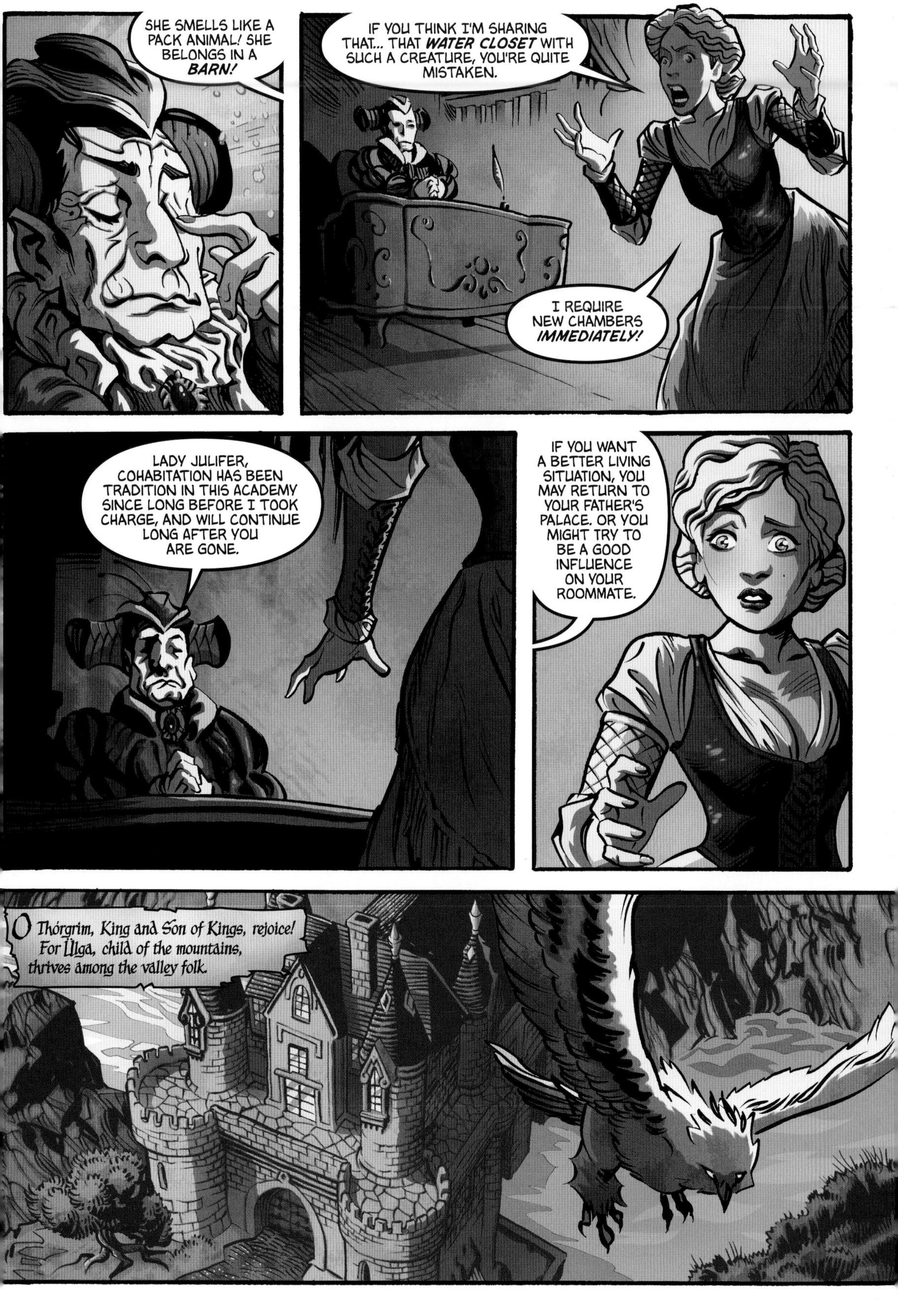
SHE SMELLS LIKE A PACK ANIMAL! SHE BELONGS IN A BARN!
IF YOU THINK I'M SHARING THAT... THAT WATER CLOSET WITH SUCH A CREATURE, YOU'RE QUITE MISTAKEN.
I REQUIRE NEW CHAMBERS IMMEDIATELY!
LADY JULIFER, COHABITATION HAS BEEN TRADITION IN THIS ACADEMY SINCE LONG BEFORE I TOOK CHARGE, AND WILL CONTINUE LONG AFTER YOU ARE GONE.
IF YOU WANT A BETTER LIVING SITUATION, YOU MAY RETURN TO YOUR FATHER'S PALACE. OR YOU MIGHT TRY TO BE A GOOD INFLUENCE ON YOUR ROOMMATE.
O Thórgrim, King and Son of Kings, rejoice! For Ülga, child of the mountains, thrives among the valley folk.

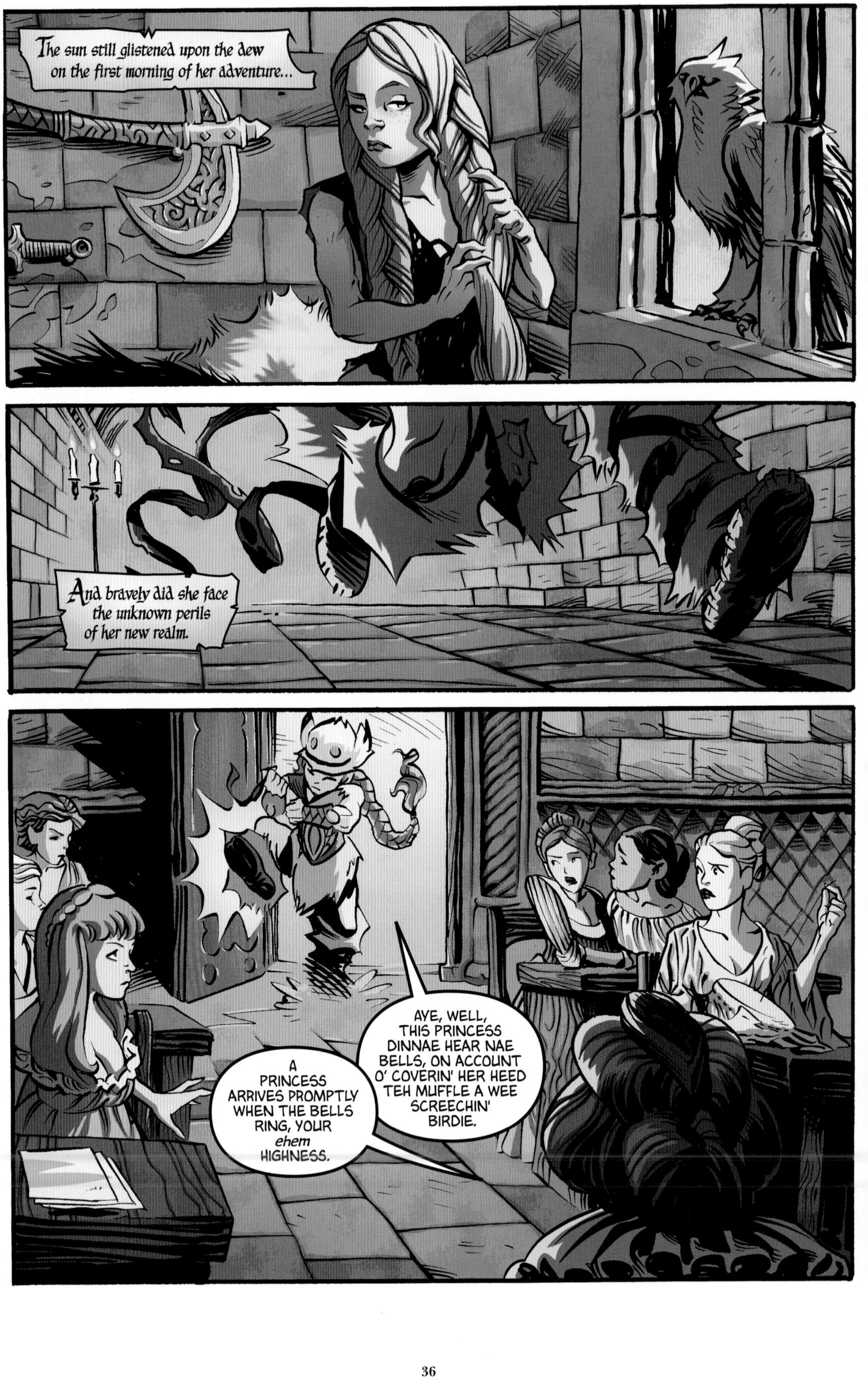
The sun still glistened upon the dew on the first morning of her adventure...
And bravely did she face the unknown perils of her new realm.
A PRINCESS ARRIVES PROMPTLY WHEN THE BELLS RING, YOUR *ehem* HIGHNESS.
AYE, WELL, THIS PRINCESS DINNAE HEAR NAE BELLS, ON ACCOUNT O' COVERIN' HER HEED TEH MUFFLE A WEE SCREECHIN' BIRDIE.

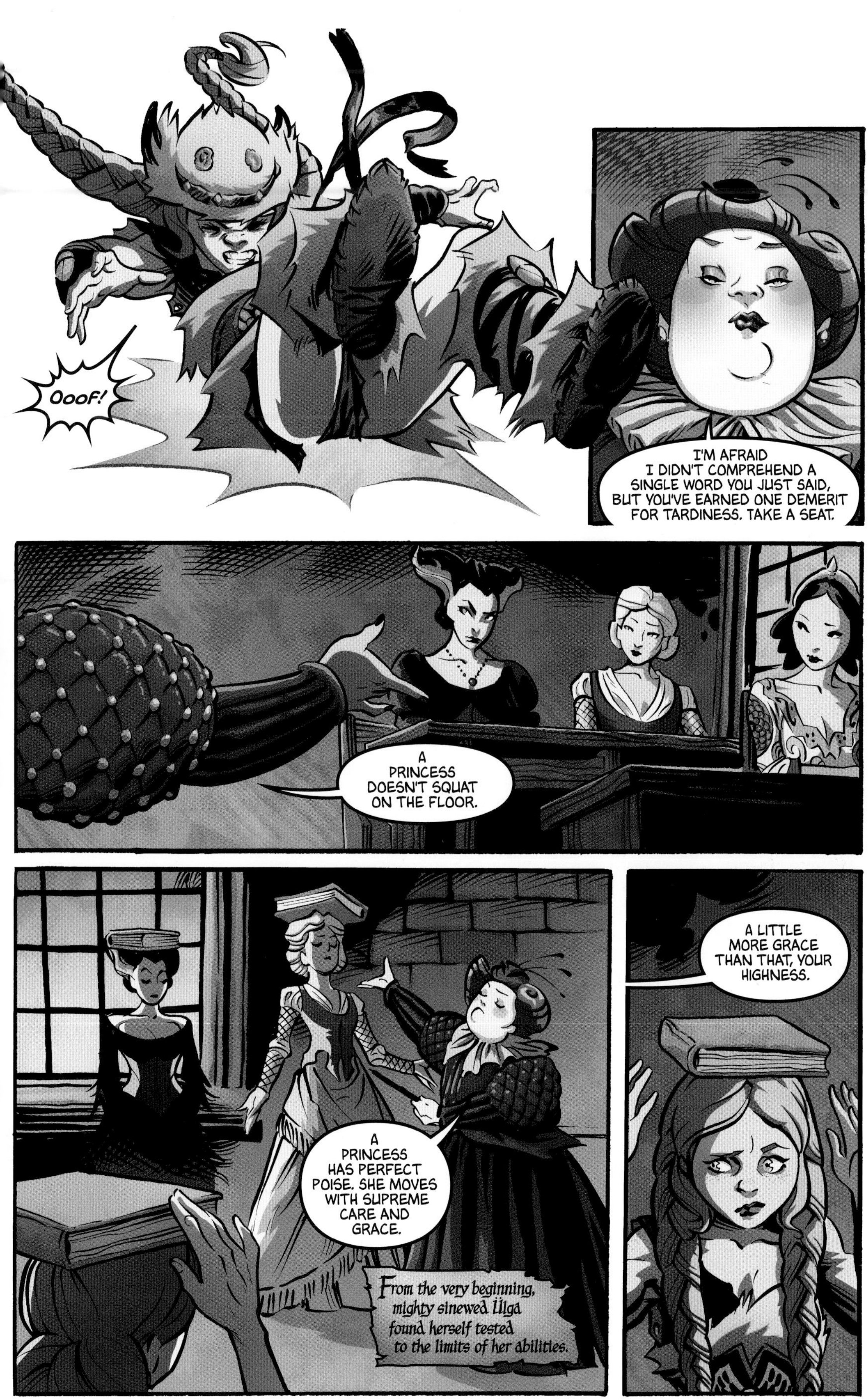
Ooof!
I'M AFRAID I DIDN'T COMPREHEND A SINGLE WORD YOU JUST SAID, BUT YOU'VE EARNED ONE DEMERIT FOR TARDINESS. TAKE A SEAT.
A PRINCESS DOESN'T SQUAT ON THE FLOOR.
A PRINCESS HAS PERFECT POISE. SHE MOVES WITH SUPREME CARE AND GRACE.
From the very beginning, mighty sinewed Ulga found herself tested to the limits of her abilities.
A LITTLE MORE GRACE THAN THAT, YOUR HIGHNESS.

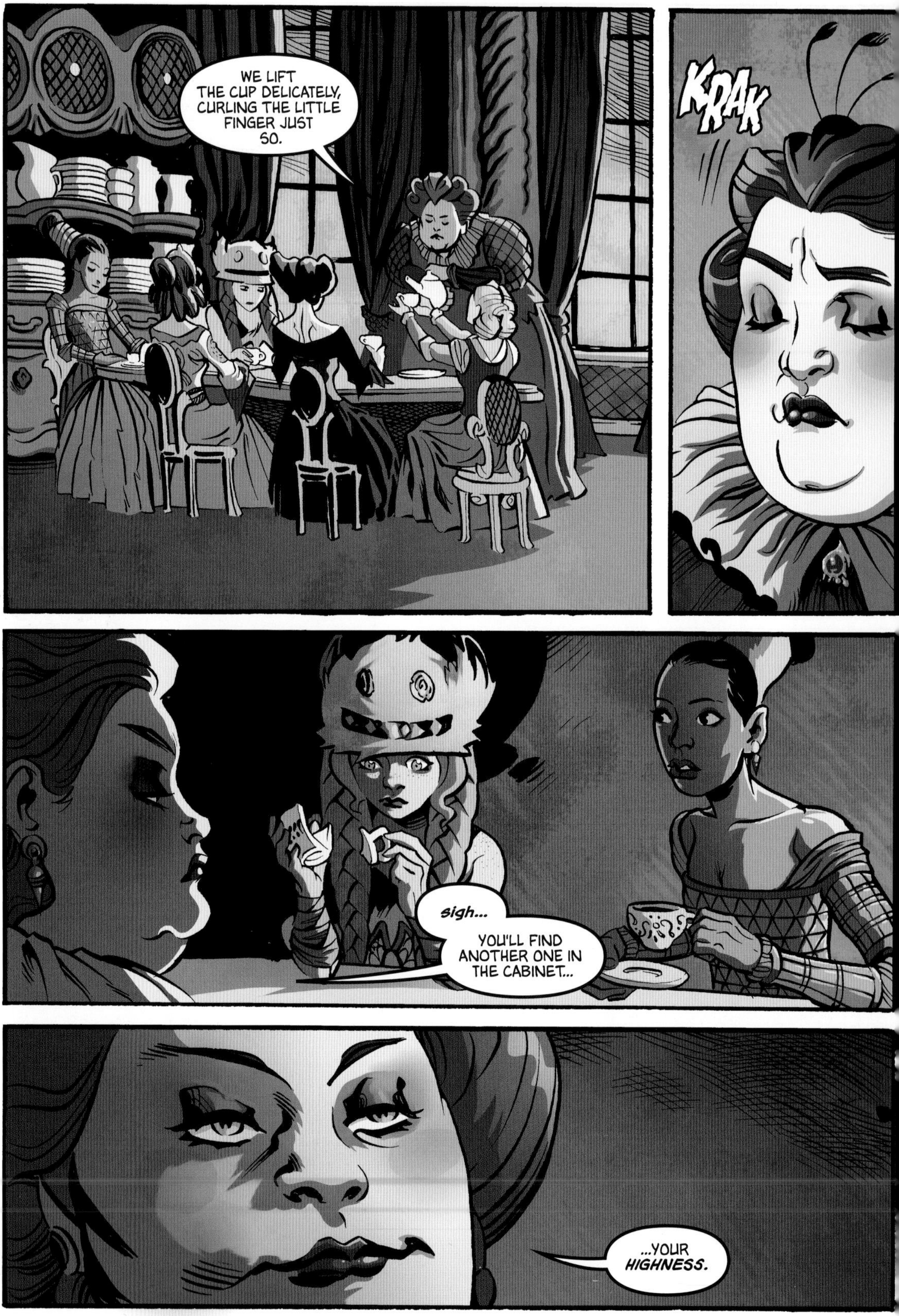
WE LIFT THE CUP DELICATELY, CURLING THE LITTLE FINGER JUST SO.
KRAK
sigh...
YOU'LL FIND ANOTHER ONE IN THE CABINET...
...YOUR *HIGHNESS.*

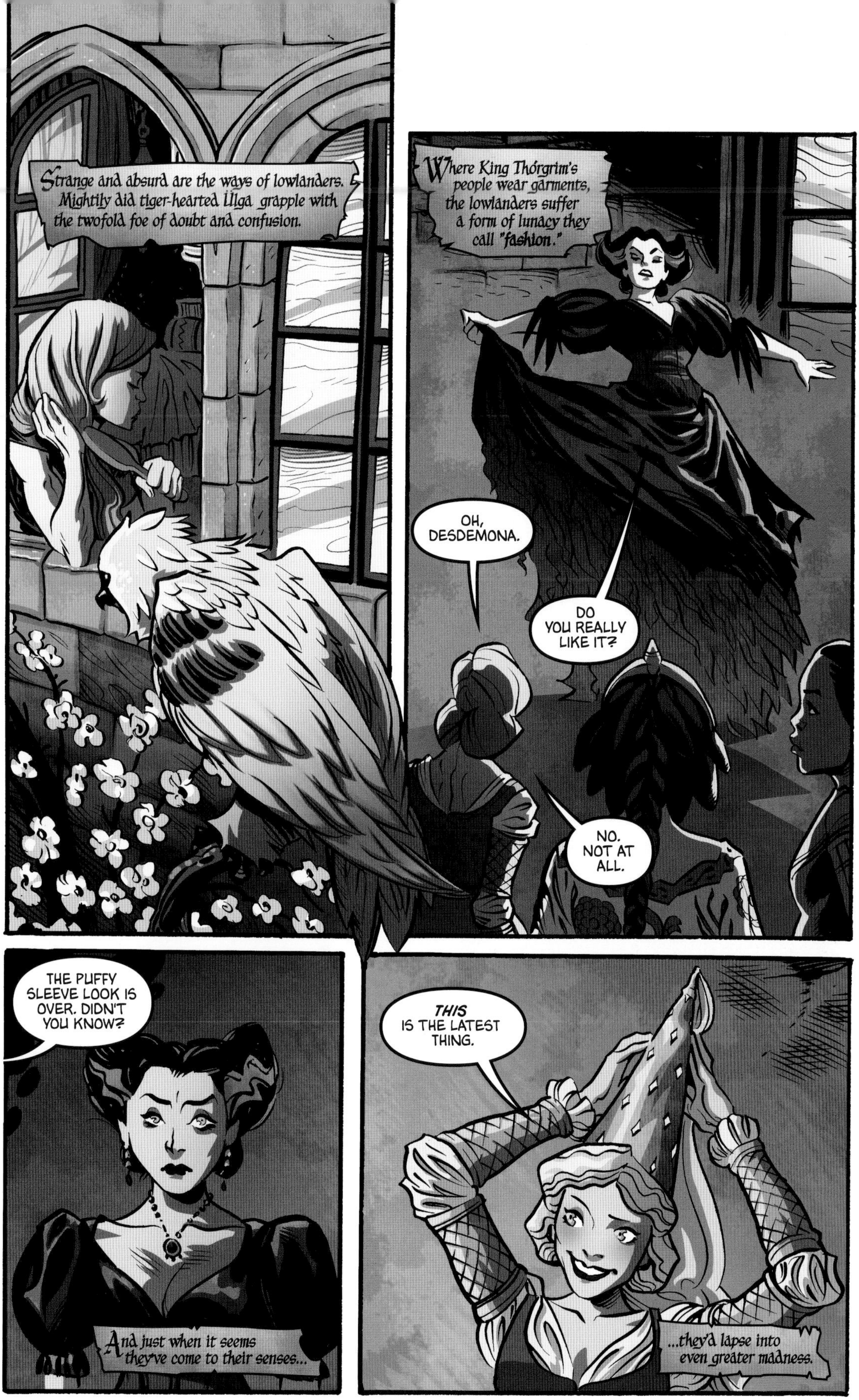
Strange and absurd are the ways of lowlanders. Mightily did tiger-hearted Ülga grapple with the twofold foe of doubt and confusion.
Where King Thórgrim's people wear garments, the lowlanders suffer a form of lunacy they call "fashion."
OH, DESDEMONA.
DO YOU REALLY LIKE IT?
NO. NOT AT ALL.
THE PUFFY SLEEVE LOOK IS OVER. DIDN'T YOU KNOW?
And just when it seems they've come to their senses...
THIS IS THE LATEST THING.
...they'd lapse into even greater madness.

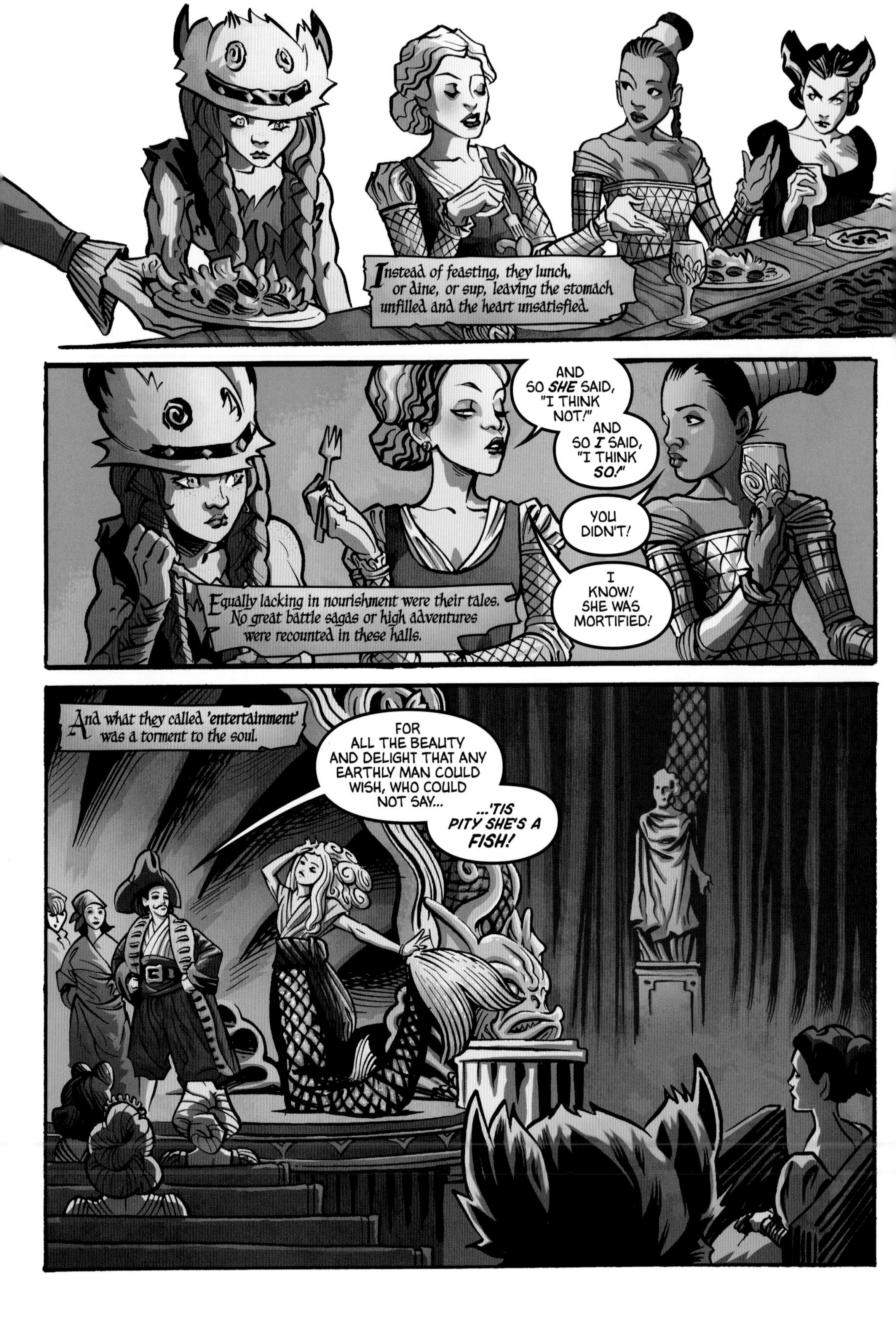
Instead of feasting, they lunch, or dine, or sup, leaving the stomach unfilled and the heart unsatisfied.
Equally lacking in nourishment were their tales. No great battle sagas or high adventures were recounted in these halls.
AND SO SHE SAID, "I THINK NOT!" AND SO I SAID, "I THINK SO!"
YOU DIDN'T!
I KNOW! SHE WAS MORTIFIED!
And what they called 'entertainment' was a torment to the soul.
FOR ALL THE BEAUTY AND DELIGHT THAT ANY EARTHLY MAN COULD WISH, WHO COULD NOT SAY...
...'TIS PITY SHE'S A FISH!

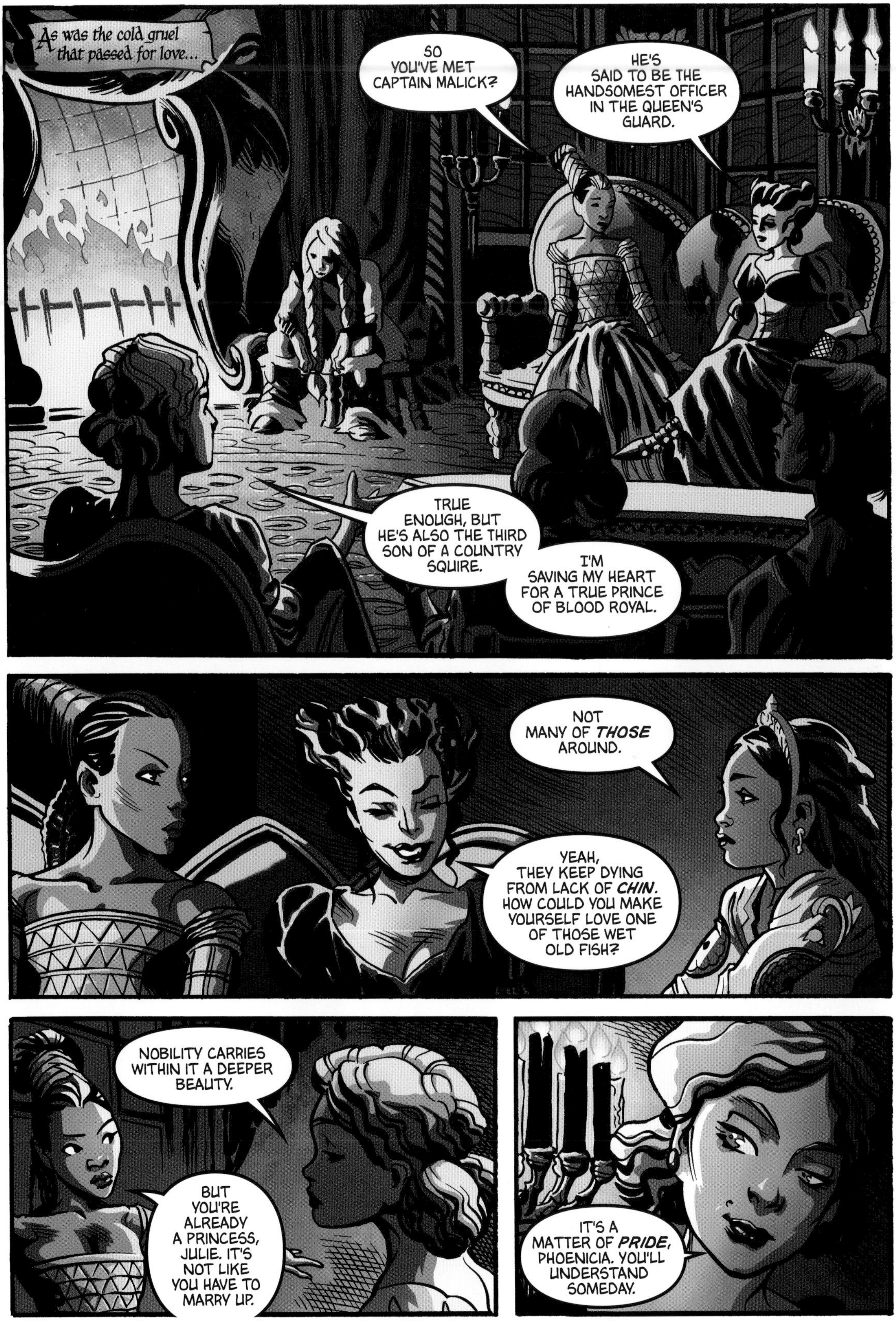

As was the cold gruel that passed for love...
SO YOU'VE MET CAPTAIN MALICK?
HE'S SAID TO BE THE HANDSOMEST OFFICER IN THE QUEEN'S GUARD.
TRUE ENOUGH, BUT HE'S ALSO THE THIRD SON OF A COUNTRY SQUIRE.
I'M SAVING MY HEART FOR A TRUE PRINCE OF BLOOD ROYAL.
NOT MANY OF *THOSE* AROUND.
YEAH, THEY KEEP DYING FROM LACK OF *CHIN*. HOW COULD YOU MAKE YOURSELF LOVE ONE OF THOSE WET OLD FISH?
NOBILITY CARRIES WITHIN IT A DEEPER BEAUTY.
BUT YOU'RE ALREADY A PRINCESS, JULIE. IT'S NOT LIKE YOU HAVE TO MARRY UP.
IT'S A MATTER OF *PRIDE*, PHOENICIA. YOU'LL UNDERSTAND SOMEDAY.

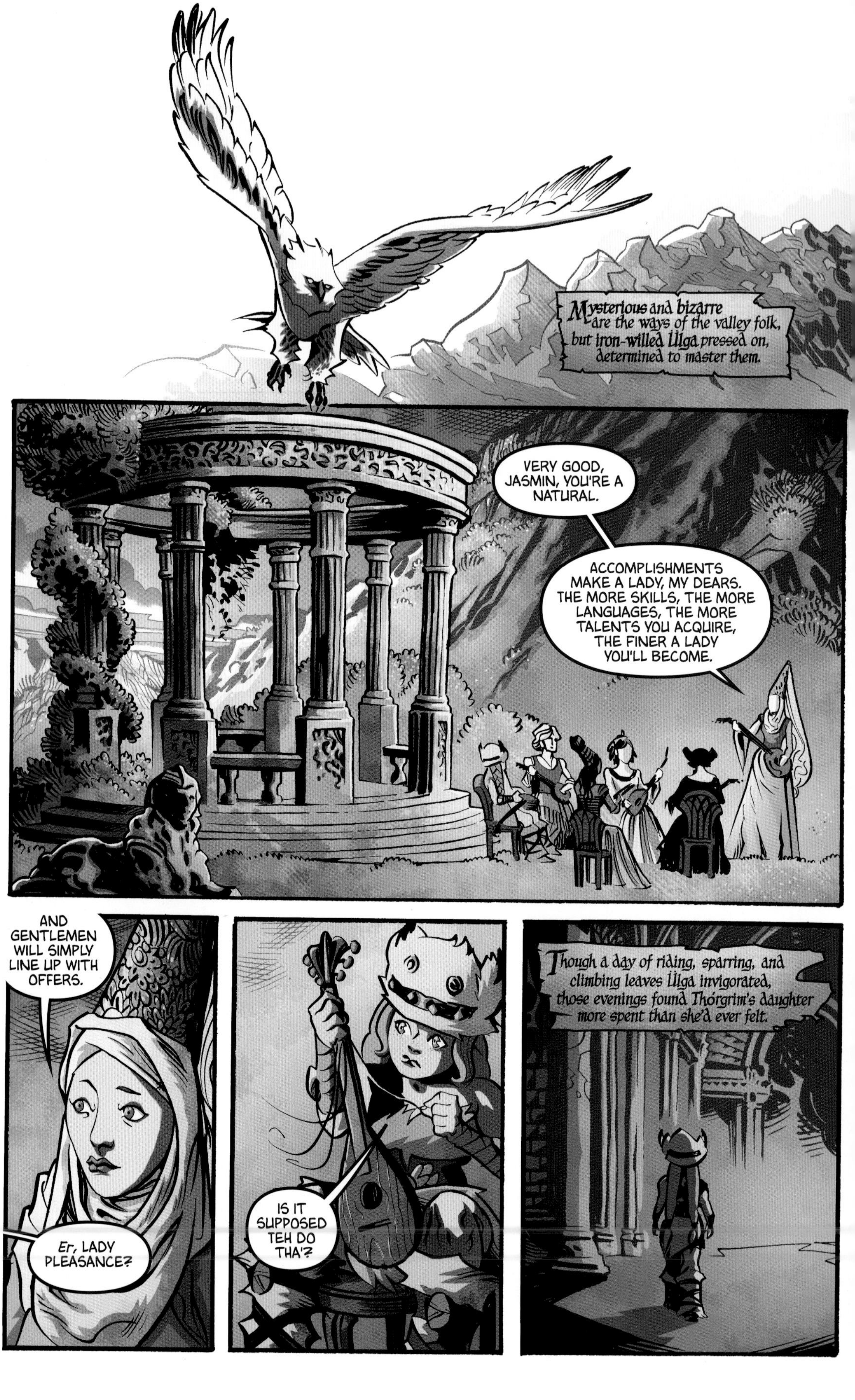
Mysterious and bizarre are the ways of the valley folk, but iron-willed Ülga pressed on, determined to master them.
VERY GOOD, JASMIN, YOU'RE A NATURAL.
ACCOMPLISHMENTS MAKE A LADY, MY DEARS. THE MORE SKILLS, THE MORE LANGUAGES, THE MORE TALENTS YOU ACQUIRE, THE FINER A LADY YOU'LL BECOME.
AND GENTLEMEN WILL SIMPLY LINE UP WITH OFFERS.
Er, LADY PLEASANCE?
IS IT SUPPOSED TEH DO THA'?
Though a day of riding, sparring, and climbing leaves Ülga invigorated, those evenings found Thórgrim's daughter more spent than she'd ever felt.

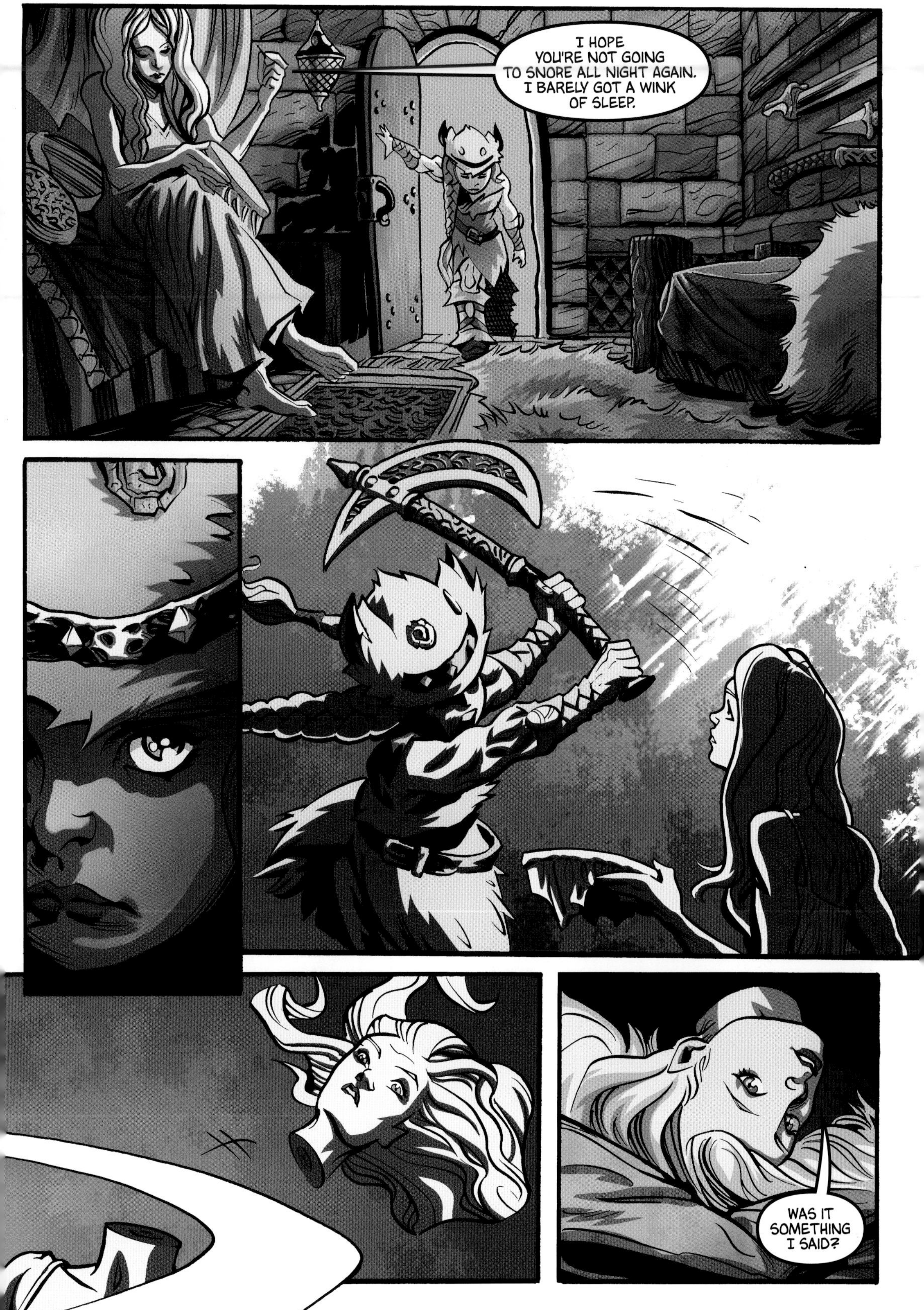
I HOPE YOU'RE NOT GOING TO SNORE ALL NIGHT AGAIN. I BARELY GOT A WINK OF SLEEP.
WAS IT SOMETHING I SAID?

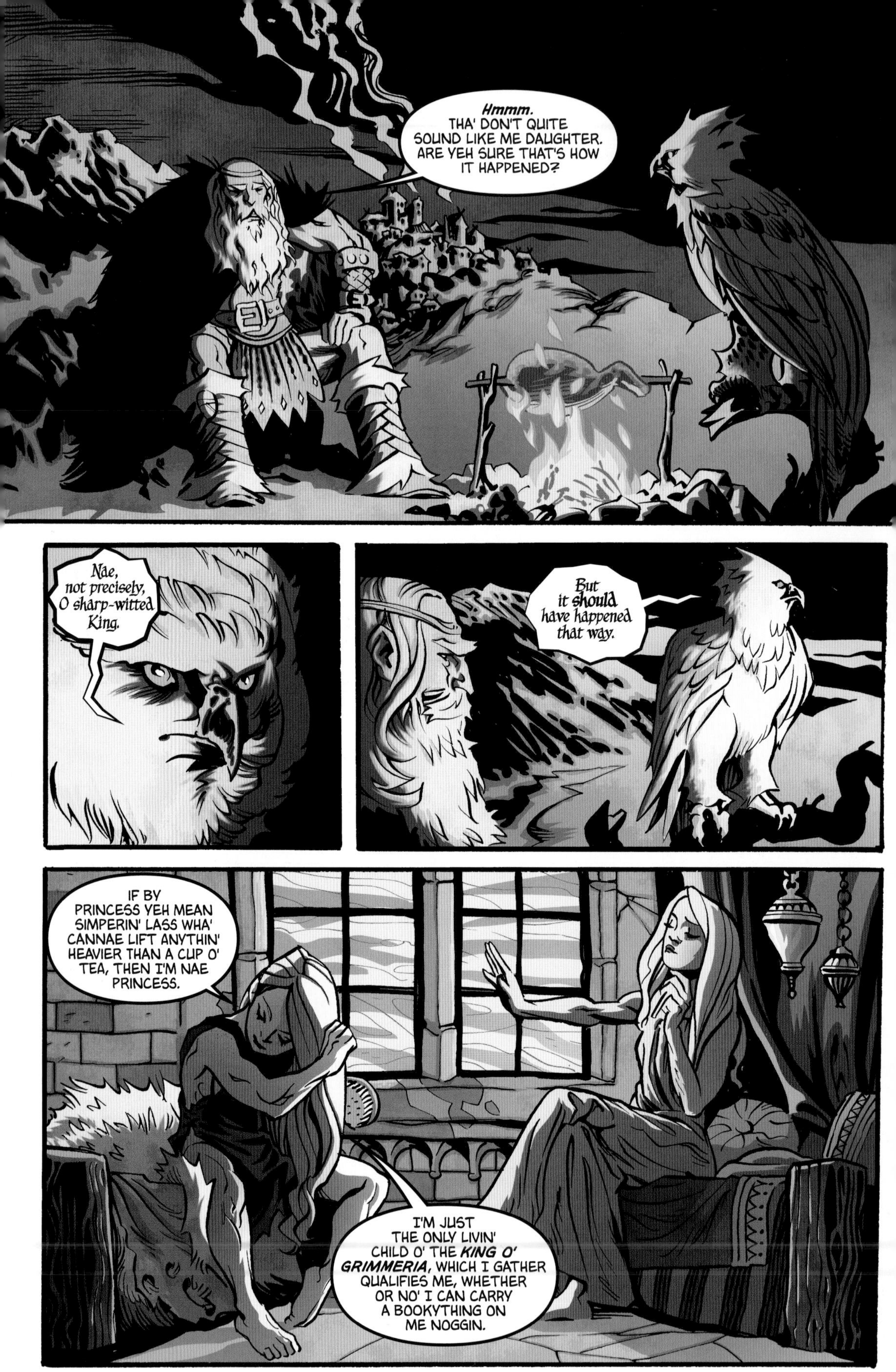
Hmmm.
THA' DON'T QUITE SOUND LIKE ME DAUGHTER. ARE YEH SURE THAT'S HOW IT HAPPENED?
Nae, not precisely, O sharp-witted King.
But it should have happened that way.
IF BY PRINCESS YEH MEAN SIMPERIN' LASS WHA' CANNAE LIFT ANYTHIN' HEAVIER THAN A CUP O' TEA, THEN I'M NAE PRINCESS.
I'M JUST THE ONLY LIVIN' CHILD O' THE KING O' GRIMMERIA, WHICH I GATHER QUALIFIES ME, WHETHER OR NO' I CAN CARRY A BOOKYTHING ON ME NOGGIN.

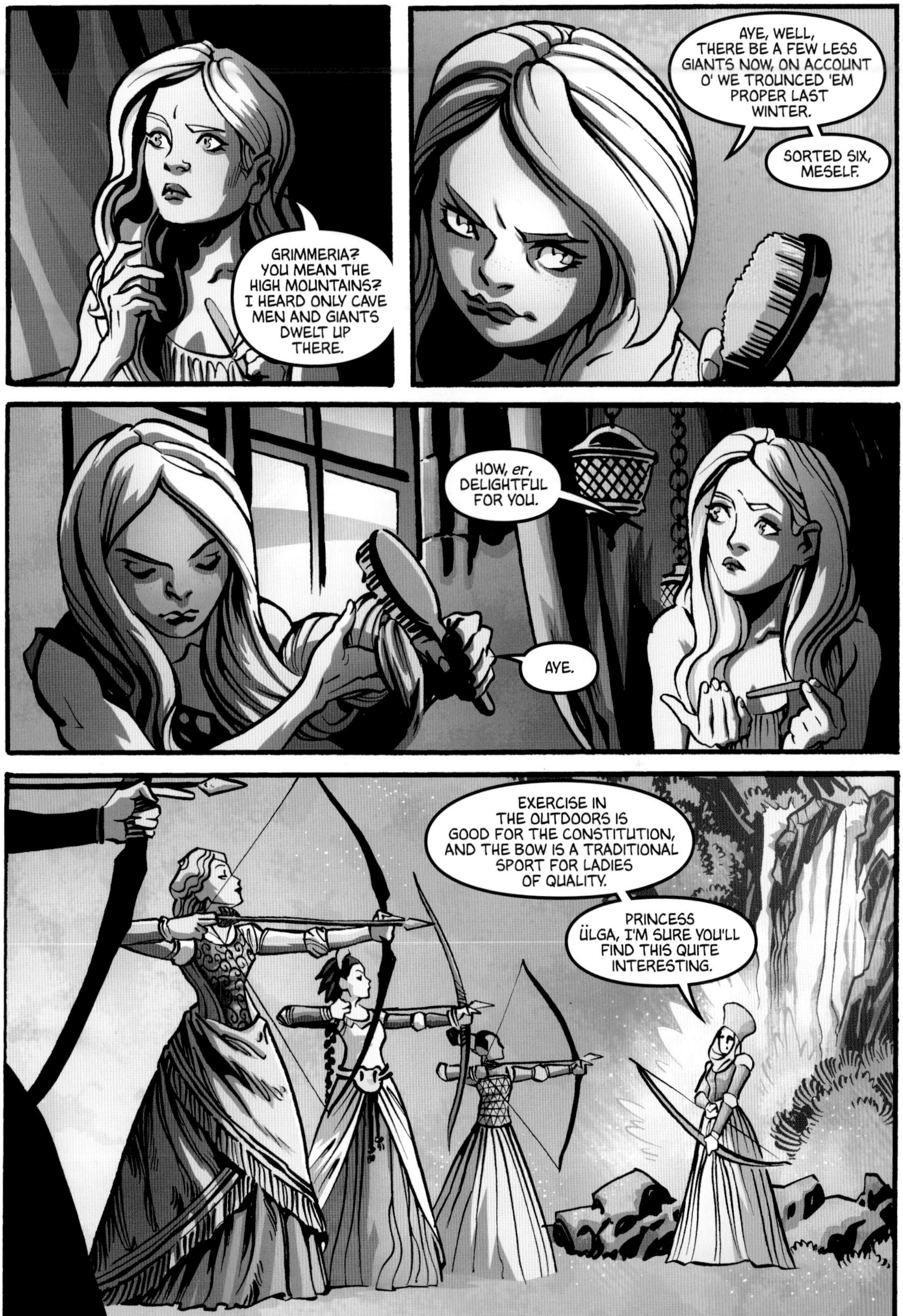
GRIMMERIA? YOU MEAN THE HIGH MOUNTAINS? I HEARD ONLY CAVE MEN AND GIANTS DWELT UP THERE.
AYE, WELL, THERE BE A FEW LESS GIANTS NOW, ON ACCOUNT O' WE TROUNCED 'EM PROPER LAST WINTER.
SORTED SIX, MESELF.
HOW, *er*, DELIGHTFUL FOR YOU.
AYE.
EXERCISE IN THE OUTDOORS IS GOOD FOR THE CONSTITUTION, AND THE BOW IS A TRADITIONAL SPORT FOR LADIES OF QUALITY.
PRINCESS ÜLGA, I'M SURE YOU'LL FIND THIS QUITE INTERESTING.

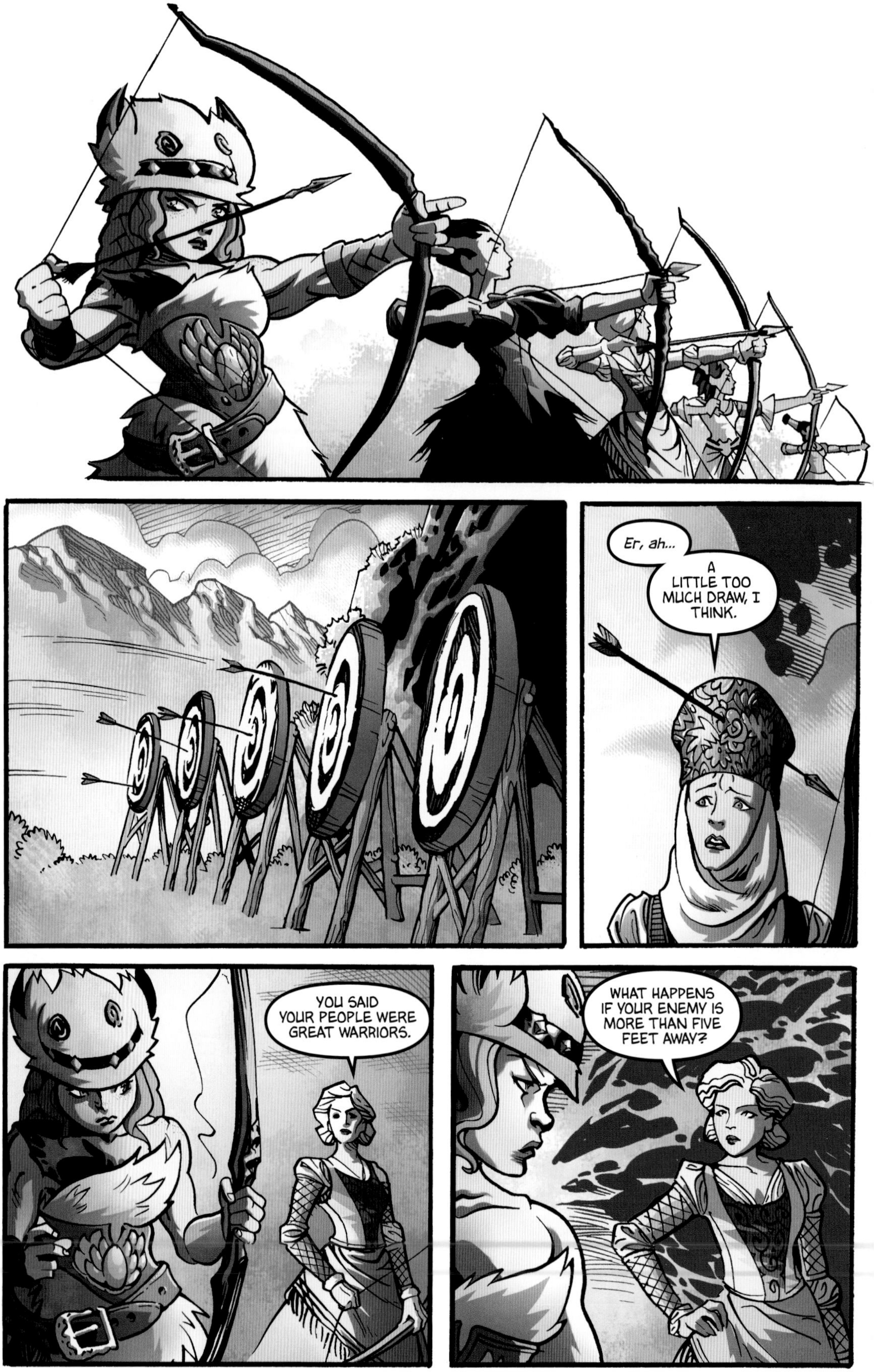
Er, ah...
A LITTLE TOO MUCH DRAW, I THINK.
YOU SAID YOUR PEOPLE WERE GREAT WARRIORS.
WHAT HAPPENS IF YOUR ENEMY IS MORE THAN FIVE FEET AWAY?

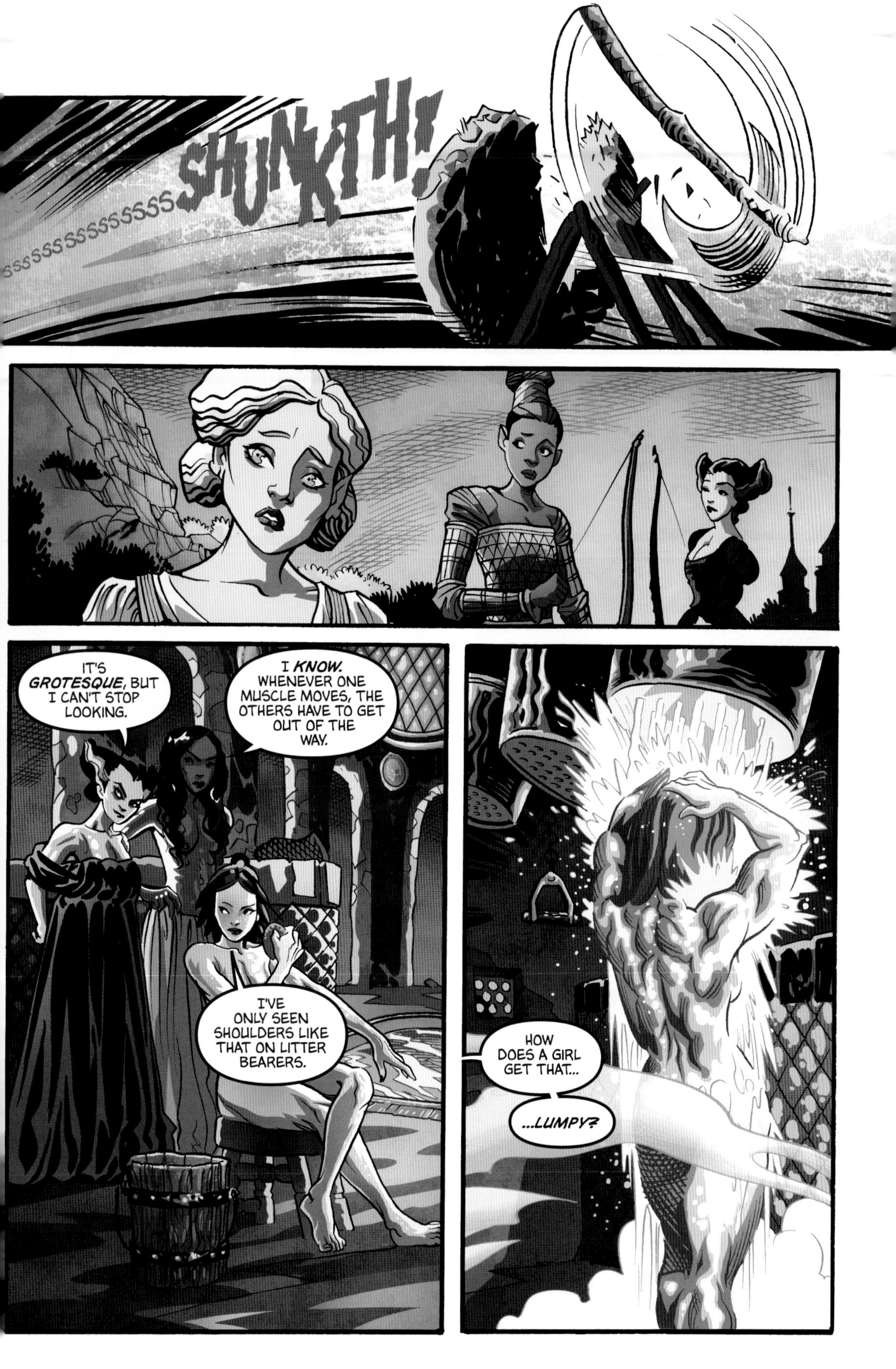
SSSSSSSSSSSSSSSSSSHUNKTH!
IT'S GROTESQUE, BUT I CAN'T STOP LOOKING.
I KNOW. WHENEVER ONE MUSCLE MOVES, THE OTHERS HAVE TO GET OUT OF THE WAY.
I'VE ONLY SEEN SHOULDERS LIKE THAT ON LITTER BEARERS.
HOW DOES A GIRL GET THAT...
...LUMPY?

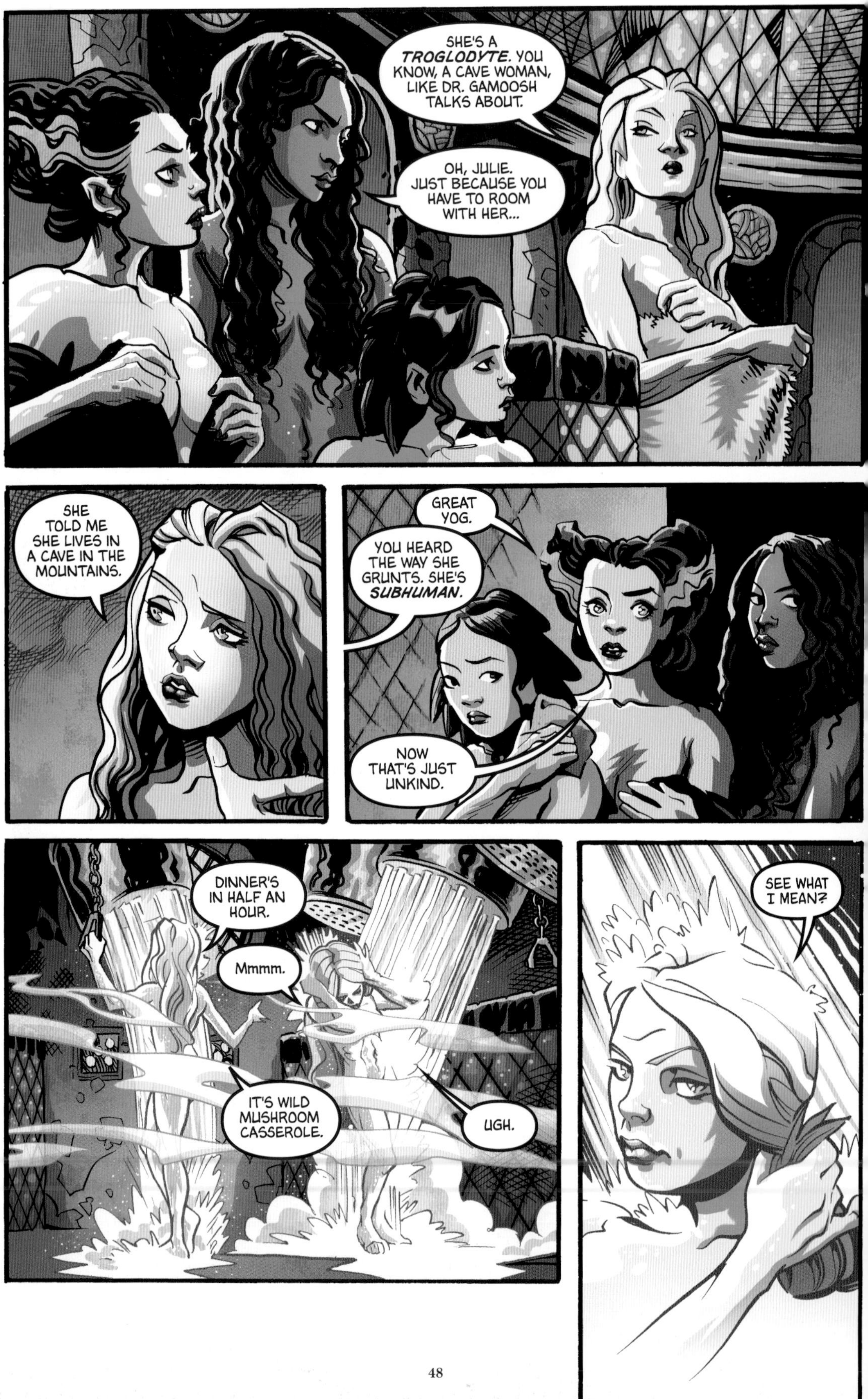
SHE'S A *TROGLODYTE.* YOU KNOW, A CAVE WOMAN, LIKE DR. GAMOOSH TALKS ABOUT.
OH, JULIE. JUST BECAUSE YOU HAVE TO ROOM WITH HER...
SHE TOLD ME SHE LIVES IN A CAVE IN THE MOUNTAINS.
GREAT YOG.
YOU HEARD THE WAY SHE GRUNTS. SHE'S *SUBHUMAN*.
NOW THAT'S JUST UNKIND.
DINNER'S IN HALF AN HOUR.
Mmmm.
IT'S WILD MUSHROOM CASSEROLE.
UGH.
SEE WHAT I MEAN?

WHAT IS SHE EVEN DOING HERE?

OH *PLEASE*, JASMIN. *YOU* DIDN'T USE A FORK WHEN YOU FIRST ARRIVED.

I *KNOW.* SHE DOESN'T EVEN KNOW HOW TO USE A FORK.

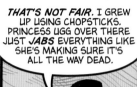

THAT'S NOT FAIR. I GREW UP USING CHOPSTICKS. PRINCESS UGG OVER THERE JUST *JABS* EVERYTHING LIKE SHE'S MAKING SURE IT'S ALL THE WAY DEAD.

The wise King knows that loneliness comes in two forms.

The loneliness of solitude sharpens the mind and nurtures the soul.

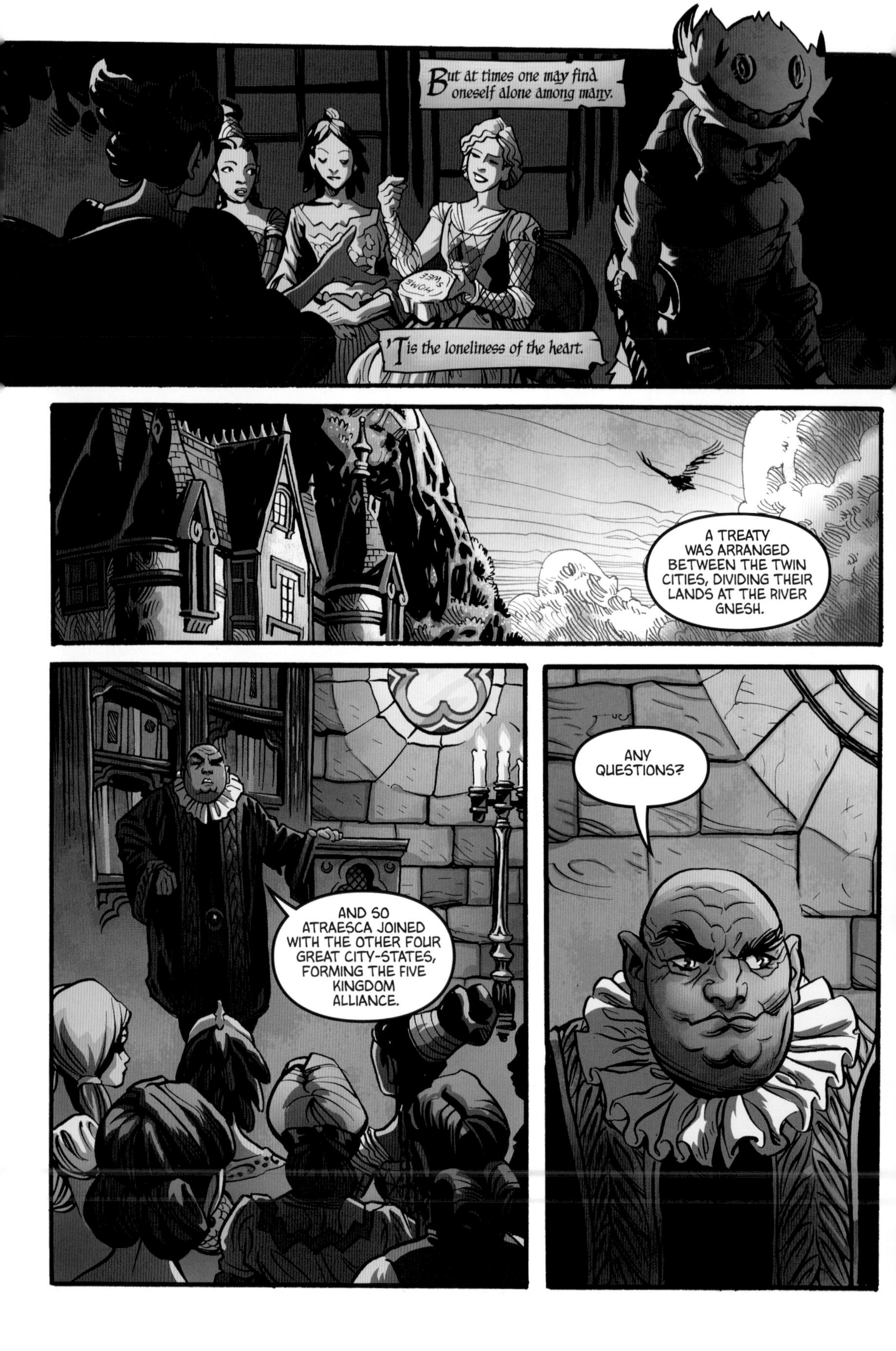
But at times one may find oneself alone among many.
'Tis the loneliness of the heart.
A TREATY WAS ARRANGED BETWEEN THE TWIN CITIES, DIVIDING THEIR LANDS AT THE RIVER GNESH.
AND SO ATRAESCA JOINED WITH THE OTHER FOUR GREAT CITY-STATES, FORMING THE FIVE KINGDOM ALLIANCE.
ANY QUESTIONS?

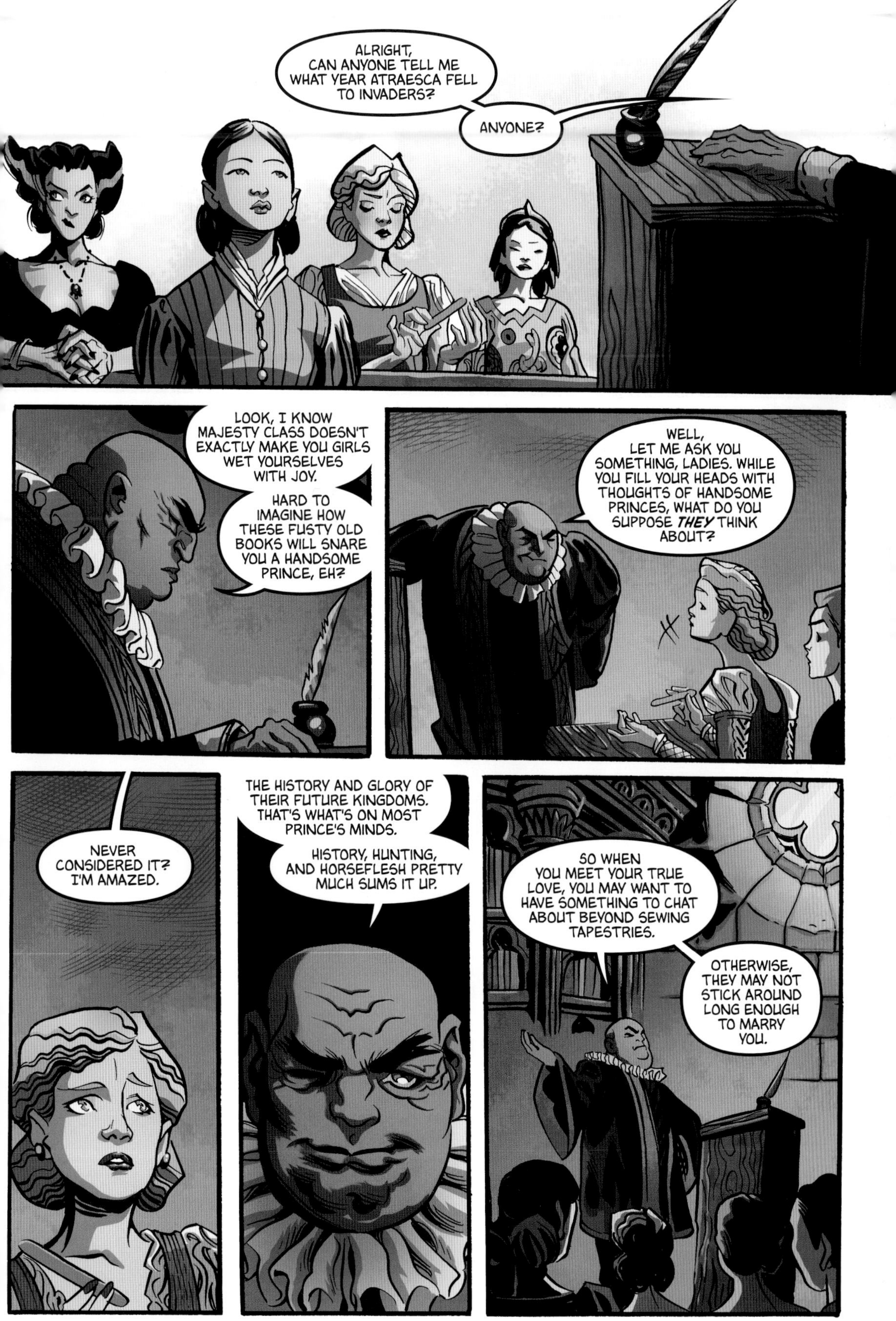
ALRIGHT, CAN ANYONE TELL ME WHAT YEAR ATRAESCA FELL TO INVADERS?
ANYONE?
LOOK, I KNOW MAJESTY CLASS DOESN'T EXACTLY MAKE YOU GIRLS WET YOURSELVES WITH JOY.
HARD TO IMAGINE HOW THESE FUSTY OLD BOOKS WILL SNARE YOU A HANDSOME PRINCE, EH?
WELL, LET ME ASK YOU SOMETHING, LADIES. WHILE YOU FILL YOUR HEADS WITH THOUGHTS OF HANDSOME PRINCES, WHAT DO YOU SUPPOSE *THEY* THINK ABOUT?
NEVER CONSIDERED IT? I'M AMAZED.
THE HISTORY AND GLORY OF THEIR FUTURE KINGDOMS. THAT'S WHAT'S ON MOST PRINCE'S MINDS.
HISTORY, HUNTING, AND HORSEFLESH PRETTY MUCH SUMS IT UP.
SO WHEN YOU MEET YOUR TRUE LOVE, YOU MAY WANT TO HAVE SOMETHING TO CHAT ABOUT BEYOND SEWING TAPESTRIES.
OTHERWISE, THEY MAY NOT STICK AROUND LONG ENOUGH TO MARRY YOU.

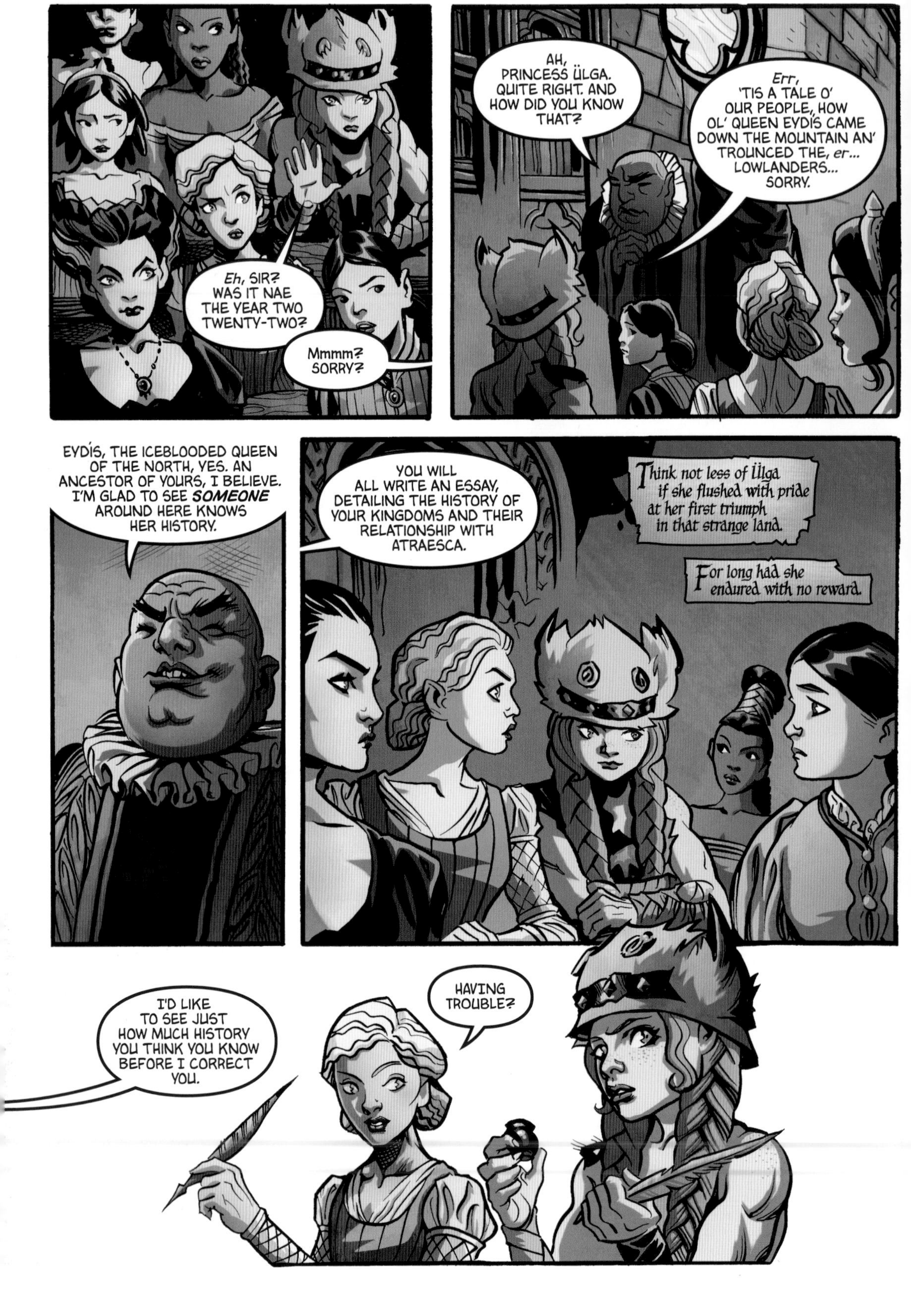

Eh, SIR? WAS IT NAE THE YEAR TWO TWENTY-TWO?
Mmmm? SORRY?
AH, PRINCESS ÜLGA. QUITE RIGHT. AND HOW DID YOU KNOW THAT?
Err, 'TIS A TALE O' OUR PEOPLE,, HOW OL' QUEEN EYDÍS CAME DOWN THE MOUNTAIN AN' TROUNCED THE, er... LOWLANDERS... SORRY.
EYDÍS, THE ICEBLOODED QUEEN OF THE NORTH, YES. AN ANCESTOR OF YOURS, I BELIEVE. I'M GLAD TO SEE SOMEONE AROUND HERE KNOWS HER HISTORY.
YOU WILL ALL WRITE AN ESSAY, DETAILING THE HISTORY OF YOUR KINGDOMS AND THEIR RELATIONSHIP WITH ATRAESCA.
Think not less of Ülga if she flushed with pride at her first triumph in that strange land.
For long had she endured with no reward.
I'D LIKE TO SEE JUST HOW MUCH HISTORY YOU THINK YOU KNOW BEFORE I CORRECT YOU.
HAVING TROUBLE?

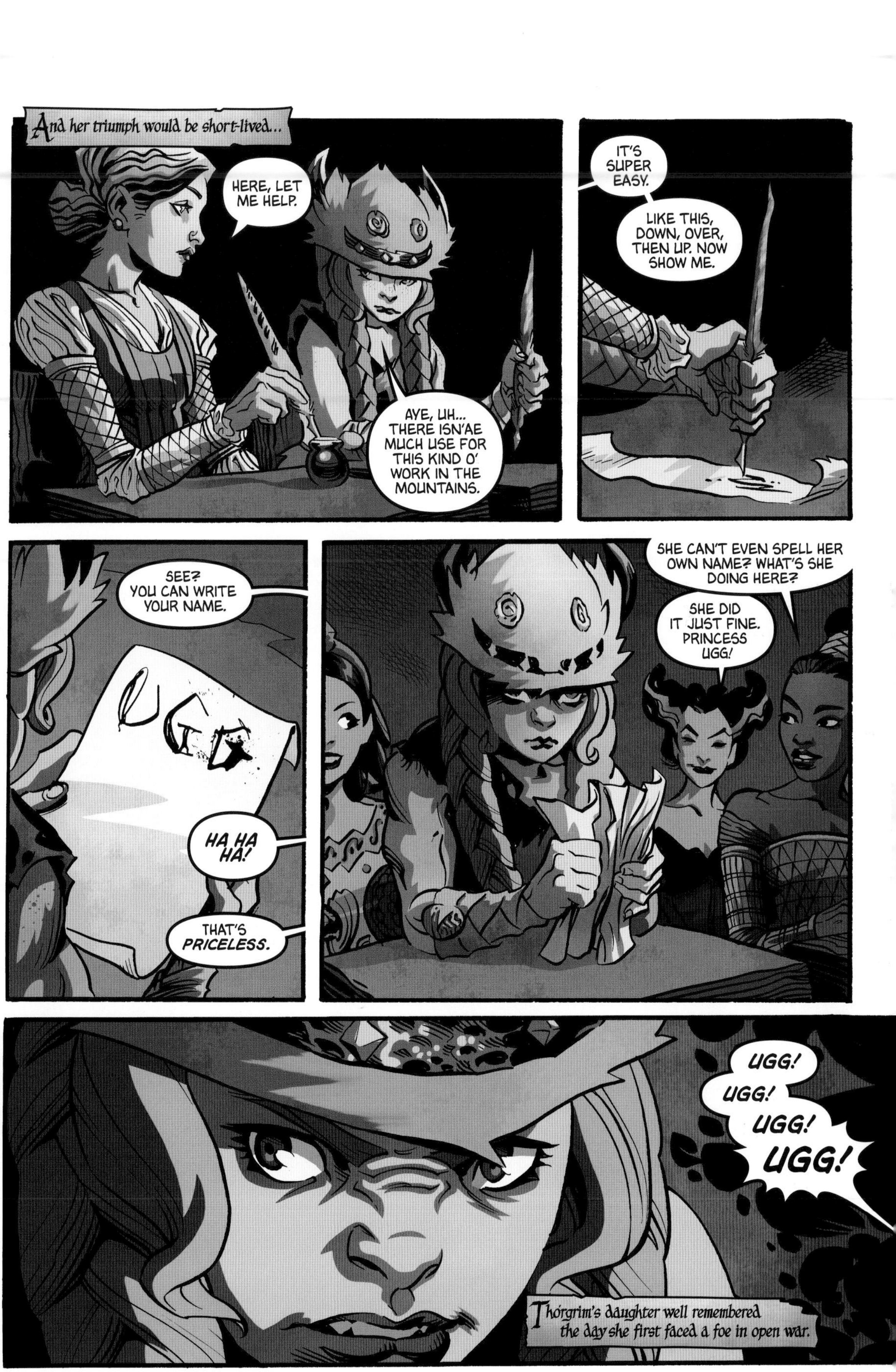
And her triumph would be short-lived...
HERE, LET ME HELP.
AYE, UH... THERE ISN'AE MUCH USE FOR THIS KIND O' WORK IN THE MOUNTAINS.
IT'S SUPER EASY.
LIKE THIS, DOWN, OVER, THEN UP. NOW SHOW ME.
SEE? YOU CAN WRITE YOUR NAME.
HA HA HA!
THAT'S *PRICELESS.*
SHE CAN'T EVEN SPELL HER OWN NAME? WHAT'S SHE DOING HERE?
SHE DID IT JUST FINE. PRINCESS UGG!
UGG!
UGG!
UGG!
UGG!
Thórgrim's daughter well remembered the day she first faced a foe in open war.

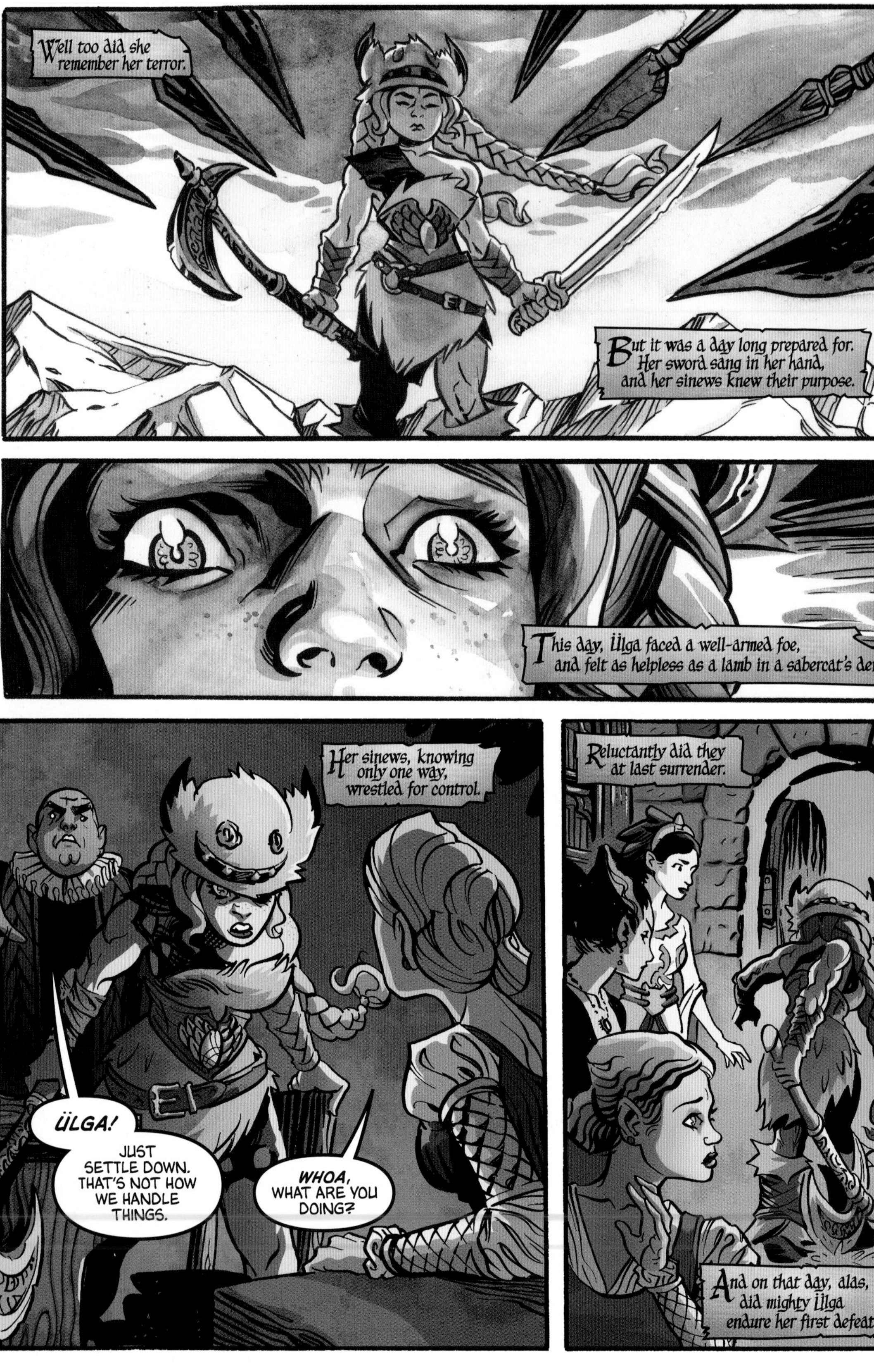

Well too did she remember her terror.
But it was a day long prepared for. Her sword sang in her hand, and her sinews knew their purpose.
This day, Ülga faced a well-armed foe, and felt as helpless as a lamb in a sabercat's den.
Her sinews, knowing only one way, wrestled for control.
ÜLGA!
JUST SETTLE DOWN. THAT'S NOT HOW WE HANDLE THINGS.
WHOA, WHAT ARE YOU DOING?
Reluctantly did they at last surrender.
And on that day, alas, did mighty Ülga endure her first defeat.

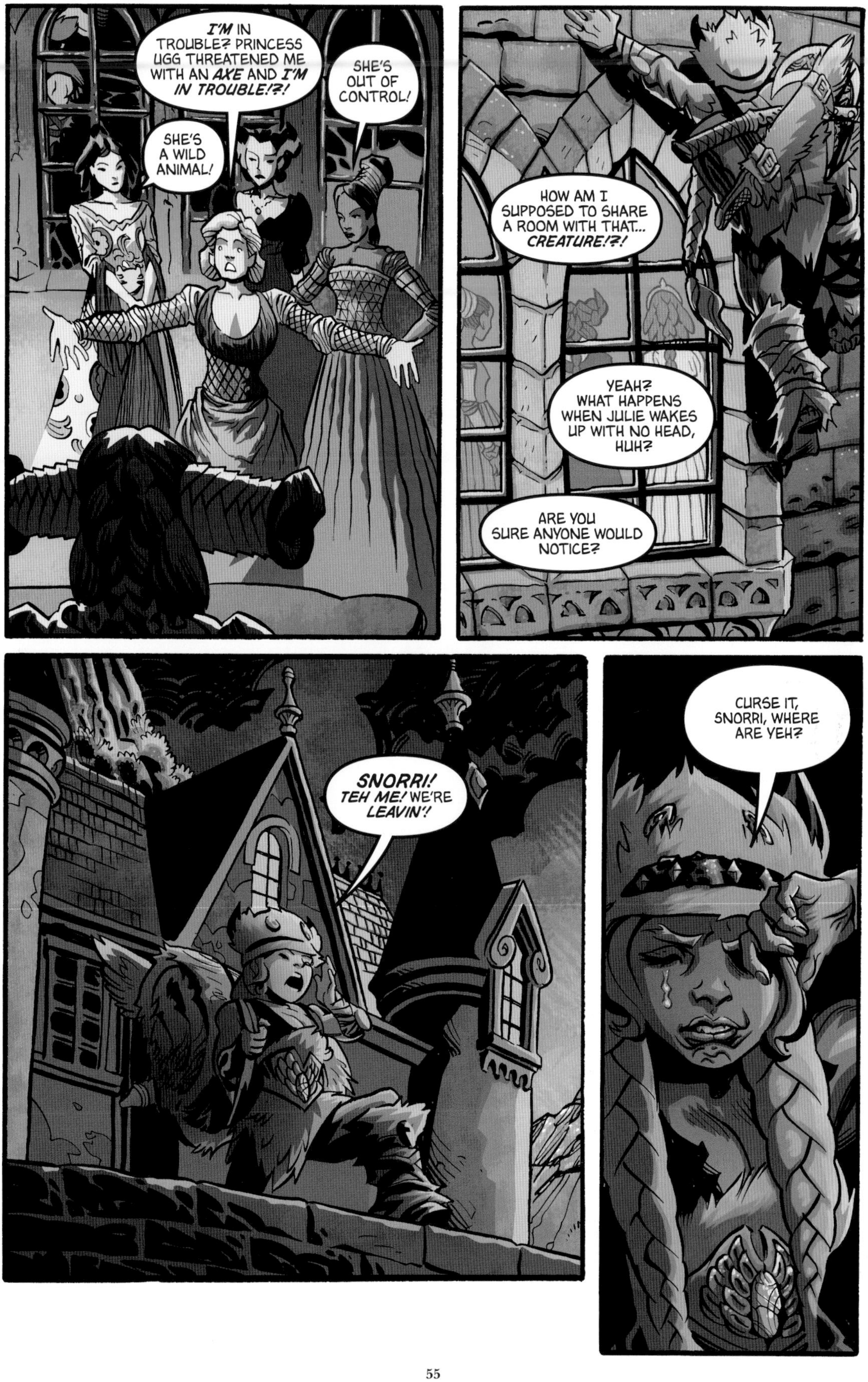
I'M IN TROUBLE? PRINCESS UGG THREATENED ME WITH AN AXE AND I'M IN TROUBLE!?!
SHE'S A WILD ANIMAL!
SHE'S OUT OF CONTROL!
HOW AM I SUPPOSED TO SHARE A ROOM WITH THAT... CREATURE!?!
YEAH? WHAT HAPPENS WHEN JULIE WAKES UP WITH NO HEAD, HUH?
ARE YOU SURE ANYONE WOULD NOTICE?
SNORRI! TEH ME! WE'RE LEAVIN'!
CURSE IT, SNORRI, WHERE ARE YEH?

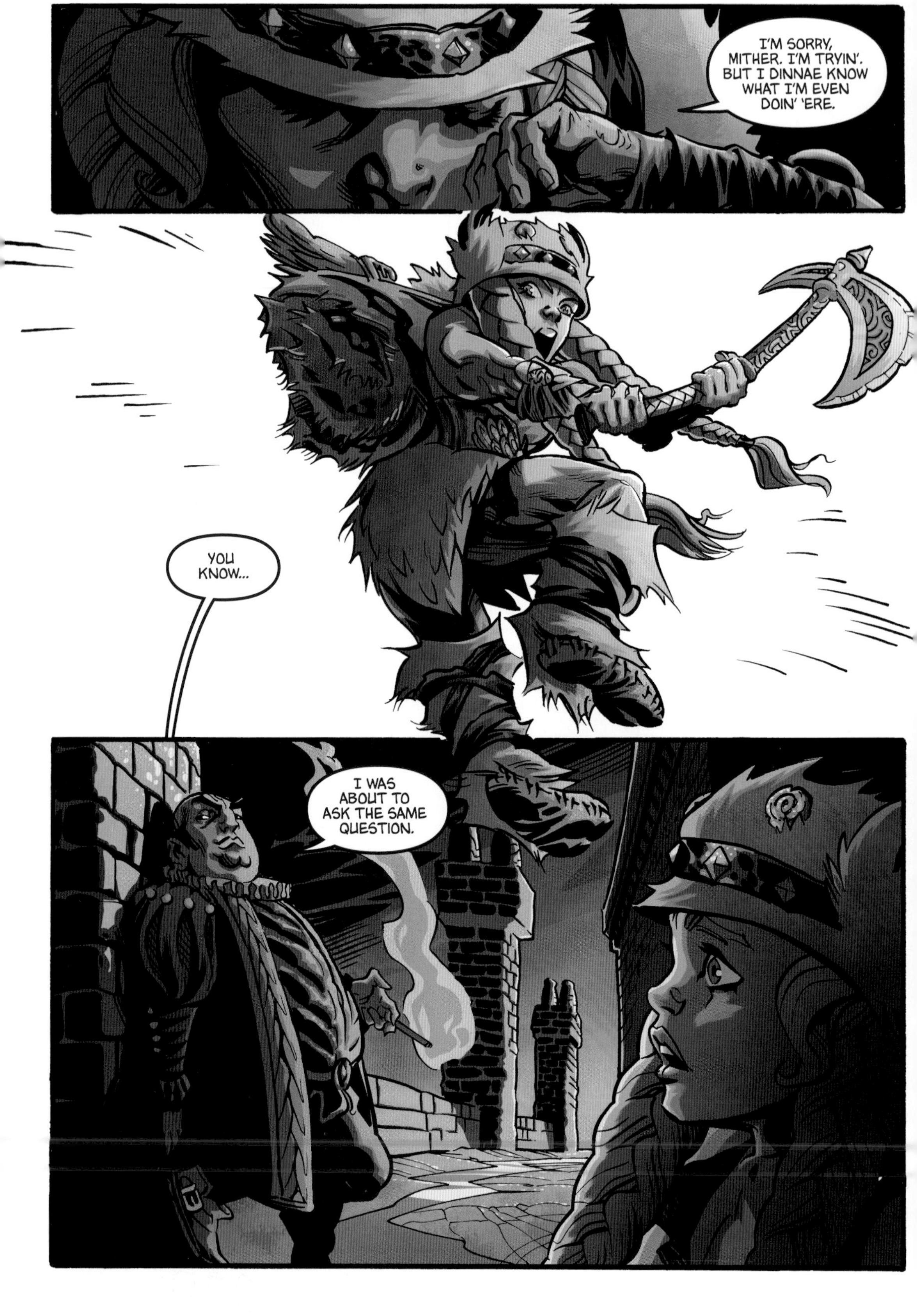
I'M SORRY, MITHER. I'M TRYIN'. BUT I DINNAE KNOW WHAT I'M EVEN DOIN' 'ERE.
YOU KNOW...
I WAS ABOUT TO ASK THE SAME QUESTION.

chapter 3

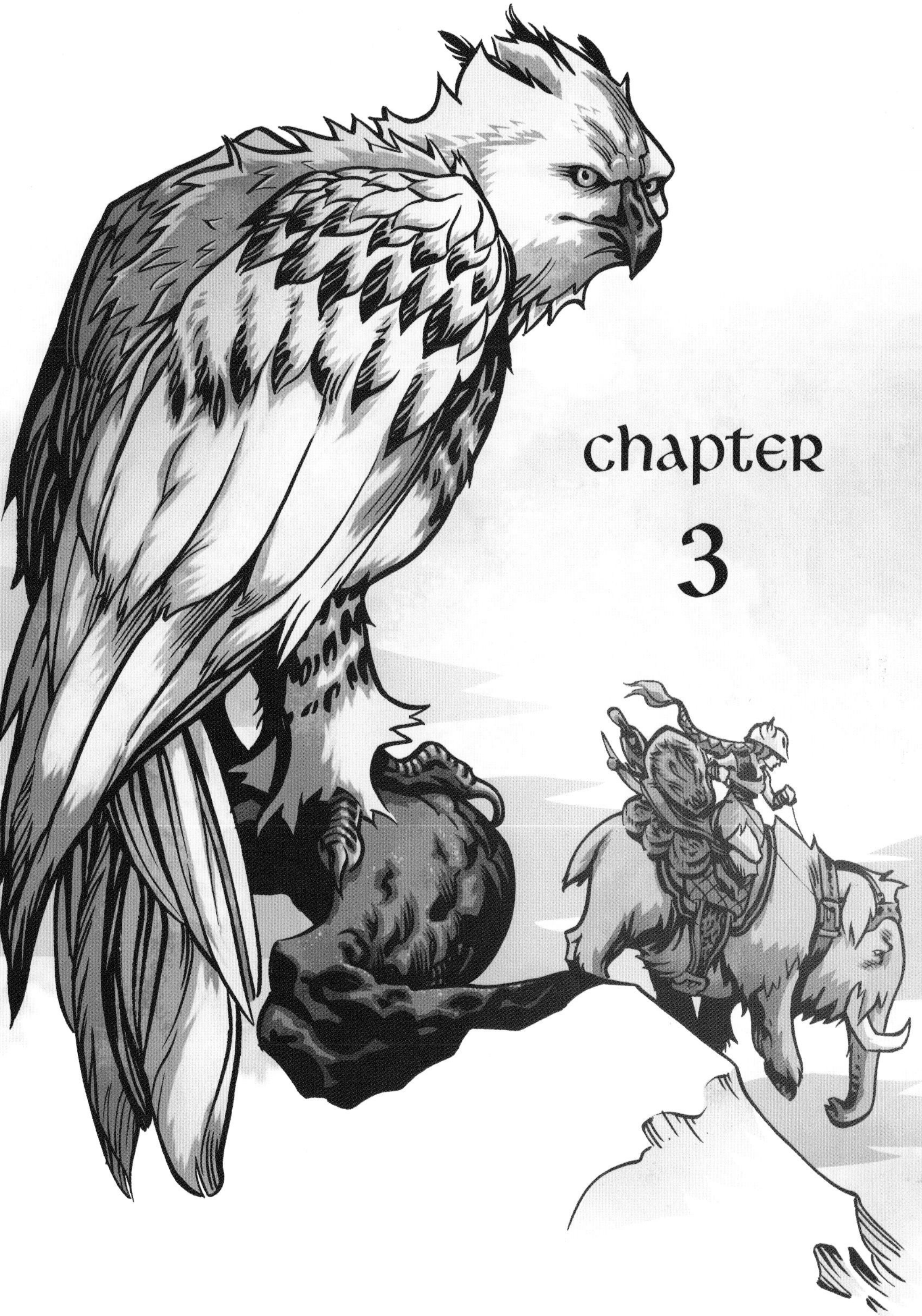

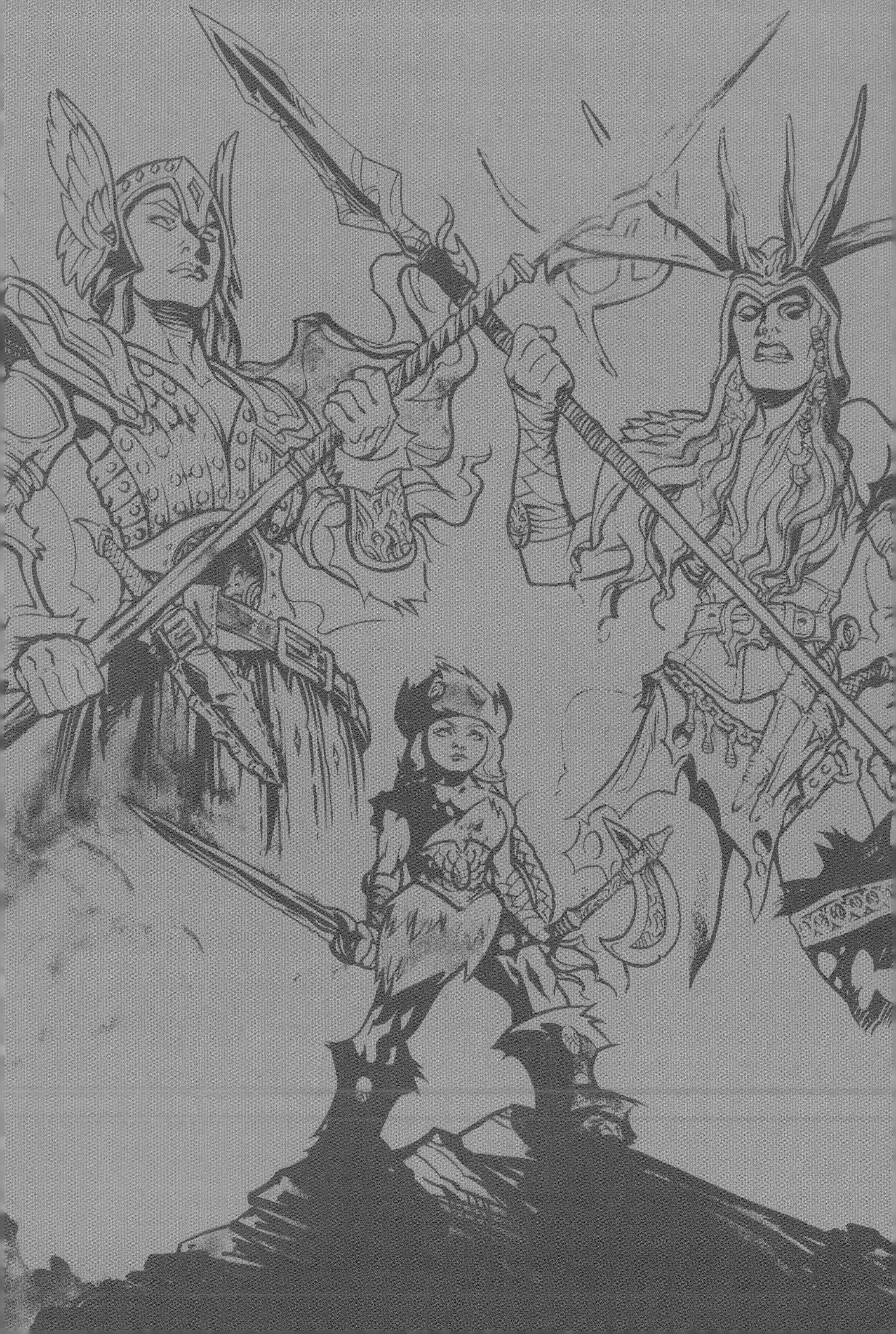

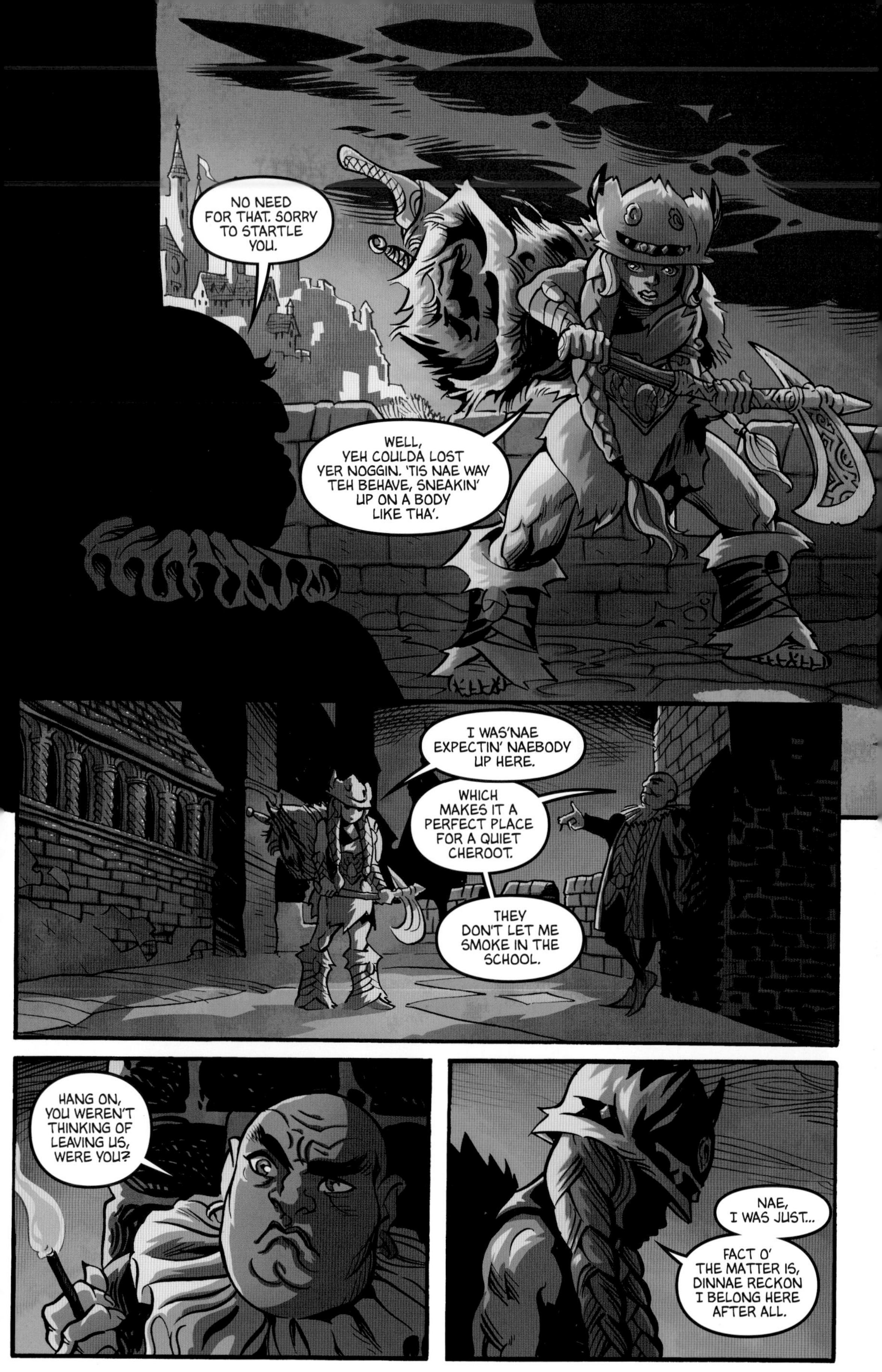
NO NEED FOR THAT. SORRY TO STARTLE YOU.
WELL, YEH COULDA LOST YER NOGGIN. 'TIS NAE WAY TEH BEHAVE, SNEAKIN' UP ON A BODY LIKE THA'.
I WAS'NAE EXPECTIN' NAEBODY UP HERE.
WHICH MAKES IT A PERFECT PLACE FOR A QUIET CHEROOT.
THEY DON'T LET ME SMOKE IN THE SCHOOL.
HANG ON, YOU WEREN'T THINKING OF LEAVING US, WERE YOU?
NAE, I WAS JUST...
FACT O' THE MATTER IS, DINNAE RECKON I BELONG HERE AFTER ALL.

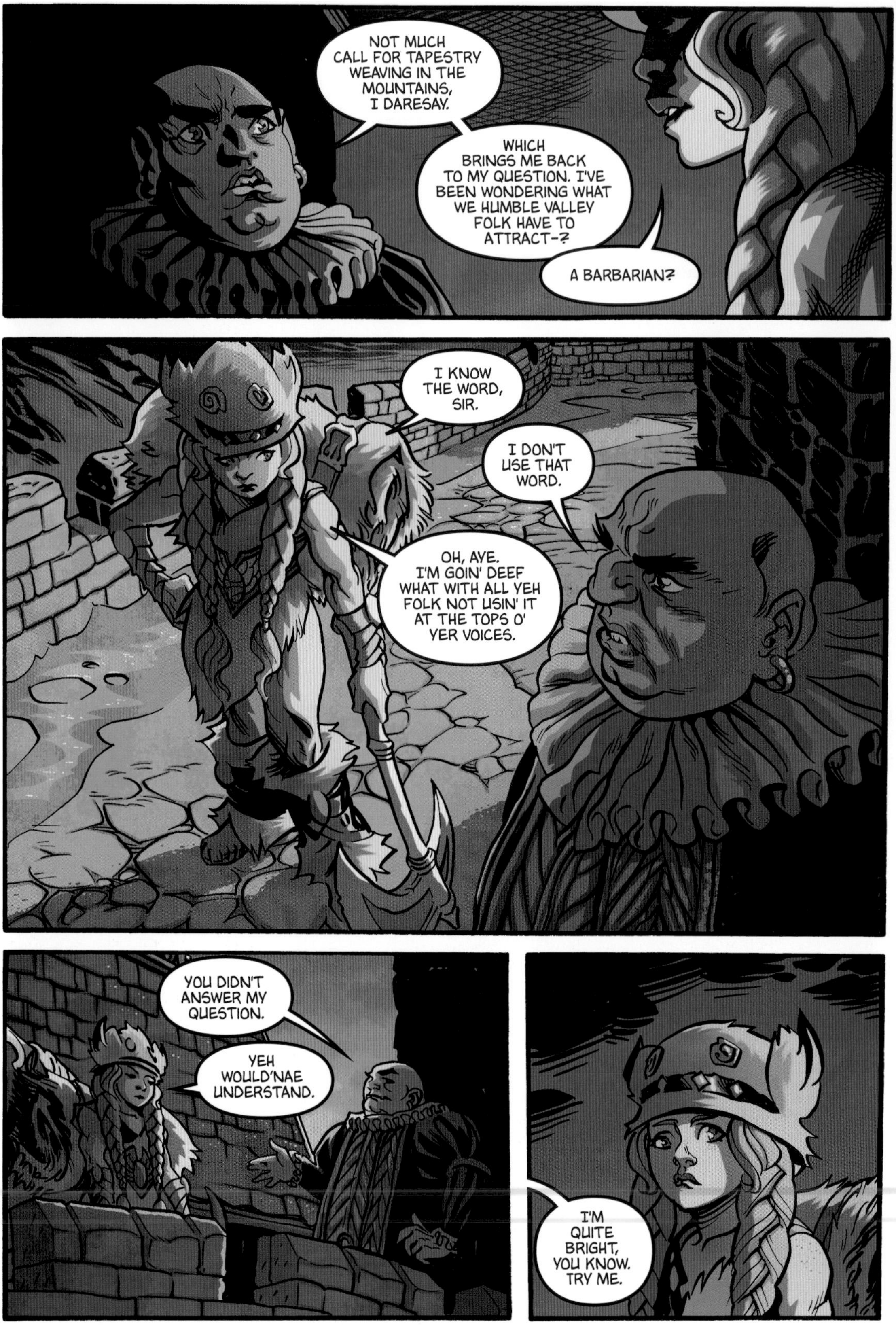
NOT MUCH CALL FOR TAPESTRY WEAVING IN THE MOUNTAINS, I DARESAY.
WHICH BRINGS ME BACK TO MY QUESTION. I'VE BEEN WONDERING WHAT WE HUMBLE VALLEY FOLK HAVE TO ATTRACT-?
A BARBARIAN?
I KNOW THE WORD, SIR.
I DON'T USE THAT WORD.
OH, AYE. I'M GOIN' DEEF WHAT WITH ALL YEH FOLK NOT USIN' IT AT THE TOPS O' YER VOICES.
YOU DIDN'T ANSWER MY QUESTION.
YEH WOULD'NAE UNDERSTAND.
I'M QUITE BRIGHT, YOU KNOW. TRY ME.

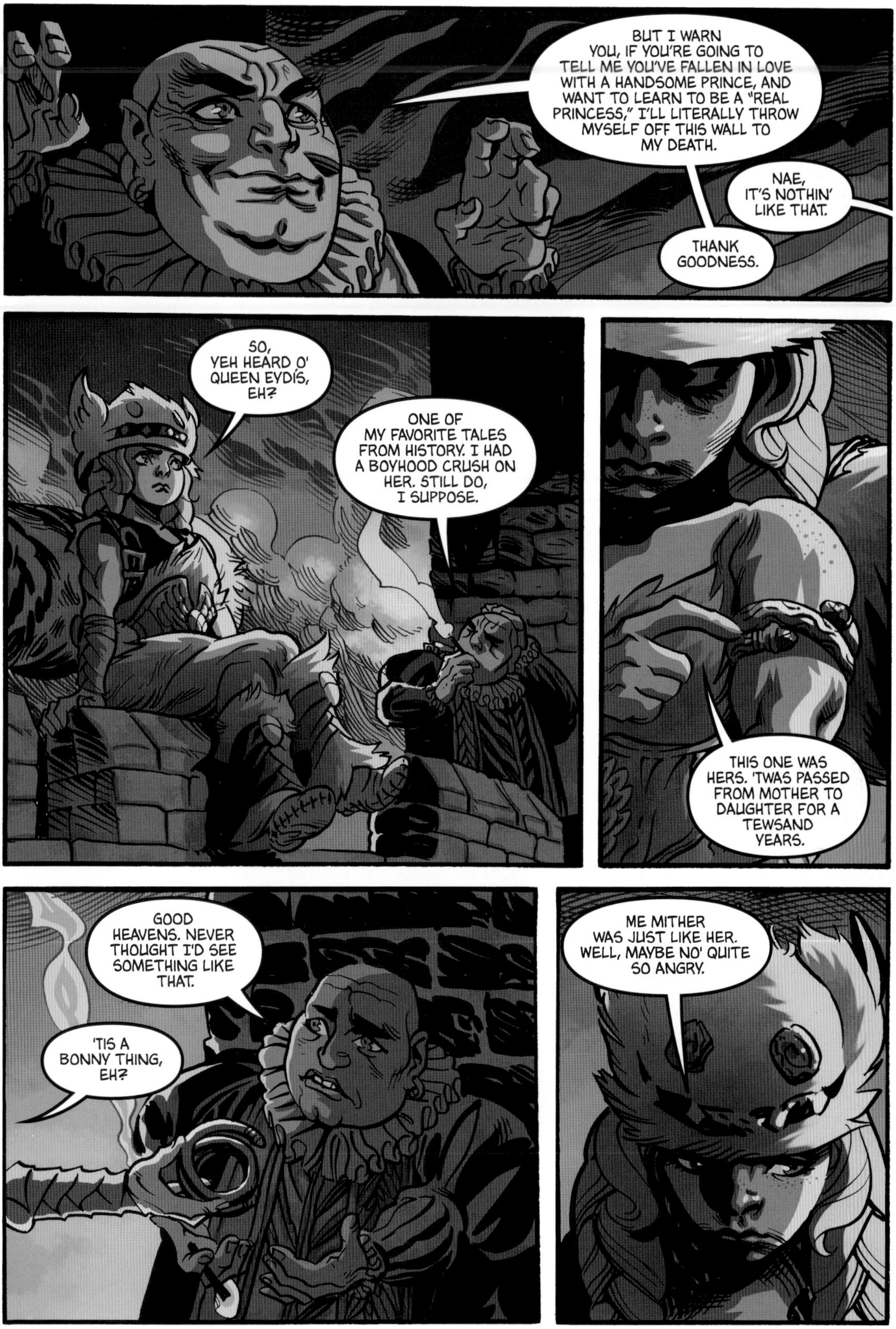
BUT I WARN YOU, IF YOU'RE GOING TO TELL ME YOU'VE FALLEN IN LOVE WITH A HANDSOME PRINCE, AND WANT TO LEARN TO BE A "REAL PRINCESS," I'LL LITERALLY THROW MYSELF OFF THIS WALL TO MY DEATH.
NAE, IT'S NOTHIN' LIKE THAT.
THANK GOODNESS.
SO, YEH HEARD O' QUEEN EYDÍS, EH?
ONE OF MY FAVORITE TALES FROM HISTORY. I HAD A BOYHOOD CRUSH ON HER. STILL DO, I SUPPOSE.
THIS ONE WAS HERS. 'TWAS PASSED FROM MOTHER TO DAUGHTER FOR A TEWSAND YEARS.
GOOD HEAVENS. NEVER THOUGHT I'D SEE SOMETHING LIKE THAT.
'TIS A BONNY THING, EH?
ME MITHER WAS JUST LIKE HER. WELL, MAYBE NO' QUITE SO ANGRY.

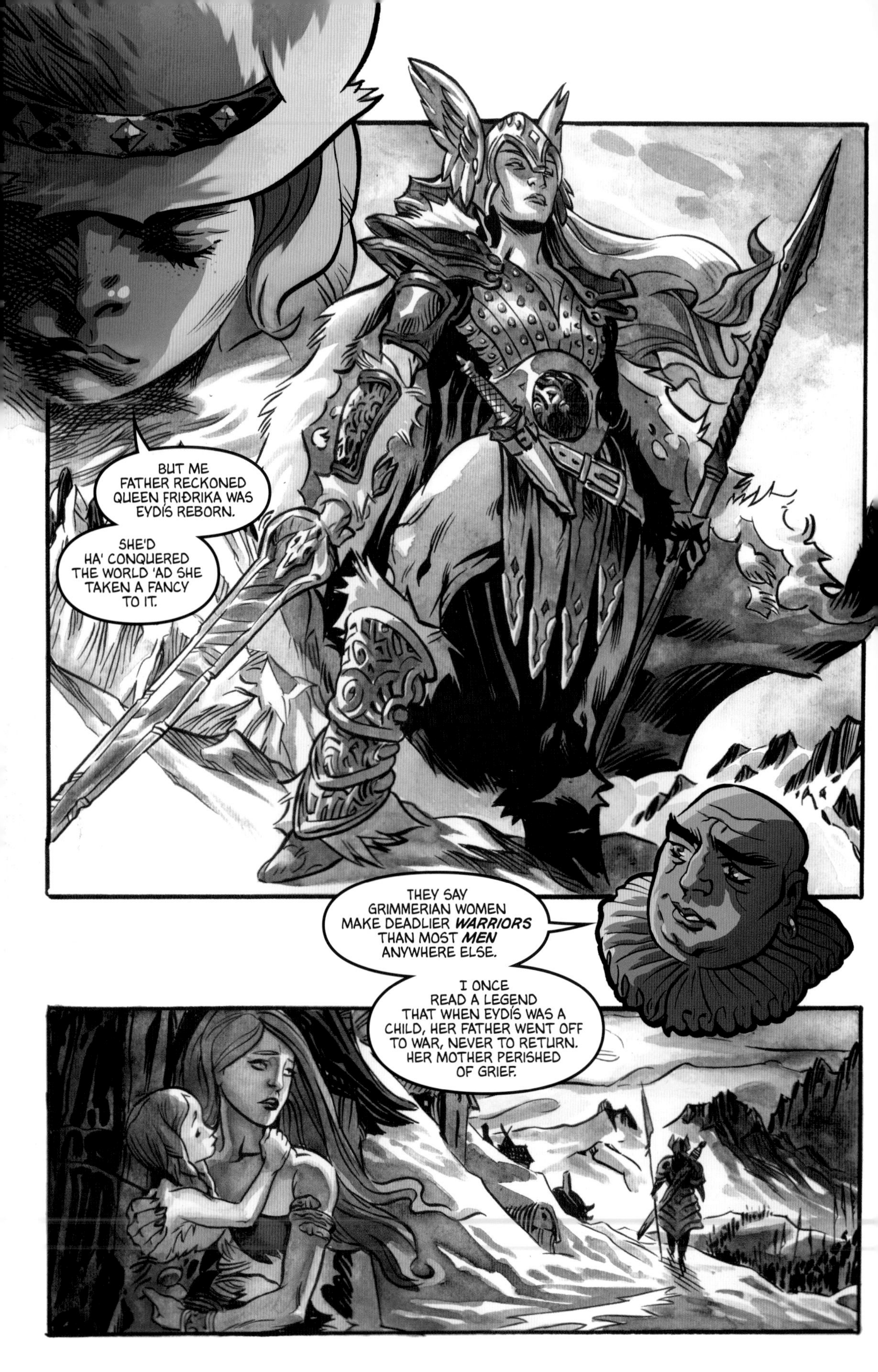
BUT ME FATHER RECKONED QUEEN FRIÐRIKA WAS EYDÍS REBORN.
SHE'D HA' CONQUERED THE WORLD 'AD SHE TAKEN A FANCY TO IT.
THEY SAY GRIMMERIAN WOMEN MAKE DEADLIER WARRIORS THAN MOST MEN ANYWHERE ELSE.
I ONCE READ A LEGEND THAT WHEN EYDÍS WAS A CHILD, HER FATHER WENT OFF TO WAR, NEVER TO RETURN. HER MOTHER PERISHED OF GRIEF.

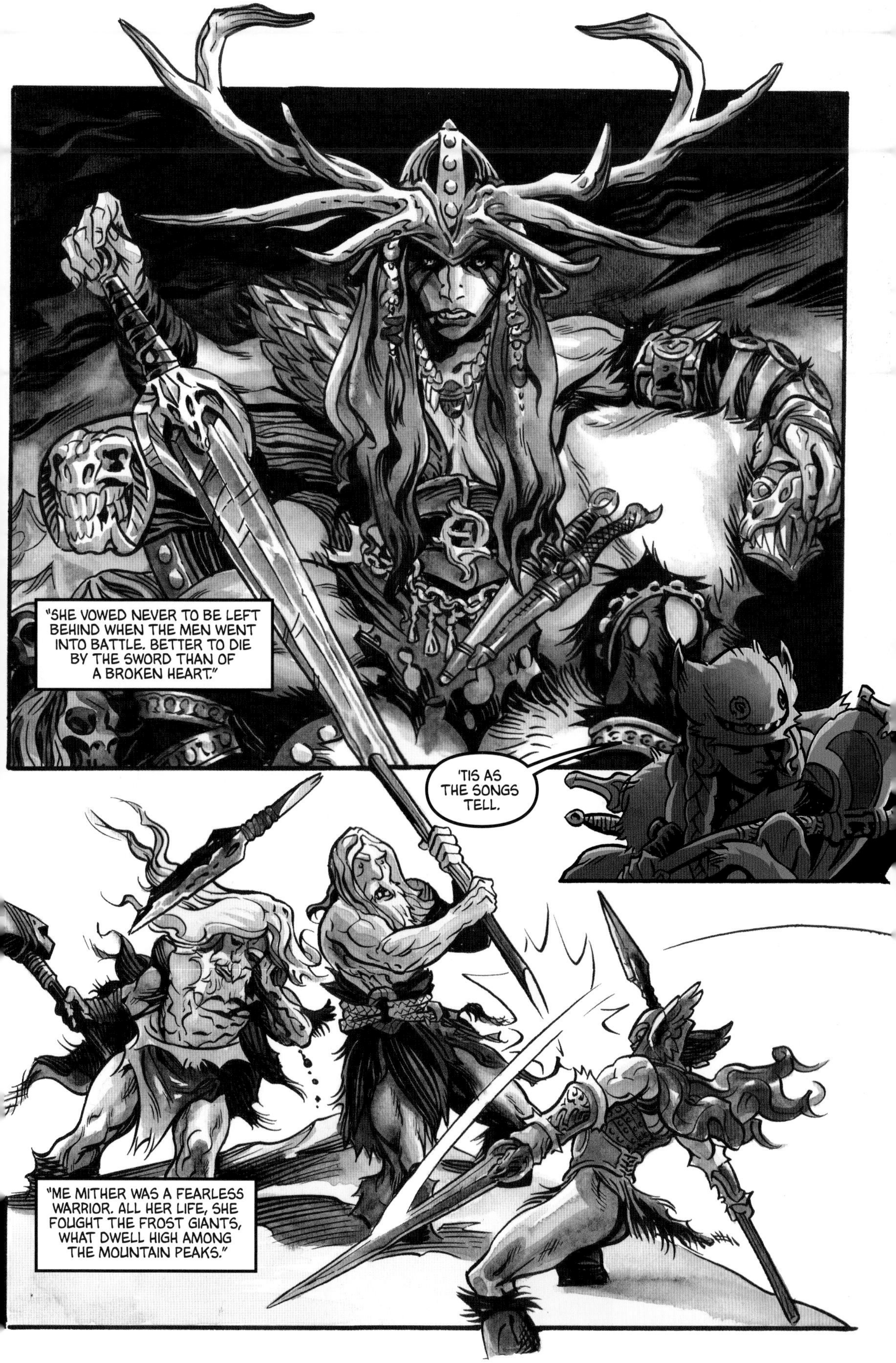
"SHE VOWED NEVER TO BE LEFT BEHIND WHEN THE MEN WENT INTO BATTLE. BETTER TO DIE BY THE SWORD THAN OF A BROKEN HEART."
'TIS AS THE SONGS TELL.
"ME MITHER WAS A FEARLESS WARRIOR. ALL HER LIFE, SHE FOUGHT THE FROST GIANTS, WHAT DWELL HIGH AMONG THE MOUNTAIN PEAKS."

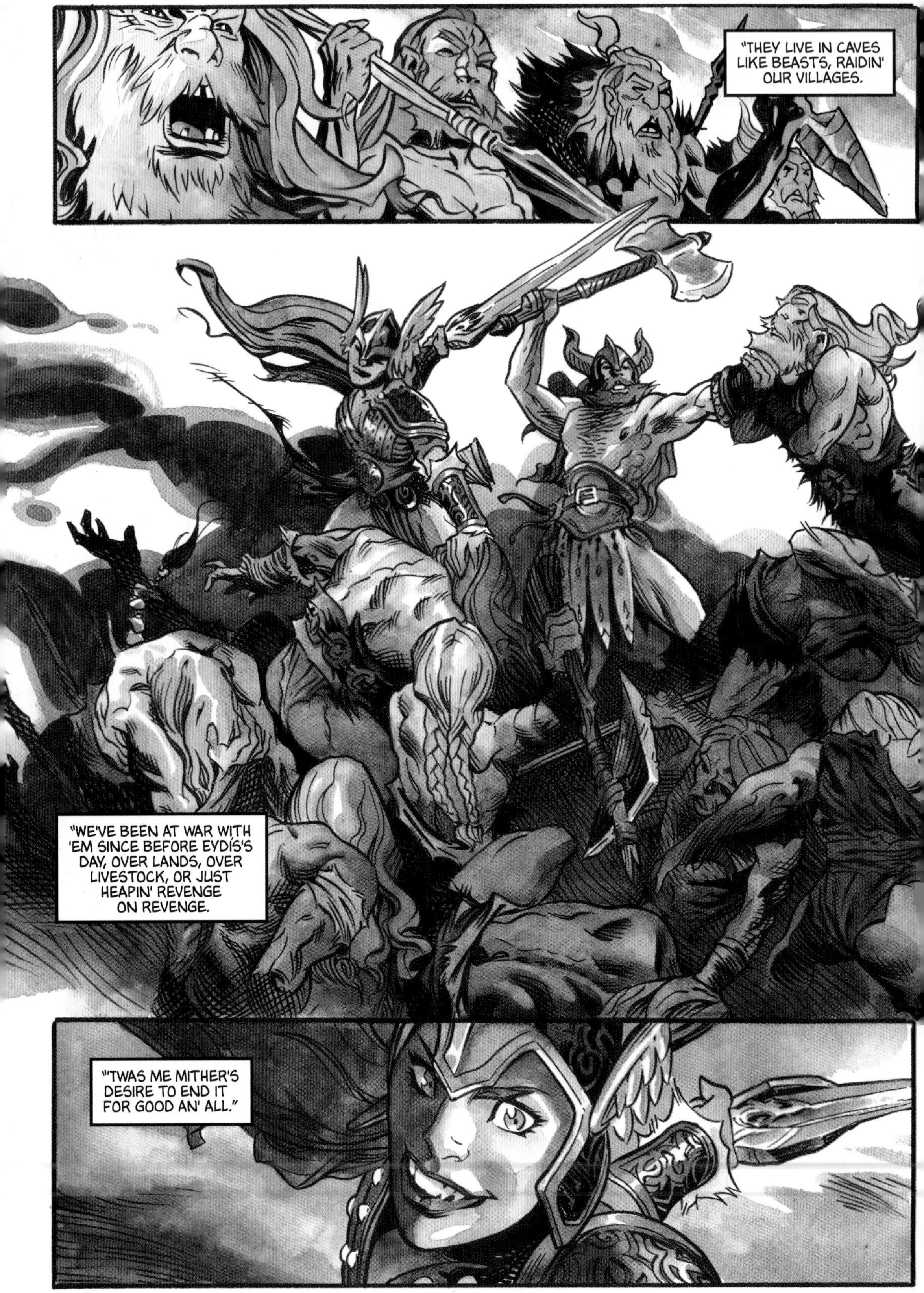
"THEY LIVE IN CAVES LIKE BEASTS, RAIDIN' OUR VILLAGES.
"WE'VE BEEN AT WAR WITH 'EM SINCE BEFORE EYDÍS'S DAY, OVER LANDS, OVER LIVESTOCK, OR JUST HEAPIN' REVENGE ON REVENGE.
"TWAS ME MITHER'S DESIRE TO END IT FOR GOOD AN' ALL."

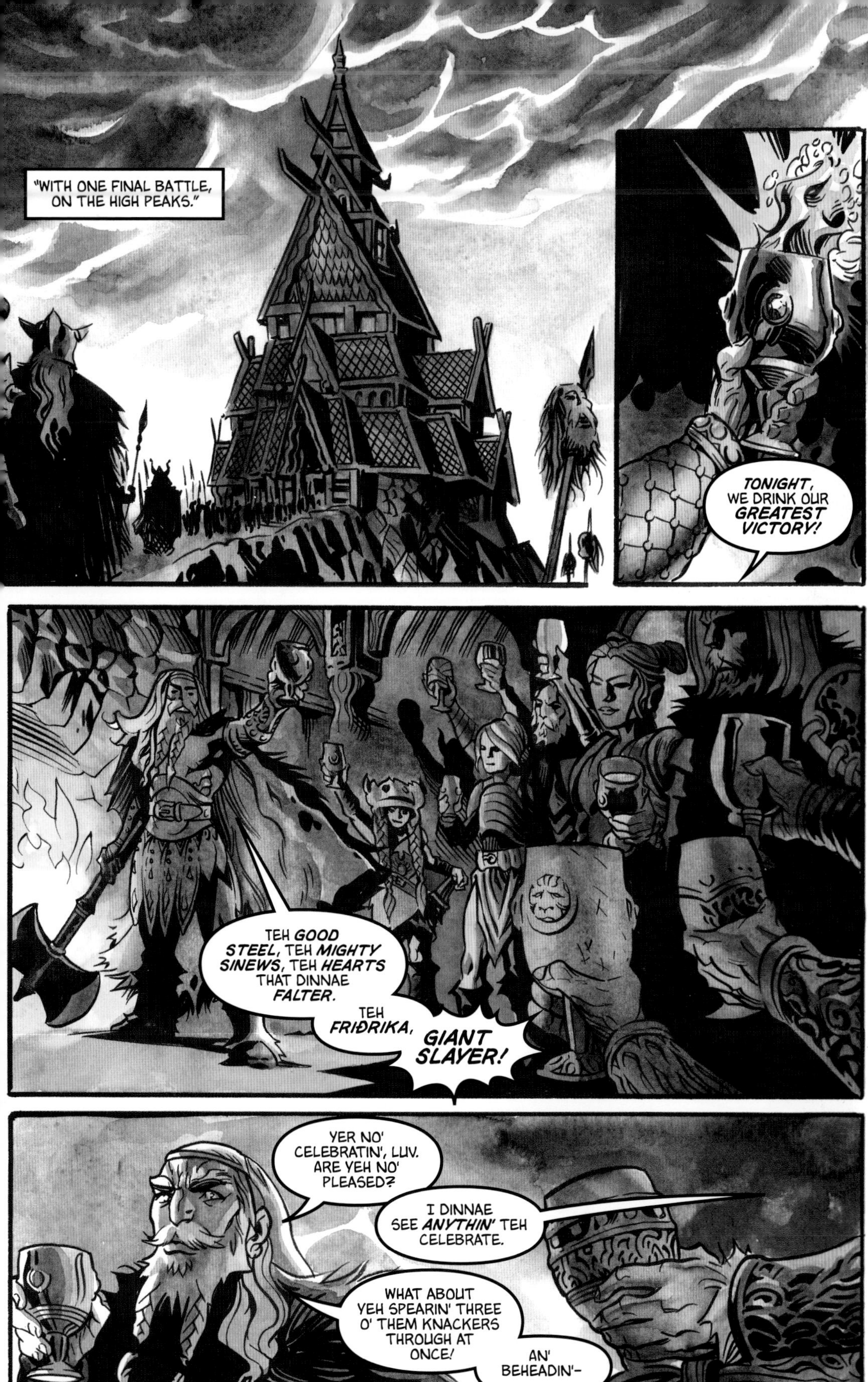
"WITH ONE FINAL BATTLE, ON THE HIGH PEAKS."
TONIGHT, WE DRINK OUR GREATEST VICTORY!
TEH GOOD STEEL, TEH MIGHTY SINEWS, TEH HEARTS THAT DINNAE FALTER.
TEH FRIÐRIKA,
GIANT SLAYER!
YER NO' CELEBRATIN', LUV. ARE YEH NO' PLEASED?
I DINNAE SEE ANYTHIN' TEH CELEBRATE.
WHAT ABOUT YEH SPEARIN' THREE O' THEM KNACKERS THROUGH AT ONCE!
AN' BEHEADIN'-

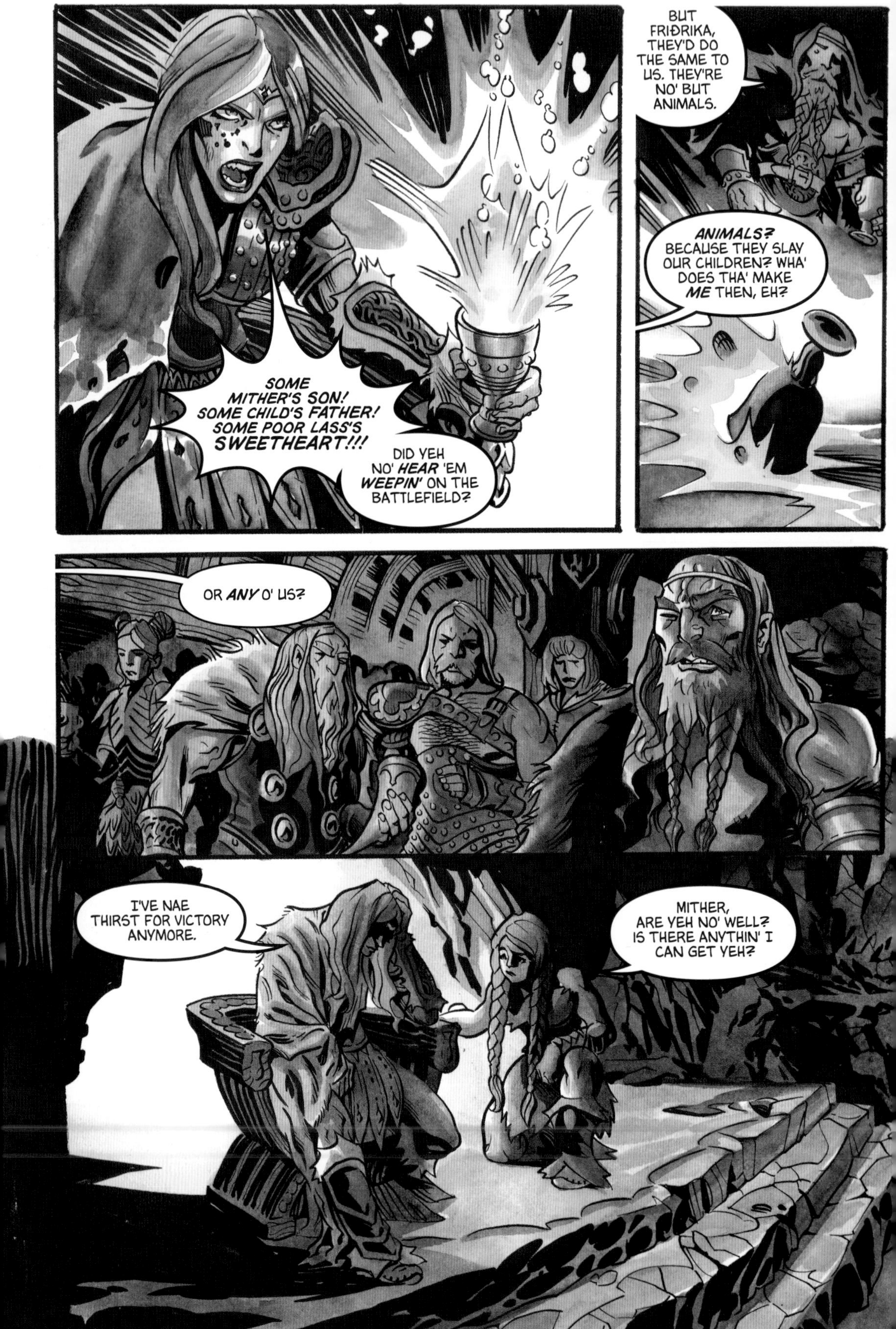
SOME MITHER'S SON! SOME CHILD'S FATHER! SOME POOR LASS'S SWEETHEART!!!
DID YEH NO' HEAR 'EM WEEPIN' ON THE BATTLEFIELD?
BUT FRIÐRIKA, THEY'D DO THE SAME TO US. THEY'RE NO' BUT ANIMALS.
ANIMALS? BECAUSE THEY SLAY OUR CHILDREN? WHA' DOES THA' MAKE ME THEN, EH?
OR ANY O' US?
I'VE NAE THIRST FOR VICTORY ANYMORE.
MITHER, ARE YEH NO' WELL? IS THERE ANYTHIN' I CAN GET YEH?

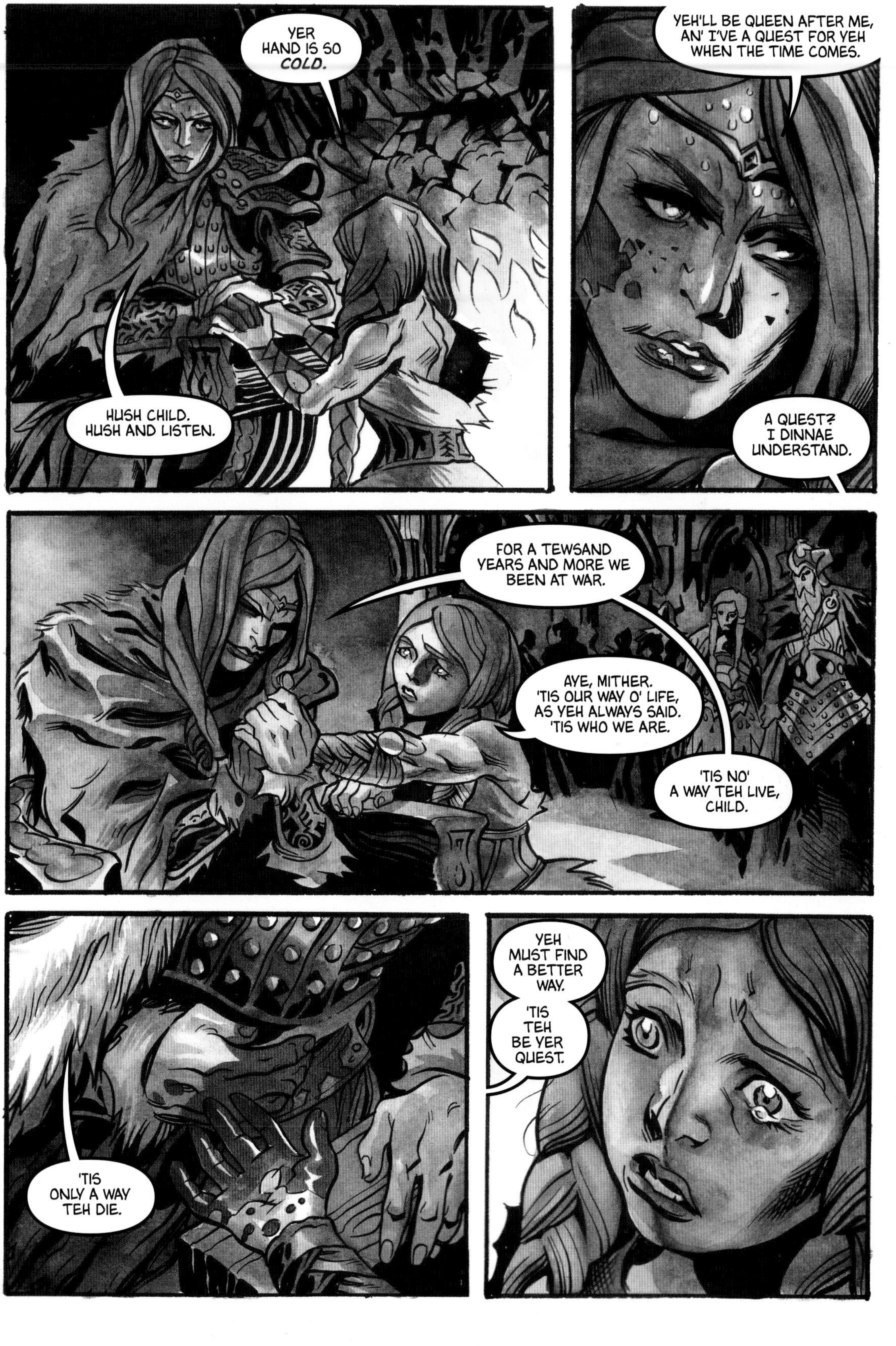
YER HAND IS SO *COLD.*
HUSH CHILD. HUSH AND LISTEN.
YEH'LL BE QUEEN AFTER ME, AN' I'VE A QUEST FOR YEH WHEN THE TIME COMES.
A QUEST? I DINNAE UNDERSTAND.
FOR A TEWSAND YEARS AND MORE WE BEEN AT WAR.
AYE, MITHER. 'TIS OUR WAY O' LIFE, AS YEH ALWAYS SAID. 'TIS WHO WE ARE.
'TIS NO' A WAY TEH LIVE, CHILD.
'TIS ONLY A WAY TEH DIE.
YEH MUST FIND A BETTER WAY.
'TIS TEH BE YER QUEST.

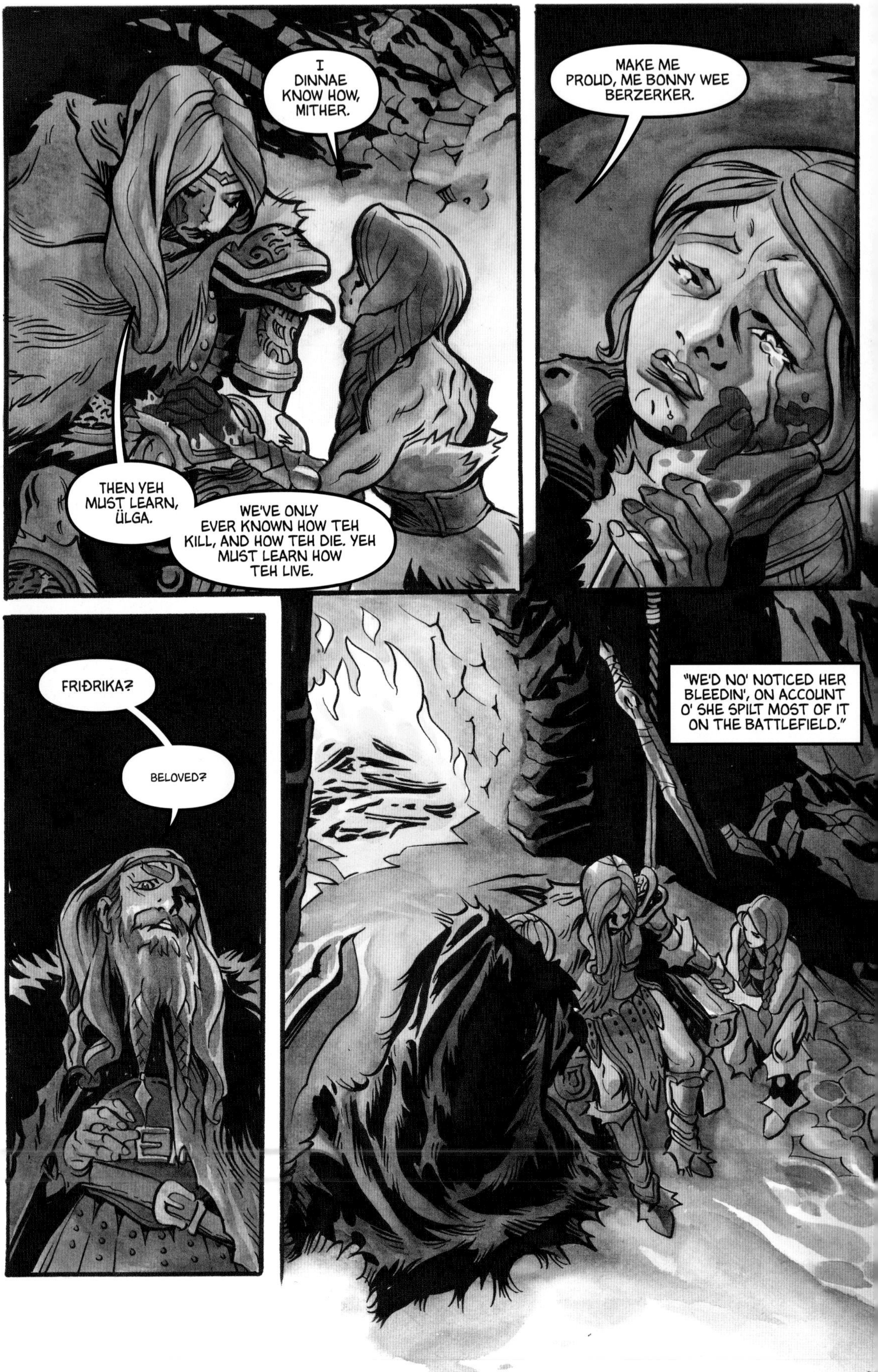
I DINNAE KNOW HOW, MITHER.
THEN YEH MUST LEARN, ÜLGA.
WE'VE ONLY EVER KNOWN HOW TEH KILL, AND HOW TEH DIE. YEH MUST LEARN HOW TEH LIVE.
MAKE ME PROUD, ME BONNY WEE BERZERKER.
FRIÐRIKA?
BELOVED?
"WE'D NO' NOTICED HER BLEEDIN', ON ACCOUNT O' SHE SPILT MOST OF IT ON THE BATTLEFIELD."

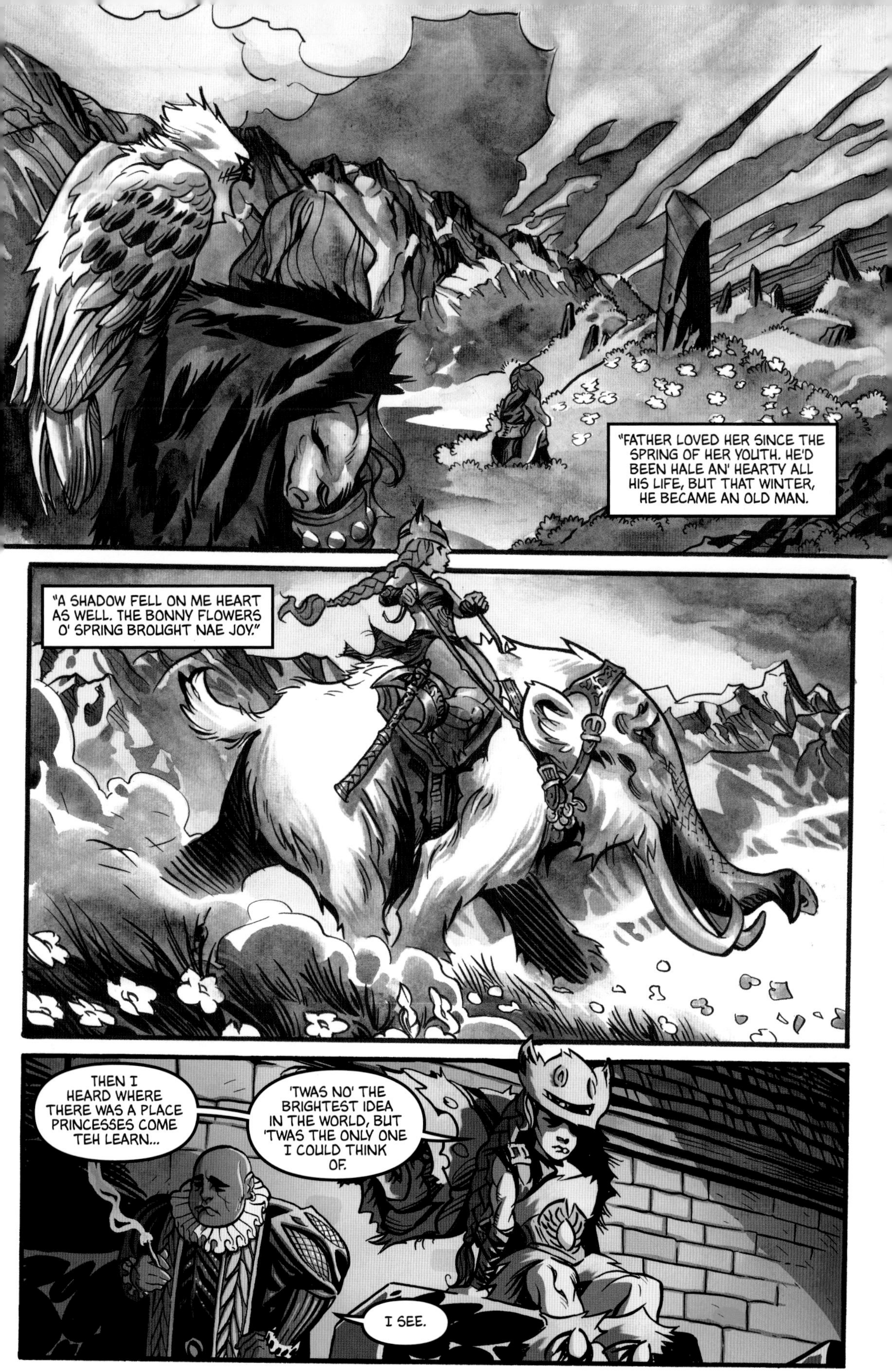
"FATHER LOVED HER SINCE THE SPRING OF HER YOUTH. HE'D BEEN HALE AN' HEARTY ALL HIS LIFE, BUT THAT WINTER, HE BECAME AN OLD MAN.
"A SHADOW FELL ON ME HEART AS WELL. THE BONNY FLOWERS O' SPRING BROUGHT NAE JOY."
THEN I HEARD WHERE THERE WAS A PLACE PRINCESSES COME TEH LEARN...
'TWAS NO' THE BRIGHTEST IDEA IN THE WORLD, BUT 'TWAS THE ONLY ONE I COULD THINK OF.
I SEE.

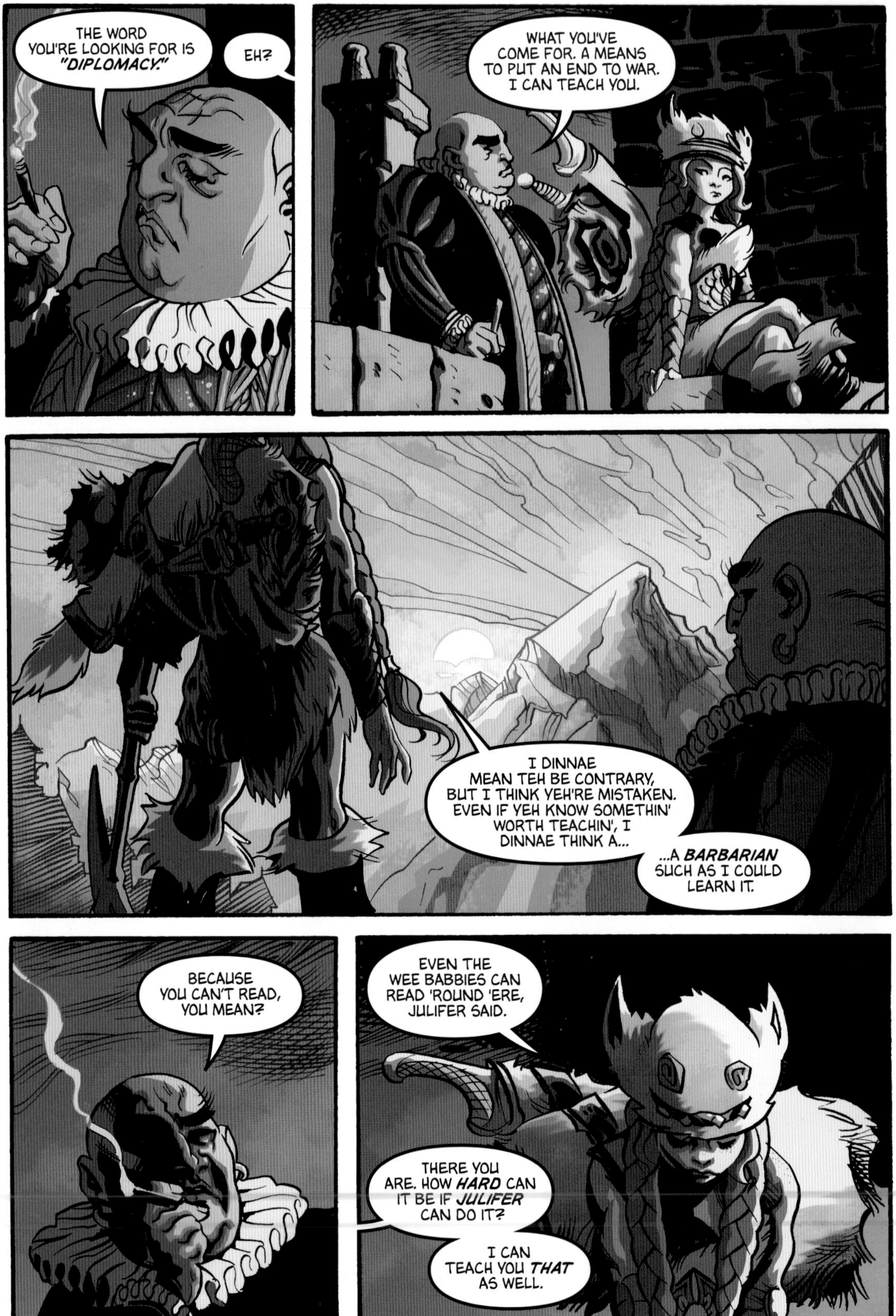

THE WORD YOU'RE LOOKING FOR IS "DIPLOMACY."
EH?
WHAT YOU'VE COME FOR. A MEANS TO PUT AN END TO WAR. I CAN TEACH YOU.
I DINNAE MEAN TEH BE CONTRARY, BUT I THINK YEH'RE MISTAKEN. EVEN IF YEH KNOW SOMETHIN' WORTH TEACHIN', I DINNAE THINK A...
...A BARBARIAN SUCH AS I COULD LEARN IT.
BECAUSE YOU CAN'T READ, YOU MEAN?
EVEN THE WEE BABBIES CAN READ 'ROUND 'ERE, JULIFER SAID.
THERE YOU ARE. HOW HARD CAN IT BE IF JULIFER CAN DO IT?
I CAN TEACH YOU THAT AS WELL.

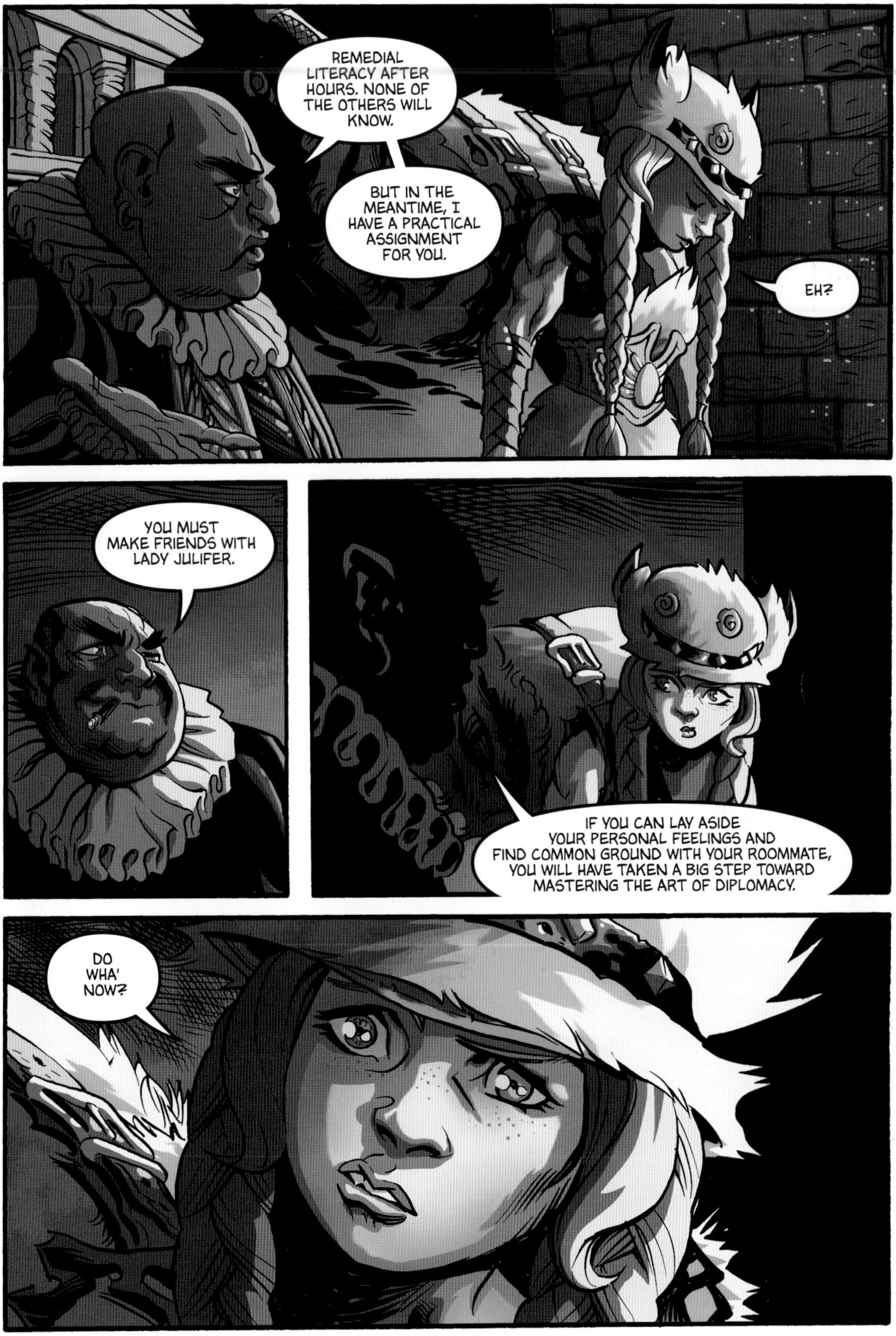
REMEDIAL LITERACY AFTER HOURS. NONE OF THE OTHERS WILL KNOW.
BUT IN THE MEANTIME, I HAVE A PRACTICAL ASSIGNMENT FOR YOU.
EH?
YOU MUST MAKE FRIENDS WITH LADY JULIFER.
IF YOU CAN LAY ASIDE YOUR PERSONAL FEELINGS AND FIND COMMON GROUND WITH YOUR ROOMMATE, YOU WILL HAVE TAKEN A BIG STEP TOWARD MASTERING THE ART OF DIPLOMACY.
DO WHA' NOW?

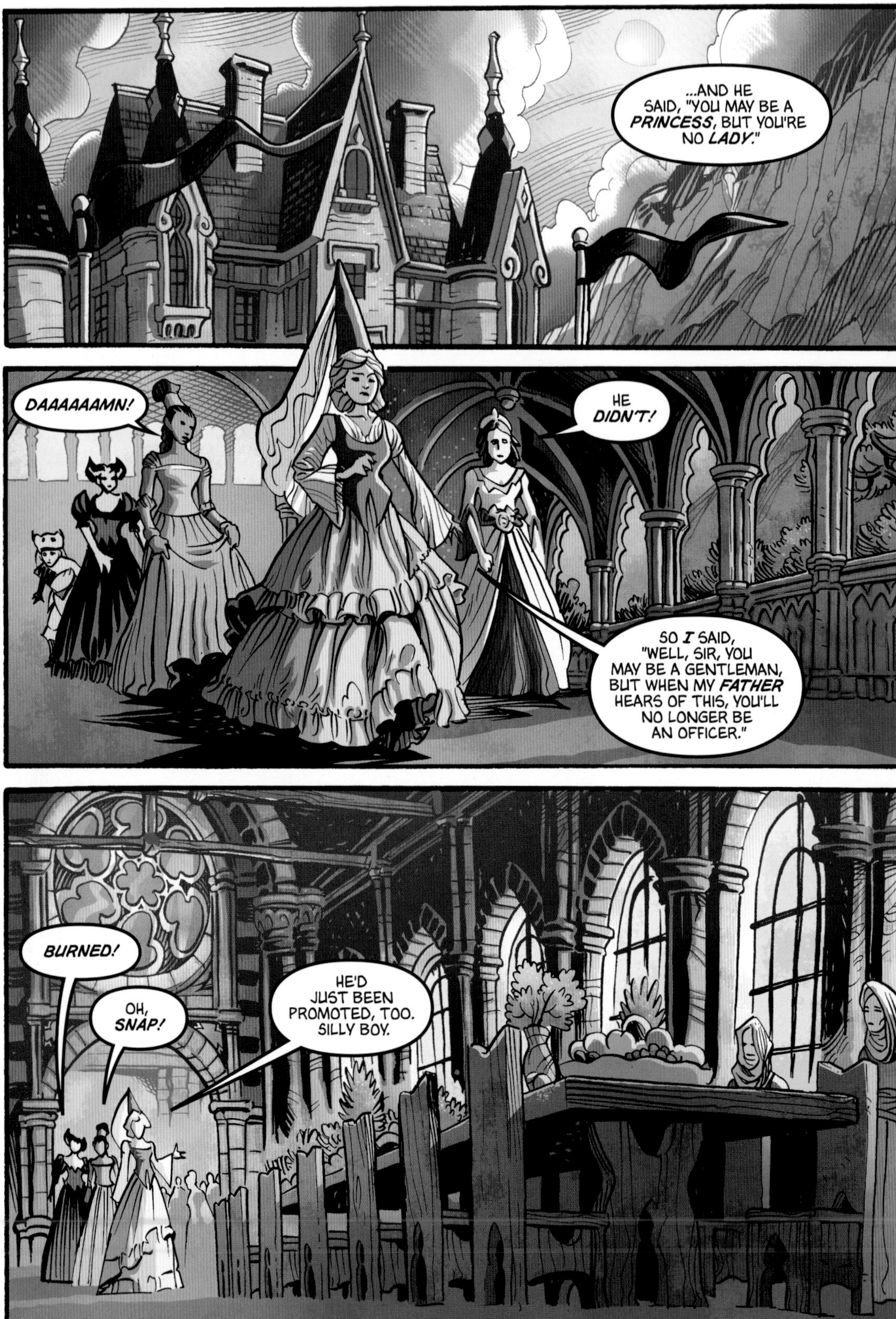
...AND HE SAID, "YOU MAY BE A *PRINCESS*, BUT YOU'RE NO *LADY*."
DAAAAAAMN!
HE *DIDN'T!*
SO *I* SAID, "WELL, SIR, YOU MAY BE A GENTLEMAN, BUT WHEN MY *FATHER* HEARS OF THIS, YOU'LL NO LONGER BE AN OFFICER."
BURNED!
OH, *SNAP!*
HE'D JUST BEEN PROMOTED, TOO. SILLY BOY.

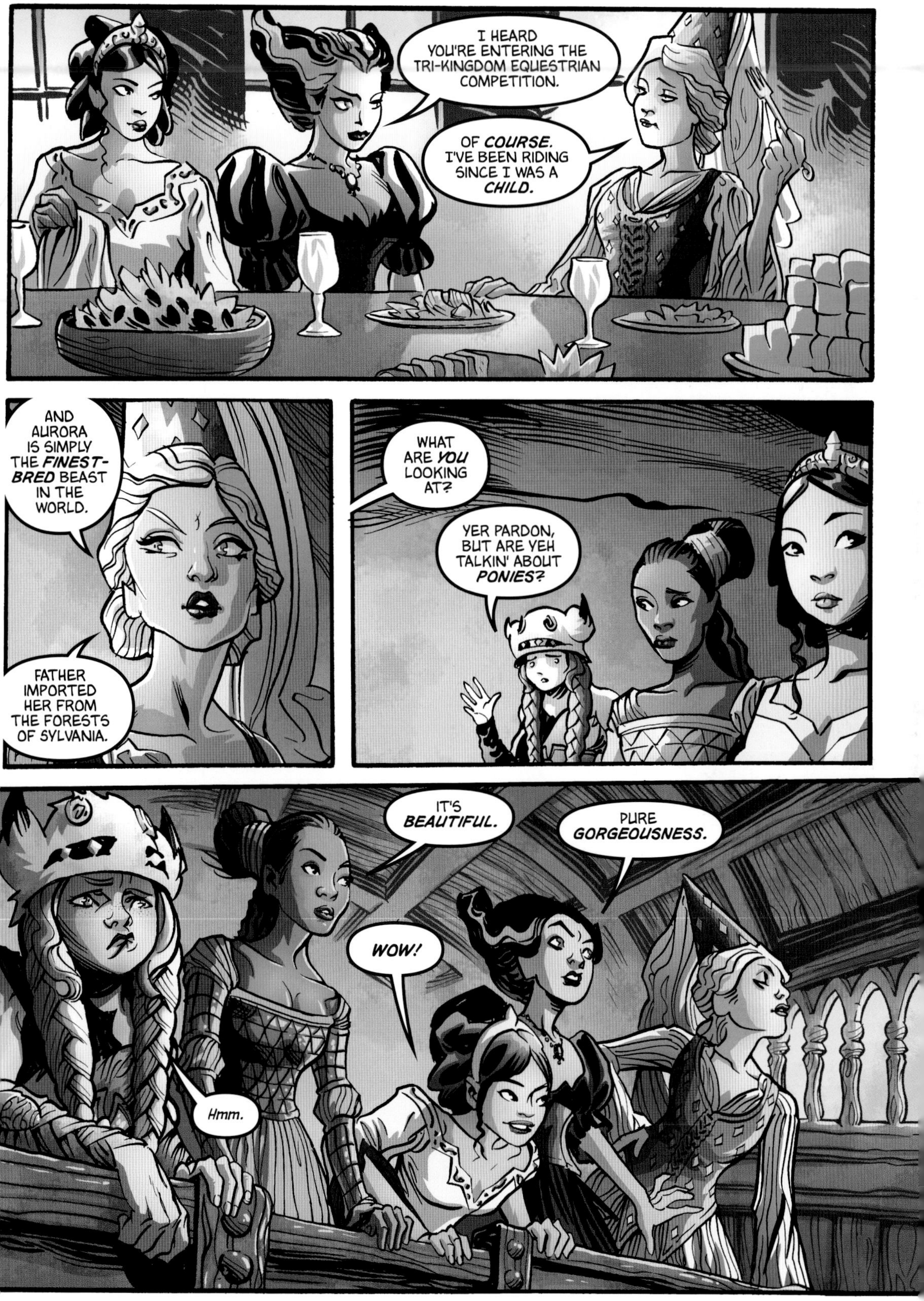
I HEARD YOU'RE ENTERING THE TRI-KINGDOM EQUESTRIAN COMPETITION.
OF *COURSE.* I'VE BEEN RIDING SINCE I WAS A *CHILD.*
AND AURORA IS SIMPLY THE *FINEST-BRED* BEAST IN THE WORLD.
FATHER IMPORTED HER FROM THE FORESTS OF SYLVANIA.
WHAT ARE *YOU* LOOKING AT?
YER PARDON, BUT ARE YEH TALKIN' ABOUT *PONIES?*
IT'S *BEAUTIFUL.*
PURE *GORGEOUSNESS.*
WOW!
Hmm.

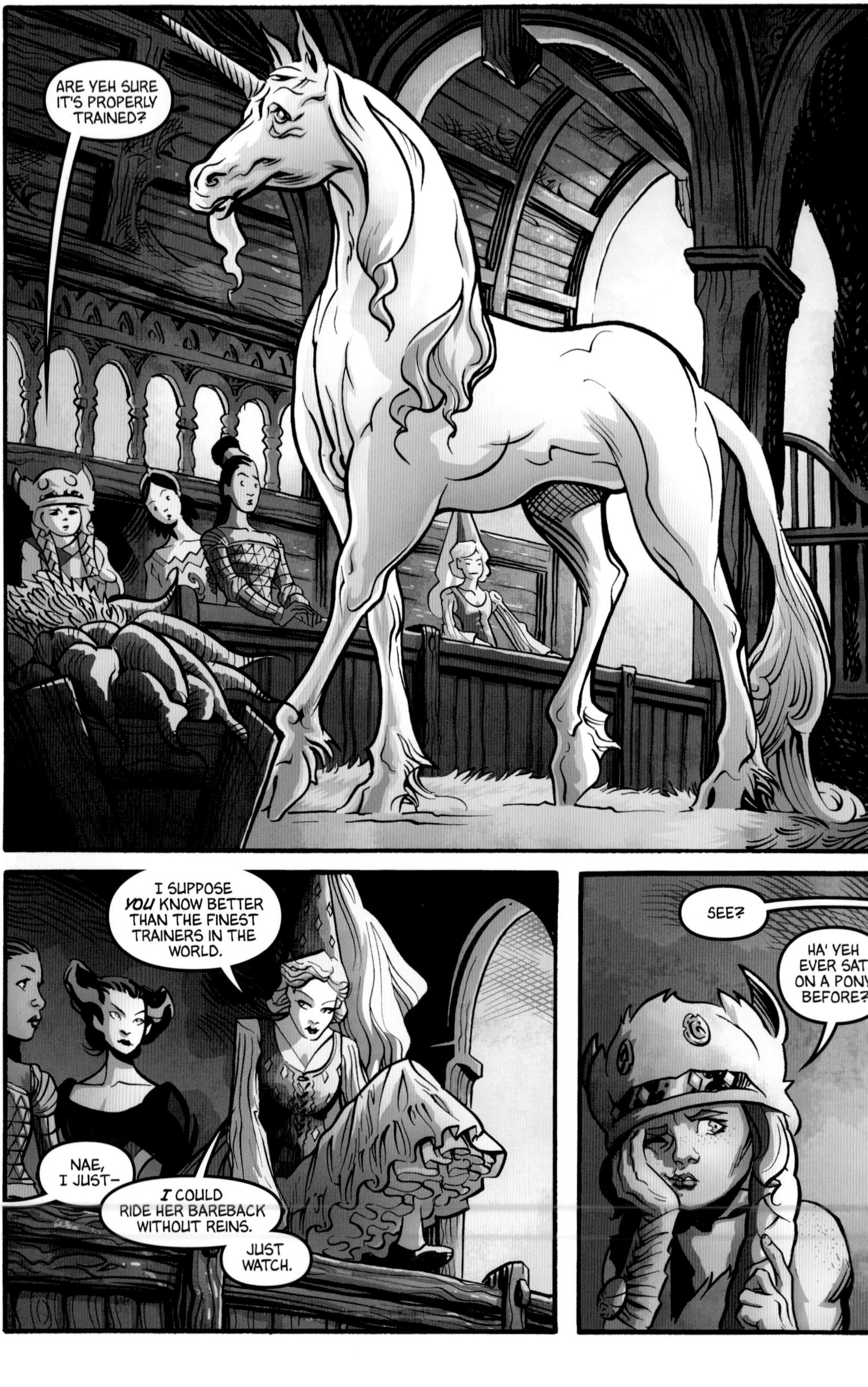
ARE YEH SURE IT'S PROPERLY TRAINED?
I SUPPOSE *YOU* KNOW BETTER THAN THE FINEST TRAINERS IN THE WORLD.
NAE, I JUST—
I COULD RIDE HER BAREBACK WITHOUT REINS.
JUST WATCH.
SEE?
HA' YEH EVER SAT ON A PONY BEFORE?

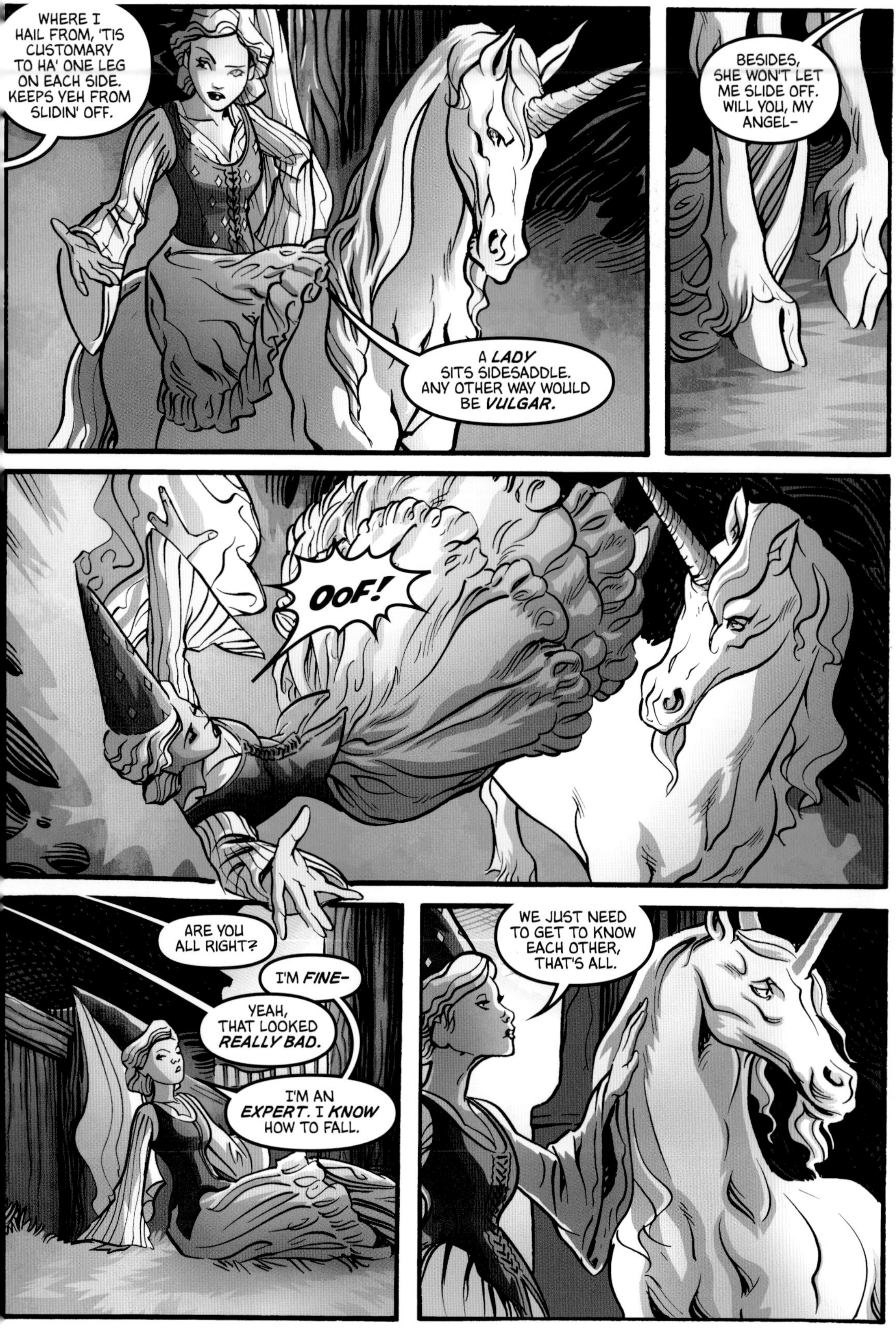
WHERE I HAIL FROM, 'TIS CUSTOMARY TO HA' ONE LEG ON EACH SIDE. KEEPS YEH FROM SLIDIN' OFF.
A LADY SITS SIDESADDLE. ANY OTHER WAY WOULD BE VULGAR.
BESIDES, SHE WON'T LET ME SLIDE OFF. WILL YOU, MY ANGEL-
OOF!
ARE YOU ALL RIGHT?
I'M FINE-
YEAH, THAT LOOKED REALLY BAD.
I'M AN EXPERT. I KNOW HOW TO FALL.
WE JUST NEED TO GET TO KNOW EACH OTHER, THAT'S ALL.

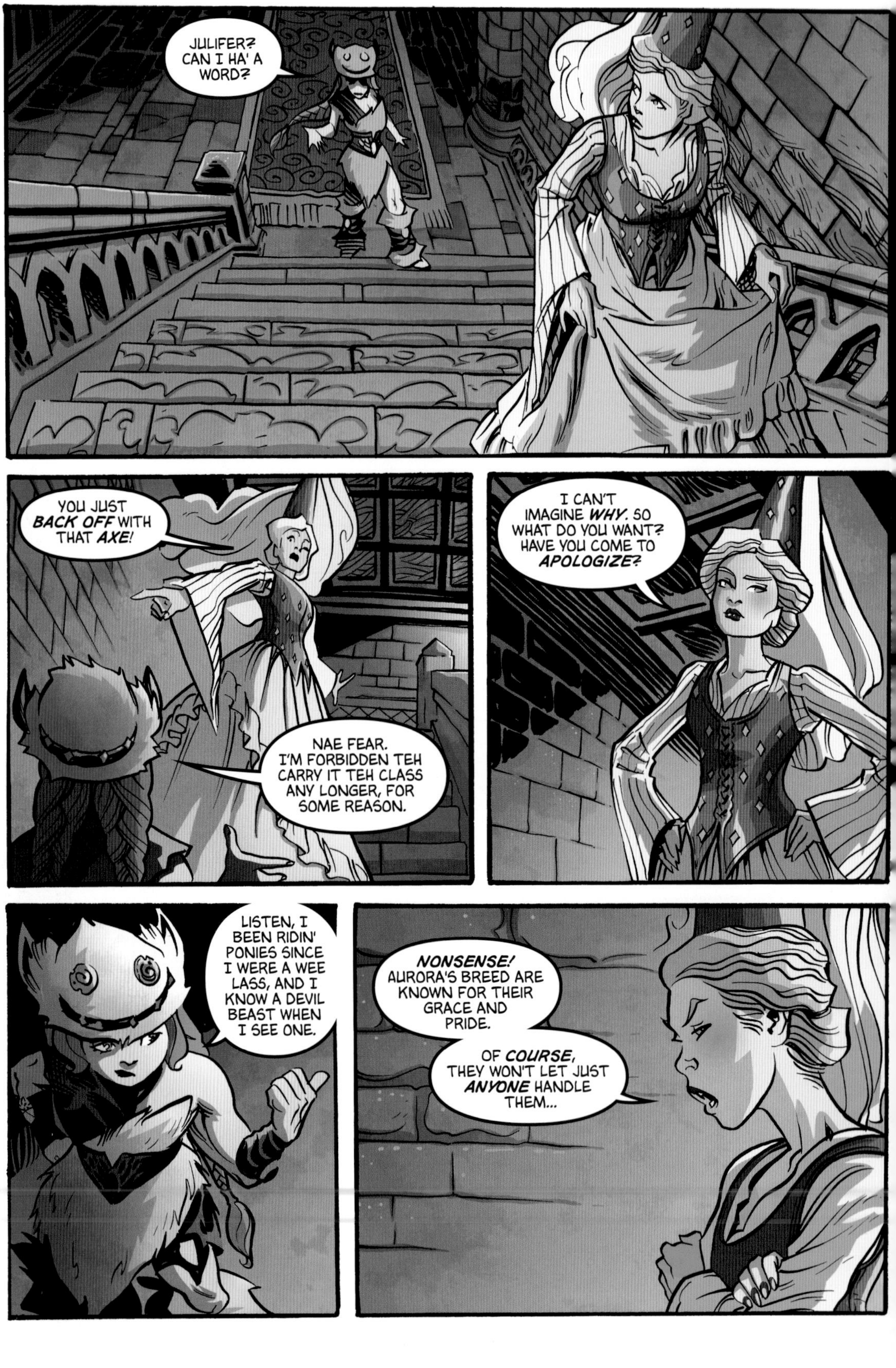
JULIFER? CAN I HA' A WORD?
YOU JUST BACK OFF WITH THAT AXE!
NAE FEAR. I'M FORBIDDEN TEH CARRY IT TEH CLASS ANY LONGER, FOR SOME REASON.
I CAN'T IMAGINE WHY. SO WHAT DO YOU WANT? HAVE YOU COME TO APOLOGIZE?
LISTEN, I BEEN RIDIN' PONIES SINCE I WERE A WEE LASS, AND I KNOW A DEVIL BEAST WHEN I SEE ONE.
NONSENSE! AURORA'S BREED ARE KNOWN FOR THEIR GRACE AND PRIDE.
OF COURSE, THEY WON'T LET JUST ANYONE HANDLE THEM...

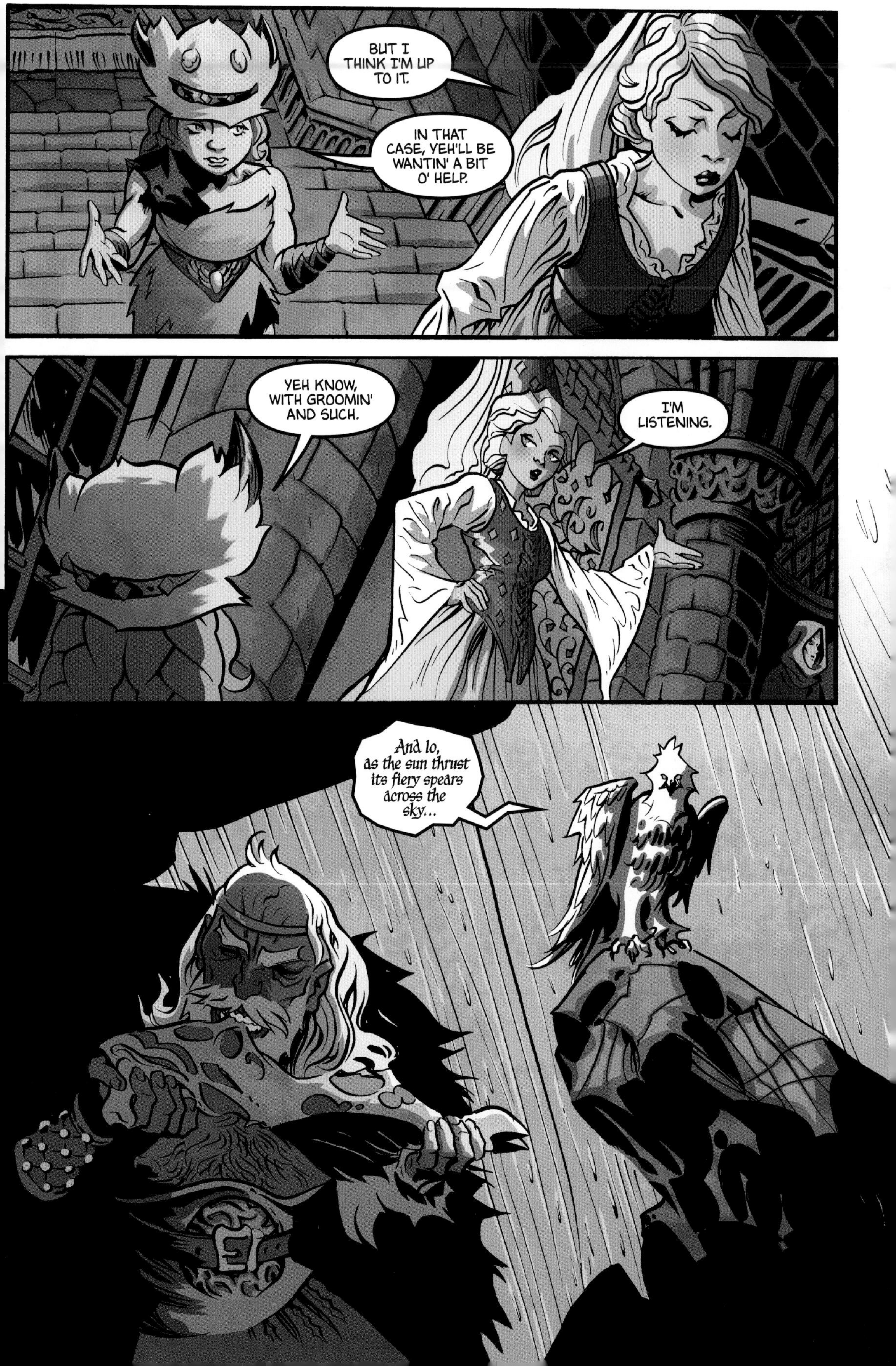
BUT I THINK I'M UP TO IT.
IN THAT CASE, YEH'LL BE WANTIN' A BIT O' HELP.
YEH KNOW, WITH GROOMIN' AND SUCH.
I'M LISTENING.
And lo, as the sun thrust its fiery spears across the sky...

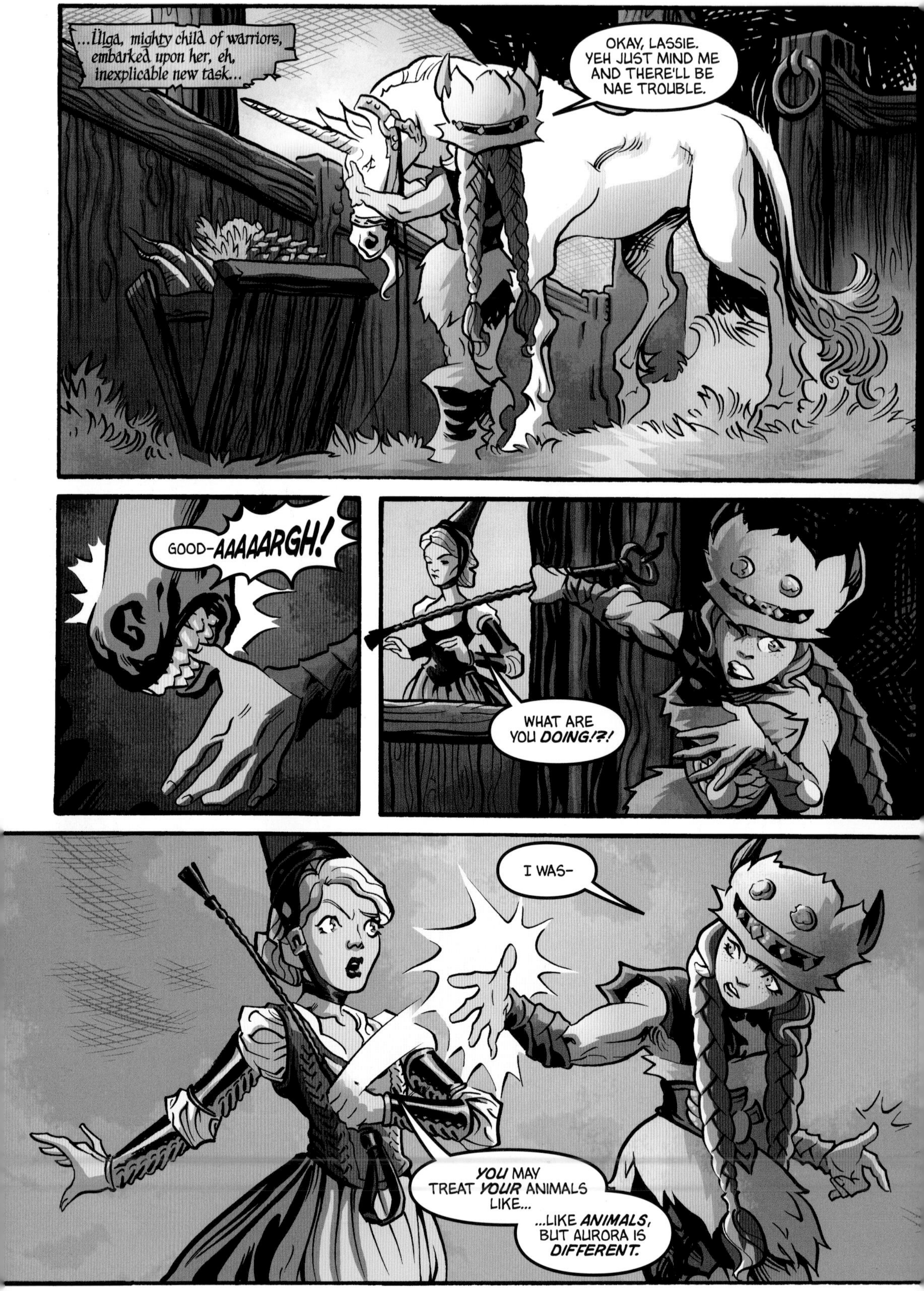
...Ulga, mighty child of warriors, embarked upon her, eh, inexplicable new task...
OKAY, LASSIE. YEH JUST MIND ME AND THERE'LL BE NAE TROUBLE.
GOOD-AAAAARGH!
WHAT ARE YOU DOING!?!
I WAS-
YOU MAY TREAT YOUR ANIMALS LIKE...
...LIKE ANIMALS, BUT AURORA IS DIFFERENT.

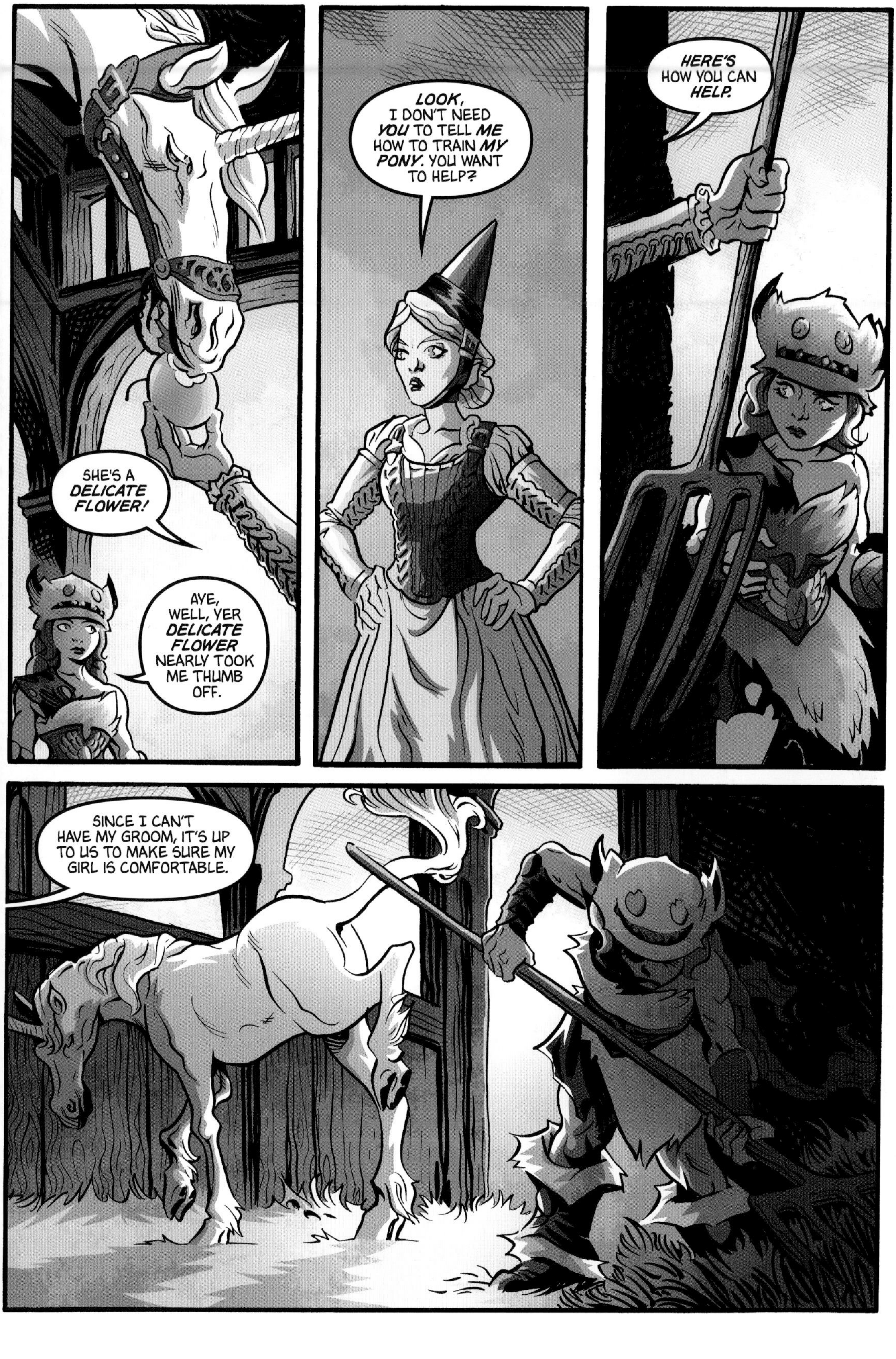
SHE'S A *DELICATE FLOWER!*
AYE, WELL, YER *DELICATE FLOWER* NEARLY TOOK ME THUMB OFF.
LOOK, I DON'T NEED *YOU* TO TELL *ME* HOW TO TRAIN *MY PONY.* YOU WANT TO HELP?
HERE'S HOW YOU CAN *HELP.*
SINCE I CAN'T HAVE MY GROOM, IT'S UP TO US TO MAKE SURE MY GIRL IS COMFORTABLE.

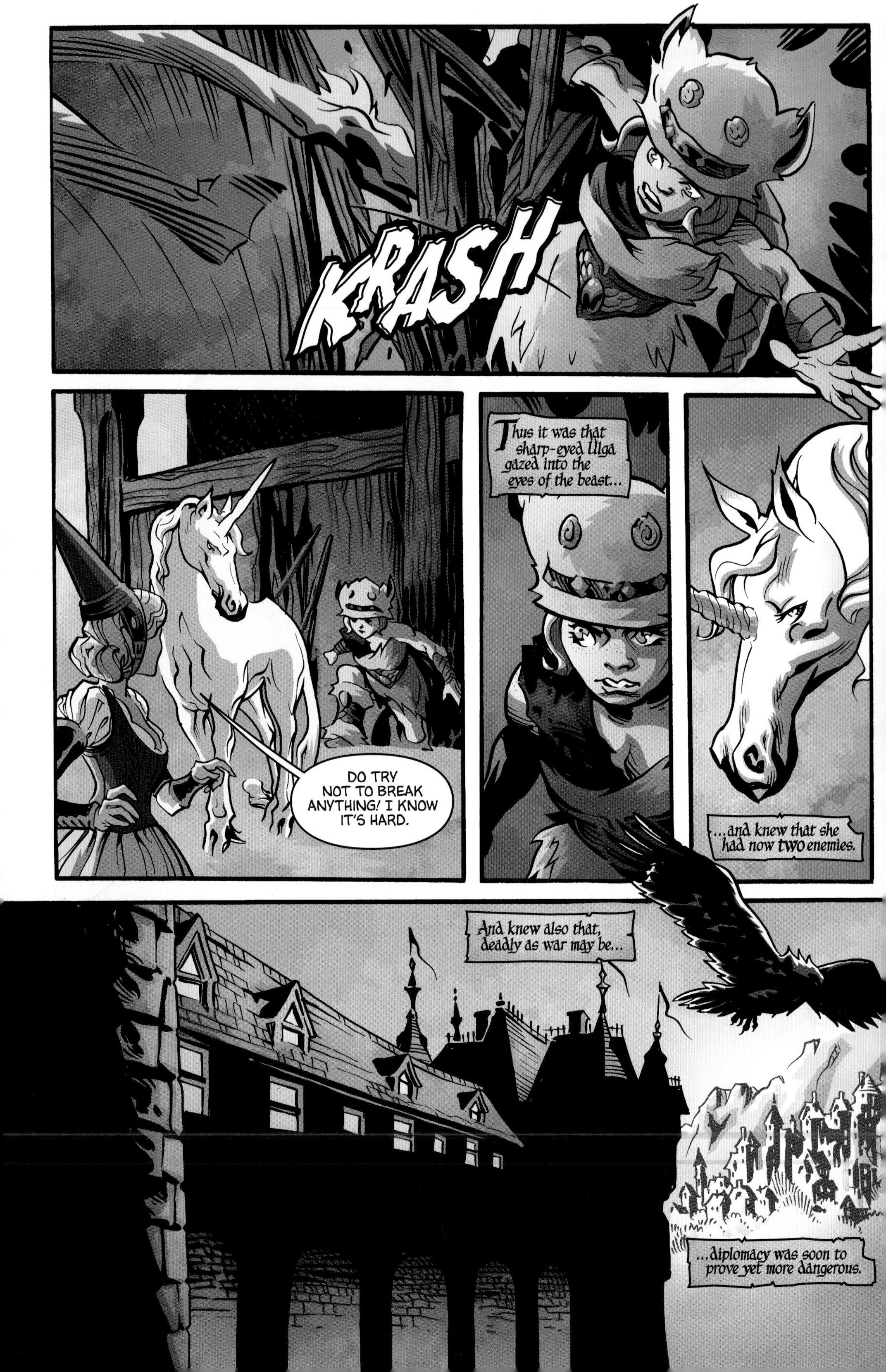
KRASH
DO TRY NOT TO BREAK ANYTHING! I KNOW IT'S HARD.
Thus it was that sharp-eyed Ulga gazed into the eyes of the beast...
...and knew that she had now two enemies.
And knew also that, deadly as war may be...
...diplomacy was soon to prove yet more dangerous.

chapter 4

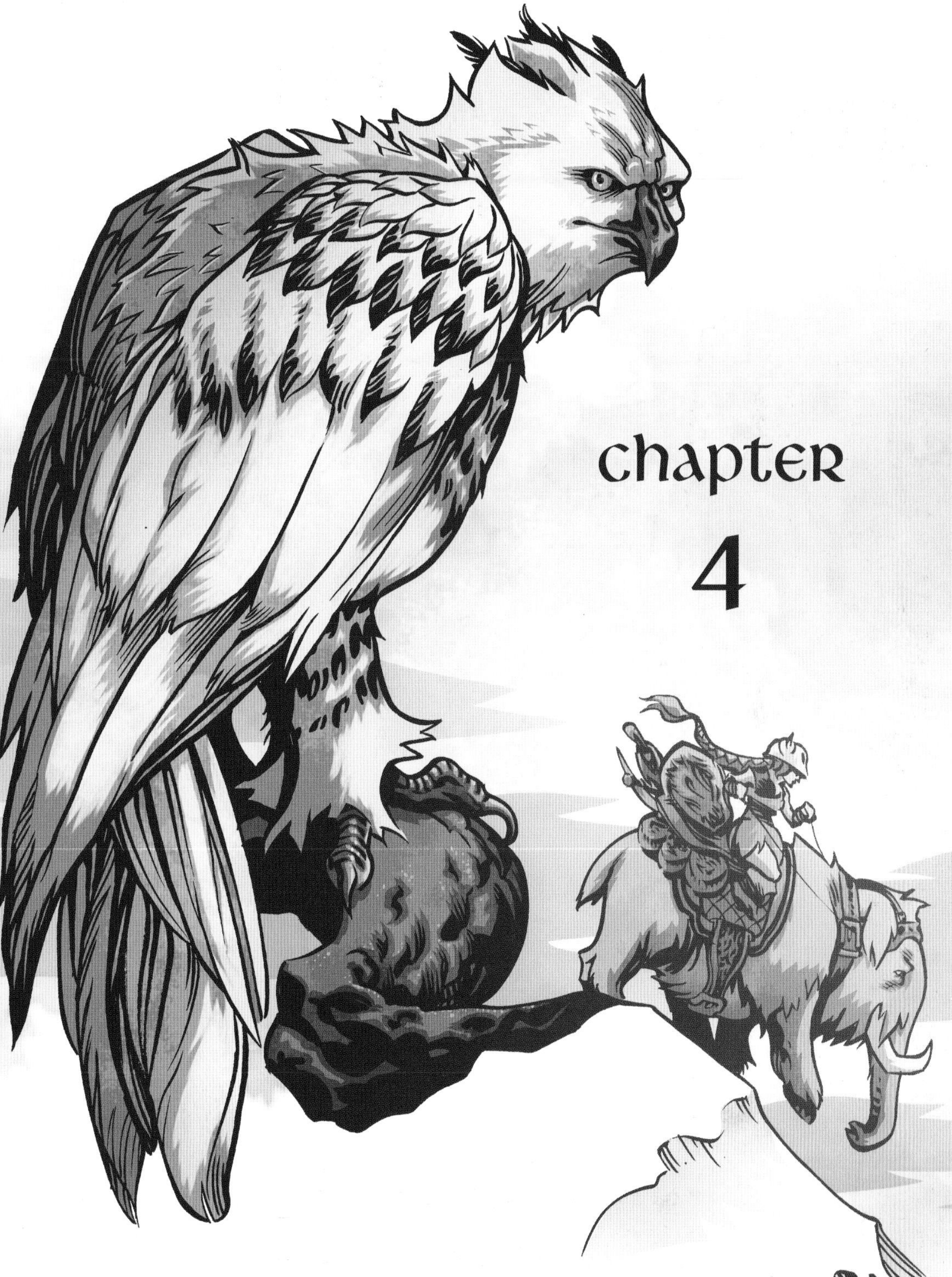

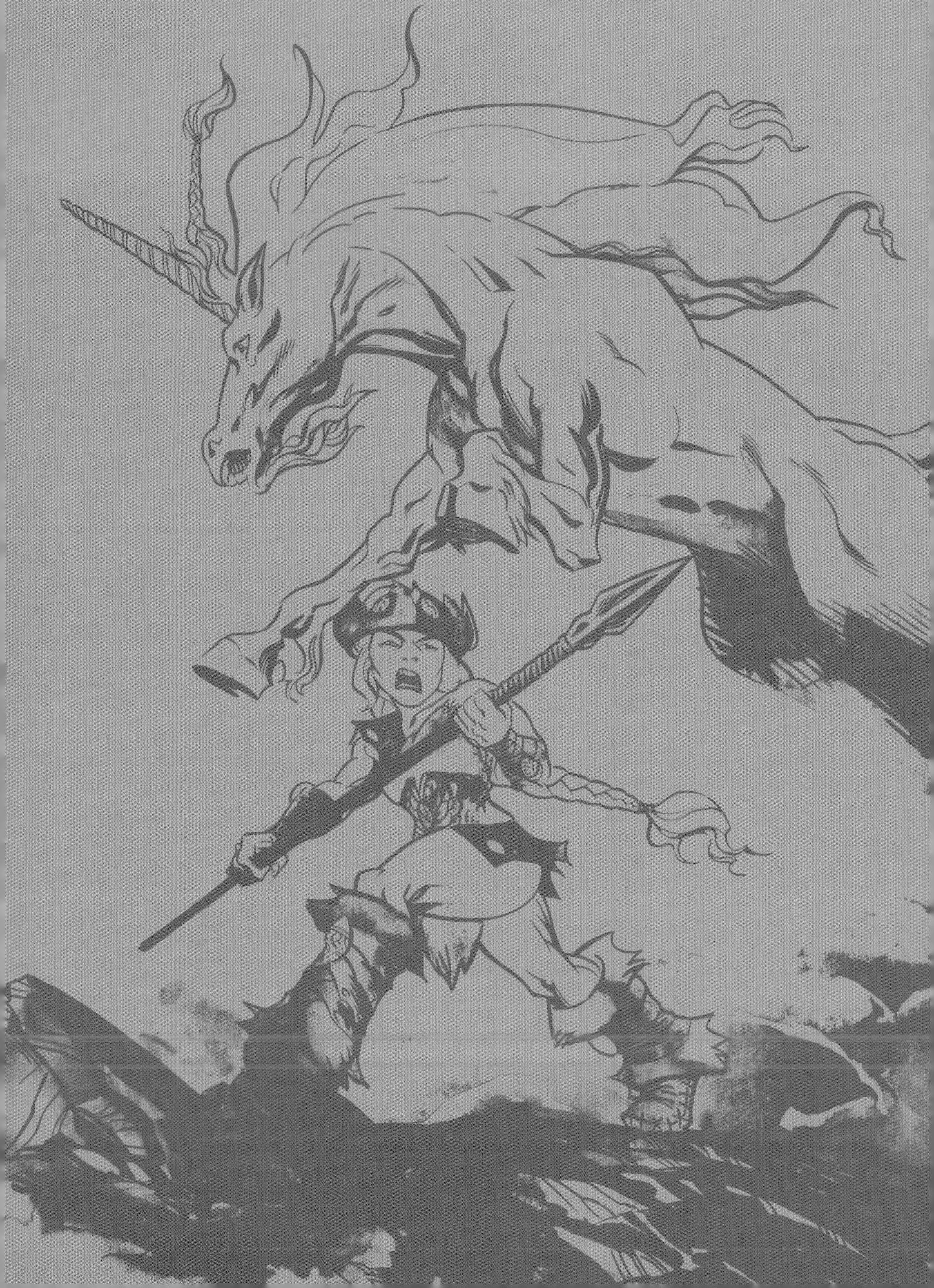

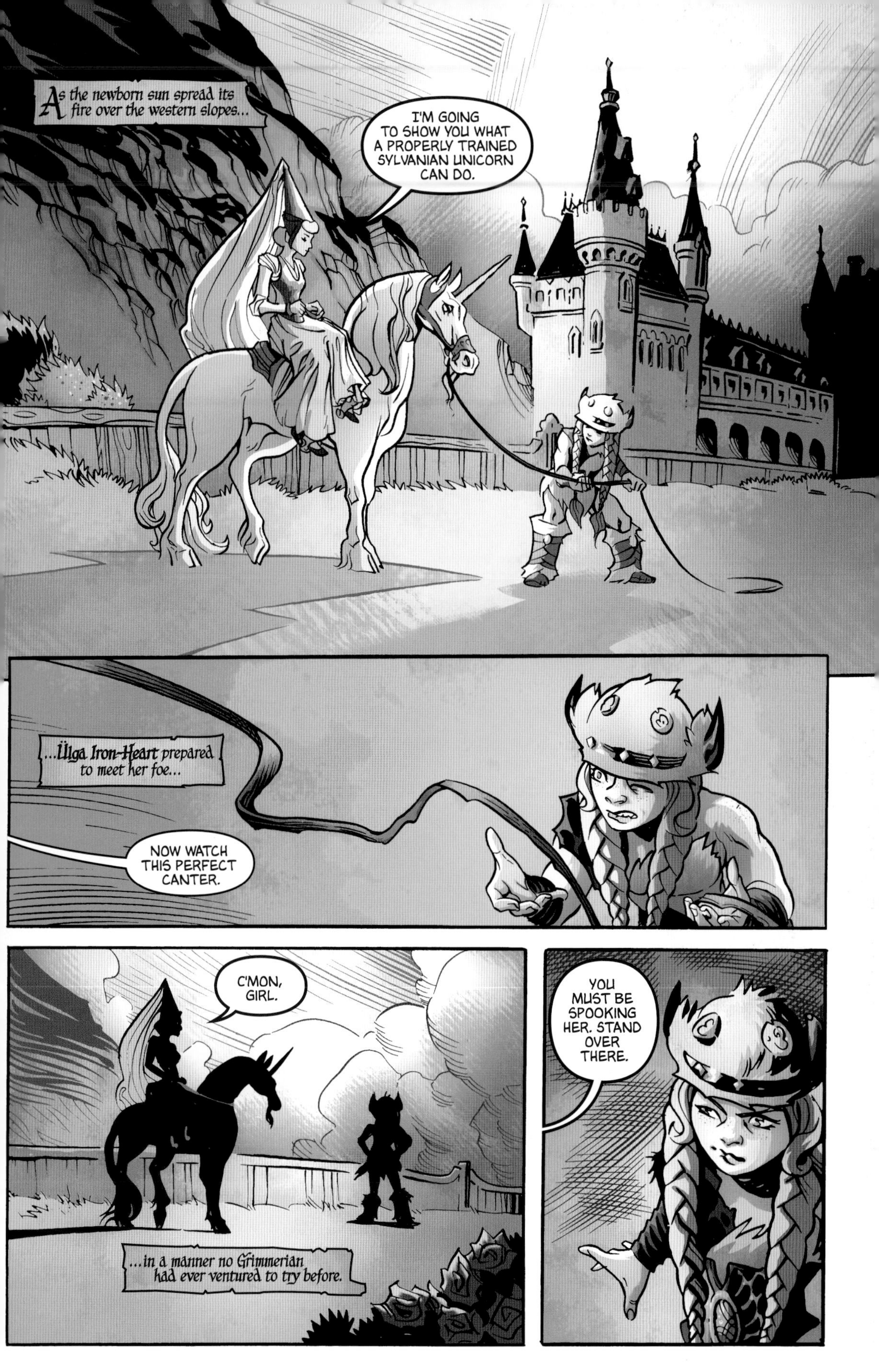
As the newborn sun spread its fire over the western slopes...
I'M GOING TO SHOW YOU WHAT A PROPERLY TRAINED SYLVANIAN UNICORN CAN DO.
...Ülga Iron-Heart prepared to meet her foe...
NOW WATCH THIS PERFECT CANTER.
C'MON, GIRL.
...in a manner no Grimmerian had ever ventured to try before.
YOU MUST BE SPOOKING HER. STAND OVER THERE.

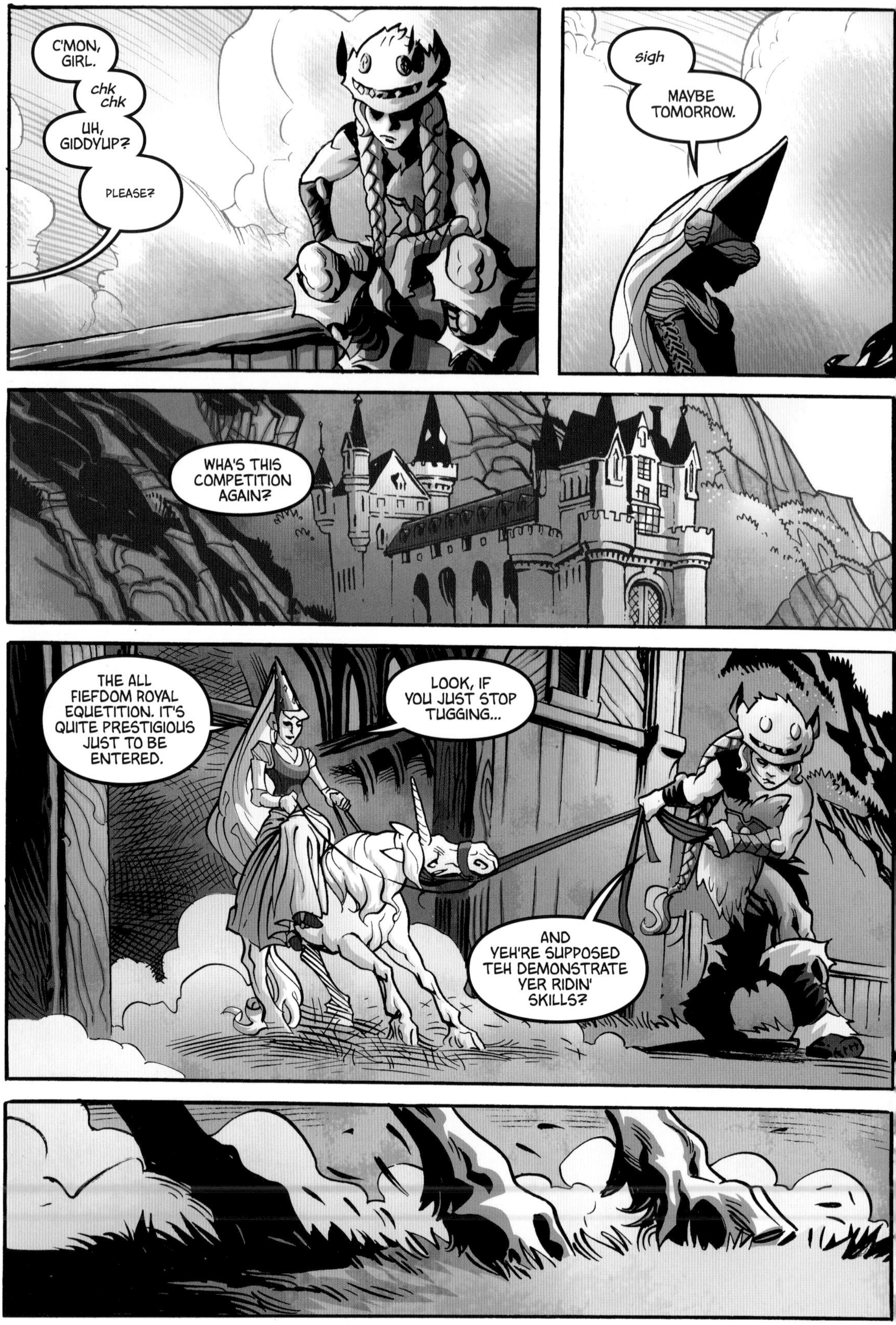
C'MON, GIRL.
chk chk
UH, GIDDYUP?
PLEASE?
sigh
MAYBE TOMORROW.
WHA'S THIS COMPETITION AGAIN?
THE ALL FIEFDOM ROYAL EQUETITION. IT'S QUITE PRESTIGIOUS JUST TO BE ENTERED.
LOOK, IF YOU JUST STOP TUGGING...
AND YEH'RE SUPPOSED TEH DEMONSTRATE YER RIDIN' SKILLS?

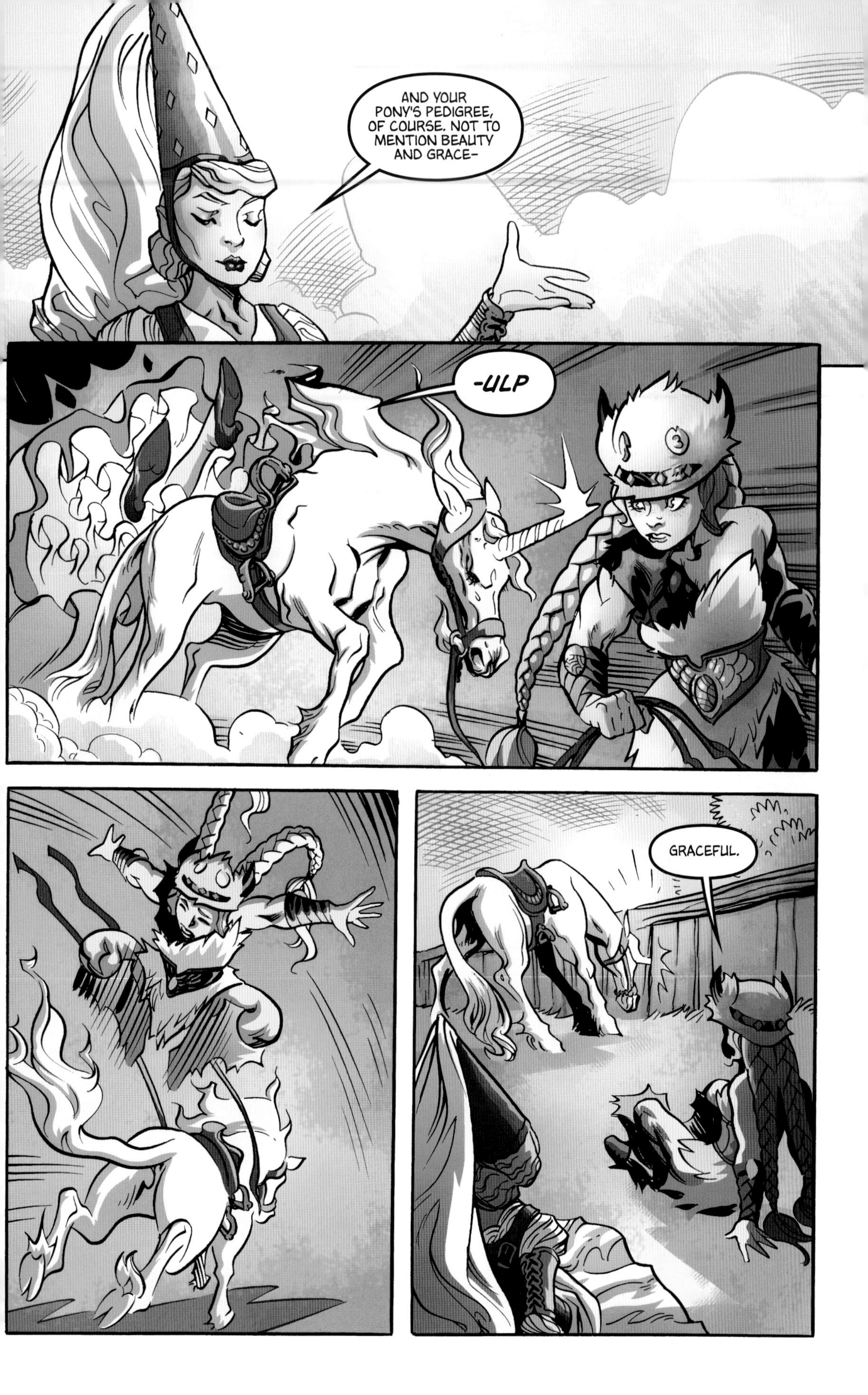
AND YOUR PONY'S PEDIGREE, OF COURSE. NOT TO MENTION BEAUTY AND GRACE-
-ULP
GRACEFUL.

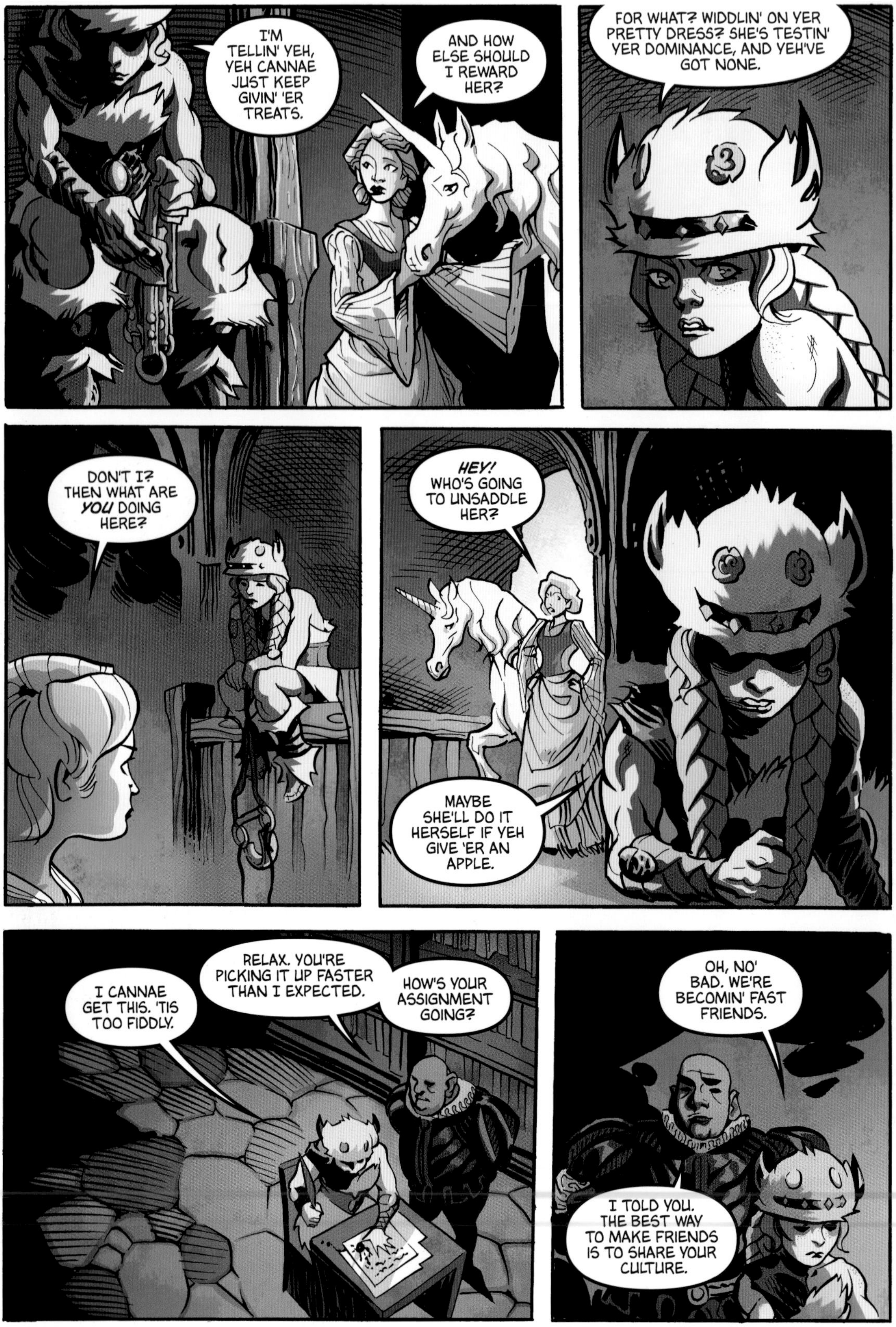
I'M TELLIN' YEH, YEH CANNAE JUST KEEP GIVIN' 'ER TREATS.
AND HOW ELSE SHOULD I REWARD HER?
FOR WHAT? WIDDLIN' ON YER PRETTY DRESS? SHE'S TESTIN' YER DOMINANCE, AND YEH'VE GOT NONE.
DON'T I? THEN WHAT ARE *YOU* DOING HERE?
HEY! WHO'S GOING TO UNSADDLE HER?
MAYBE SHE'LL DO IT HERSELF IF YEH GIVE 'ER AN APPLE.
I CANNAE GET THIS. 'TIS TOO FIDDLY.
RELAX. YOU'RE PICKING IT UP FASTER THAN I EXPECTED.
HOW'S YOUR ASSIGNMENT GOING?
OH, NO' BAD. WE'RE BECOMIN' FAST FRIENDS.
I TOLD YOU. THE BEST WAY TO MAKE FRIENDS IS TO SHARE YOUR CULTURE.

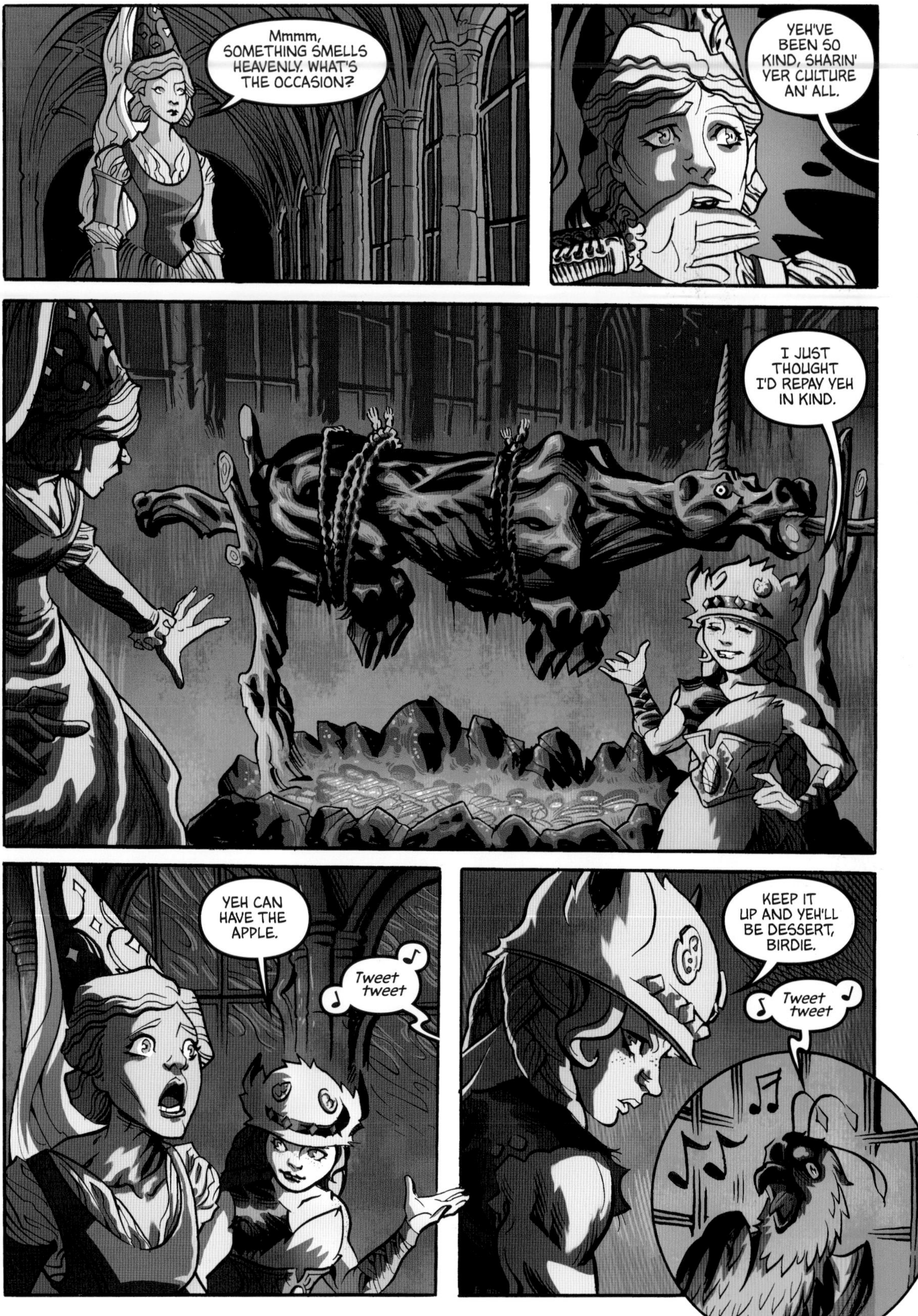
Mmmm, SOMETHING SMELLS HEAVENLY. WHAT'S THE OCCASION?
YEH'VE BEEN SO KIND, SHARIN' YER CULTURE AN' ALL.
I JUST THOUGHT I'D REPAY YEH IN KIND.
YEH CAN HAVE THE APPLE.
Tweet tweet
KEEP IT UP AND YEH'LL BE DESSERT, BIRDIE.
Tweet tweet

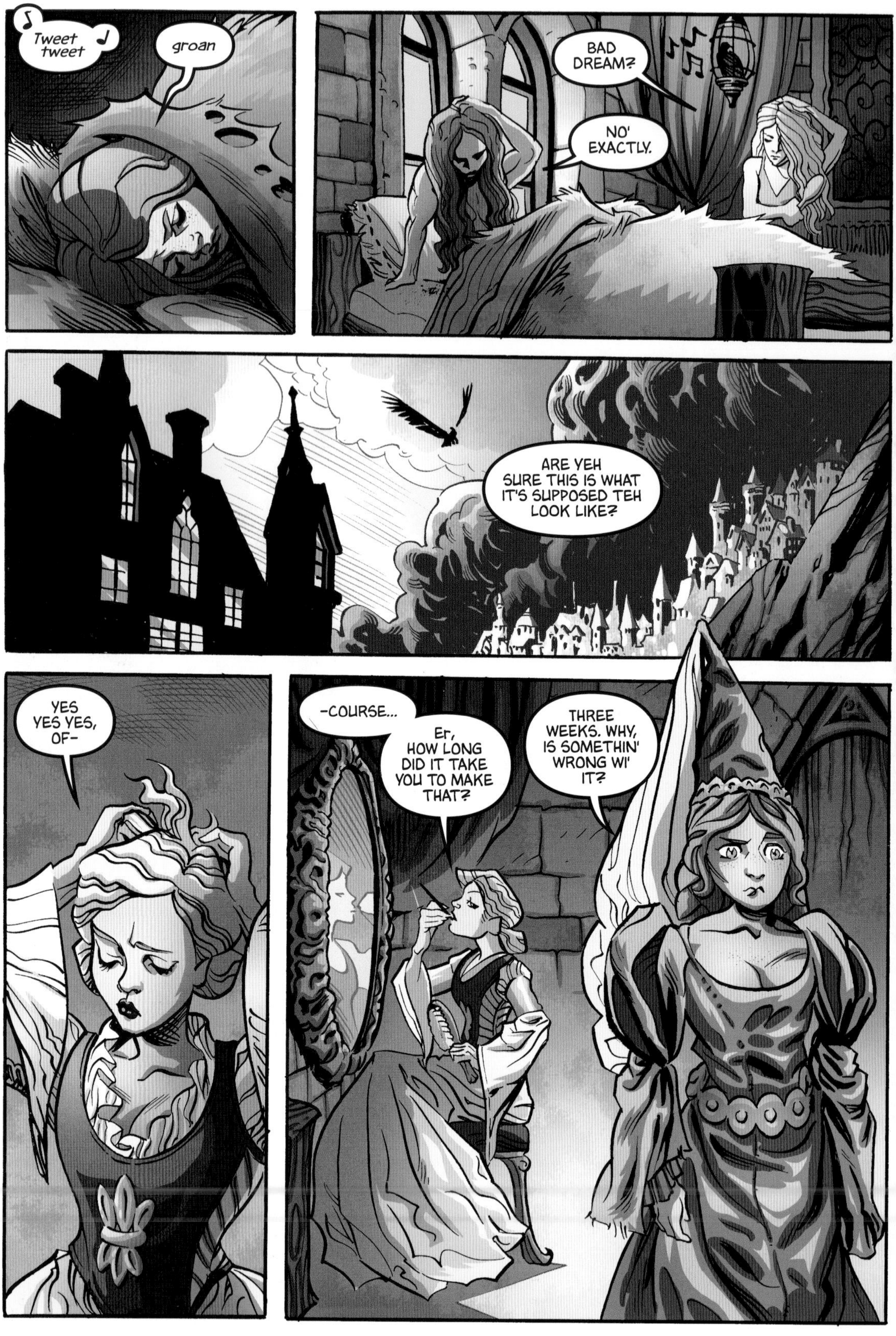
Tweet tweet
groan
BAD DREAM?
NO' EXACTLY.
ARE YEH SURE THIS IS WHAT IT'S SUPPOSED TEH LOOK LIKE?
YES YES YES, OF-
-COURSE...
Er, HOW LONG DID IT TAKE YOU TO MAKE THAT?
THREE WEEKS. WHY, IS SOMETHIN' WRONG WI' IT?

WHERE TO BEGIN?

CAN IT BE FIXED?

WITH A BONFIRE, POSSIBLY. MAYBE THE HAT'S ON BACKWARD?

YEAH, WELL, YEH TRY CHECKIN' YERSELF IN A MIRROR WI'OUT LOOKIN' YER REFLECTION IN THE EYE.

I'M RUNNING LATE. DON'T FORGET, YOU PROMISED TO BRUSH AURORA DOWN BEFORE CLASS. YOU'VE GOT HALF AN HOUR.

WHERE ARE YEH GOIN'?

LUNCH.

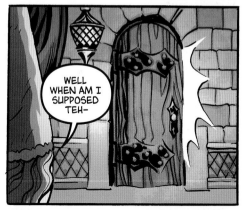

WELL WHEN AM I SUPPOSED TEH—

OKEE, LASSIE, NAE HORSEPLAY TODAY. LET'S JUST BEHAVE FOR A MOMENT AN' I'LL BE OUTTA YER HAIR.

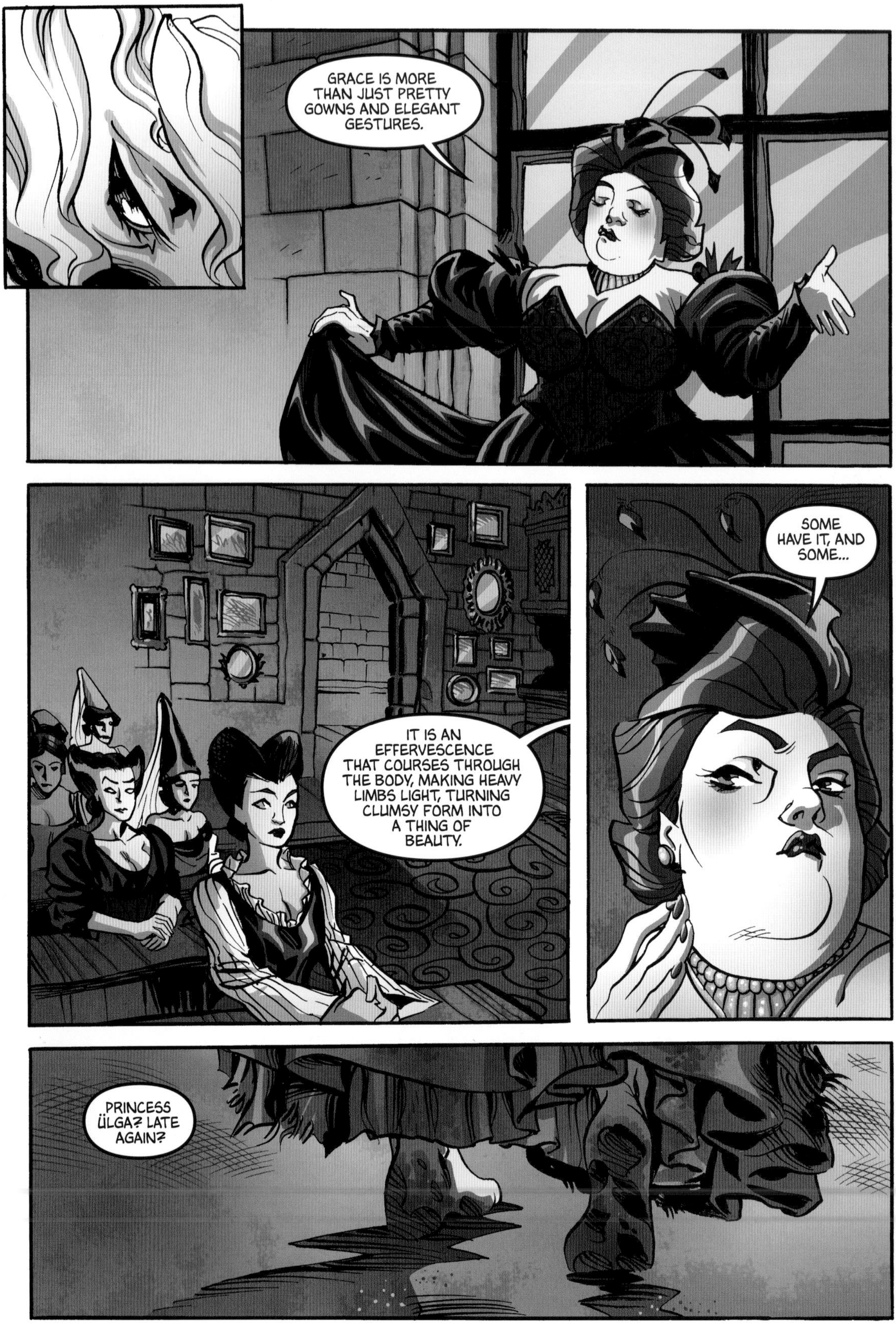
GRACE IS MORE THAN JUST PRETTY GOWNS AND ELEGANT GESTURES.
IT IS AN EFFERVESCENCE THAT COURSES THROUGH THE BODY, MAKING HEAVY LIMBS LIGHT, TURNING CLUMSY FORM INTO A THING OF BEAUTY.
SOME HAVE IT, AND SOME...
PRINCESS ÜLGA? LATE AGAIN?

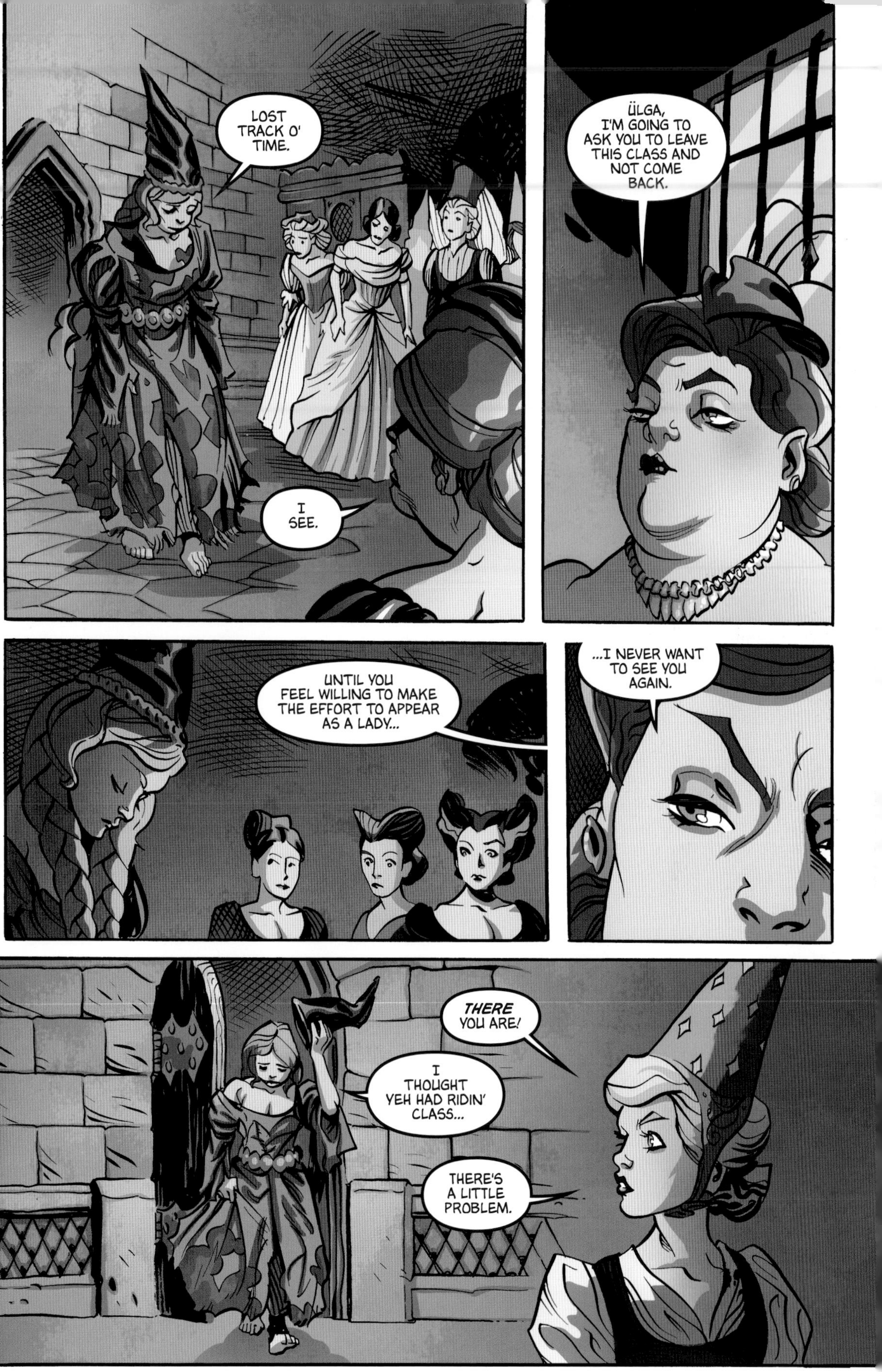
LOST TRACK O' TIME.
I SEE.
ÜLGA, I'M GOING TO ASK YOU TO LEAVE THIS CLASS AND NOT COME BACK.
UNTIL YOU FEEL WILLING TO MAKE THE EFFORT TO APPEAR AS A LADY...
...I NEVER WANT TO SEE YOU AGAIN.
THERE YOU ARE!
I THOUGHT YEH HAD RIDIN' CLASS...
THERE'S A LITTLE PROBLEM.

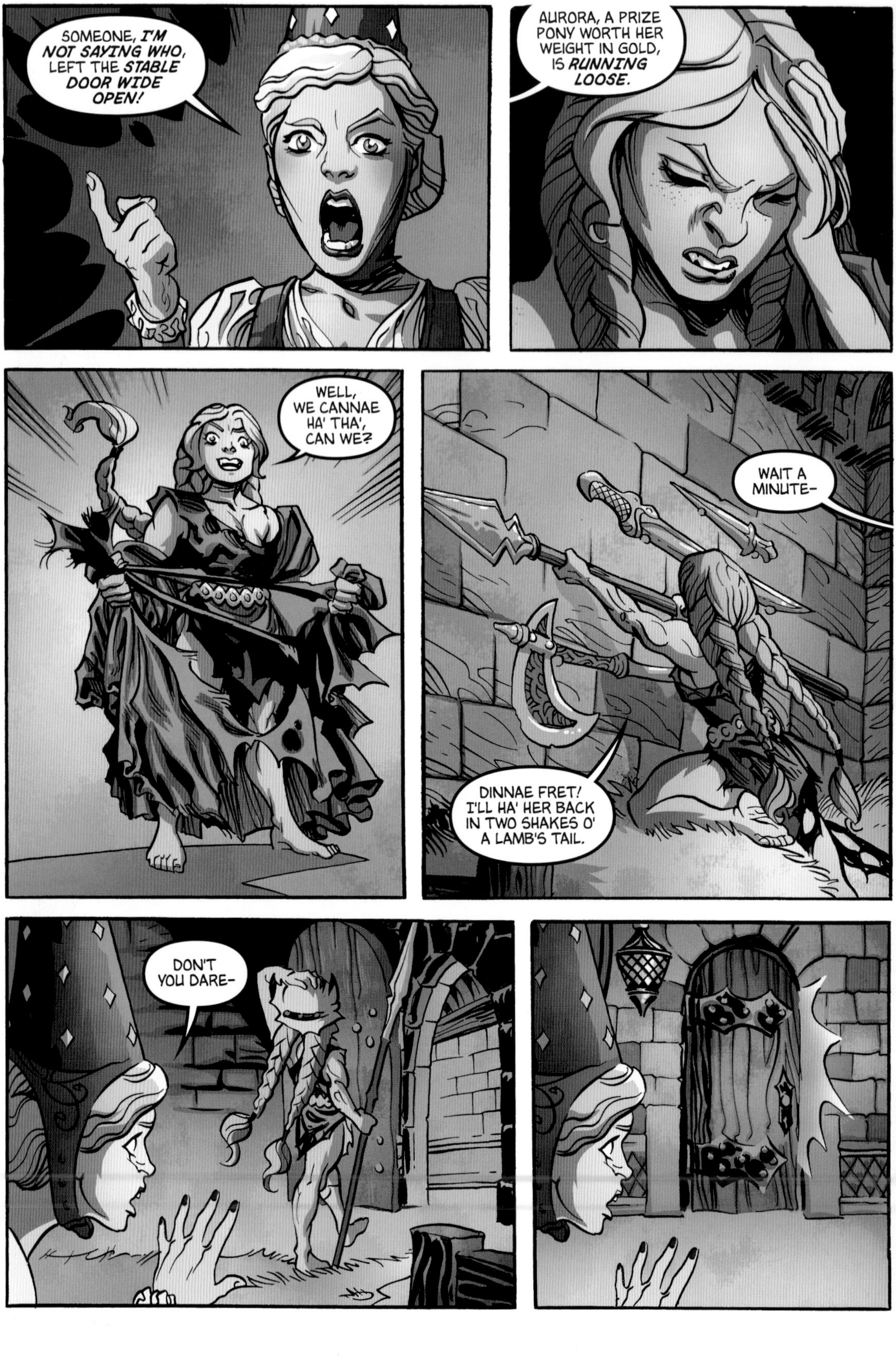
SOMEONE, *I'M NOT SAYING WHO,* LEFT THE *STABLE DOOR WIDE OPEN!*
AURORA, A PRIZE PONY WORTH HER WEIGHT IN GOLD, IS *RUNNING LOOSE.*
WELL, WE CANNAE HA' THA', CAN WE?
WAIT A MINUTE-
DINNAE FRET! I'LL HA' HER BACK IN TWO SHAKES O' A LAMB'S TAIL.
DON'T YOU DARE-

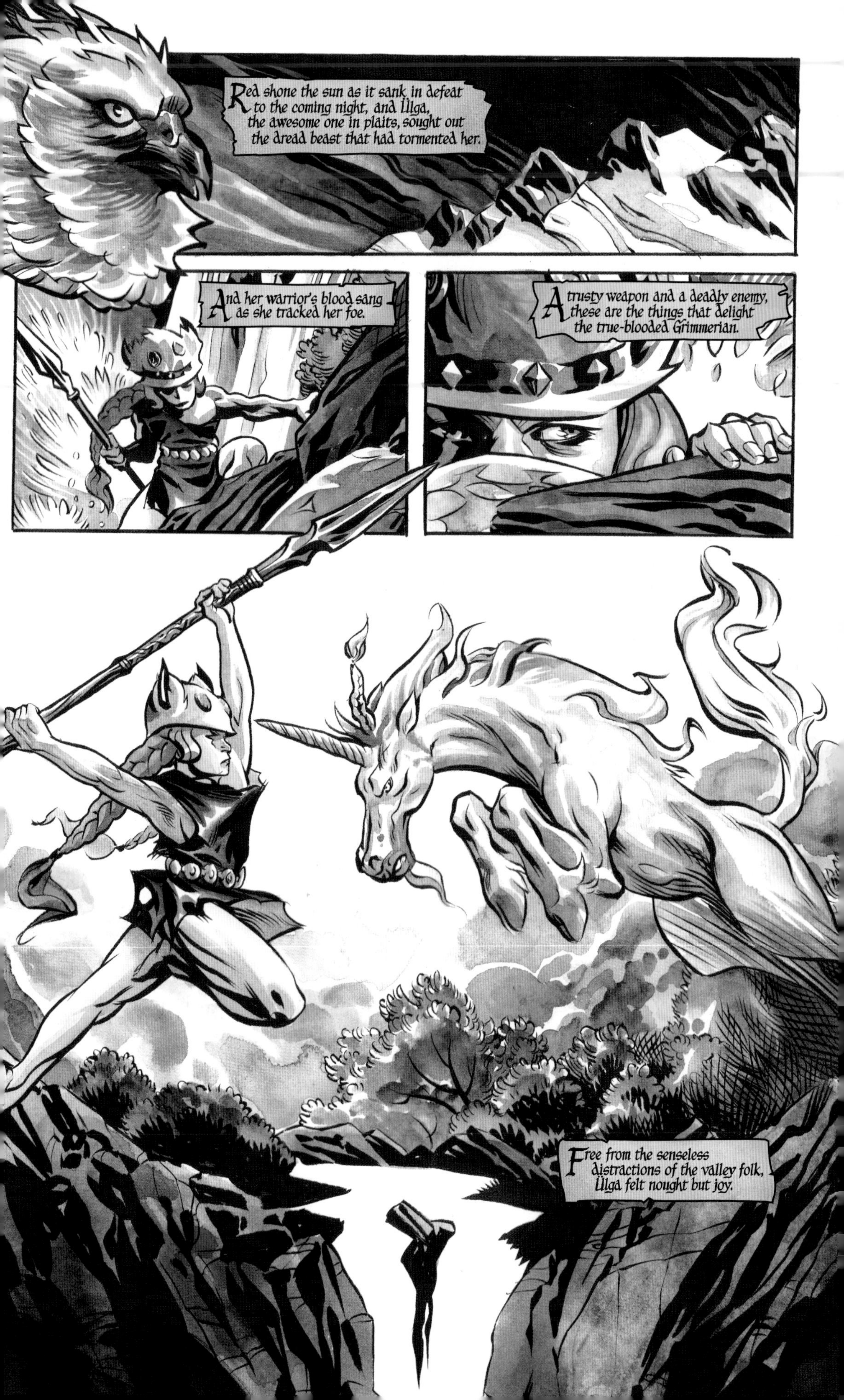
Red shone the sun as it sank in defeat to the coming night, and Ulga, the awesome one in plaits, sought out the dread beast that had tormented her.
And her warrior's blood sang as she tracked her foe.
A trusty weapon and a deadly enemy, these are the things that delight the true-blooded Grimmerian.
Free from the senseless distractions of the valley folk, Ulga felt nought but joy.

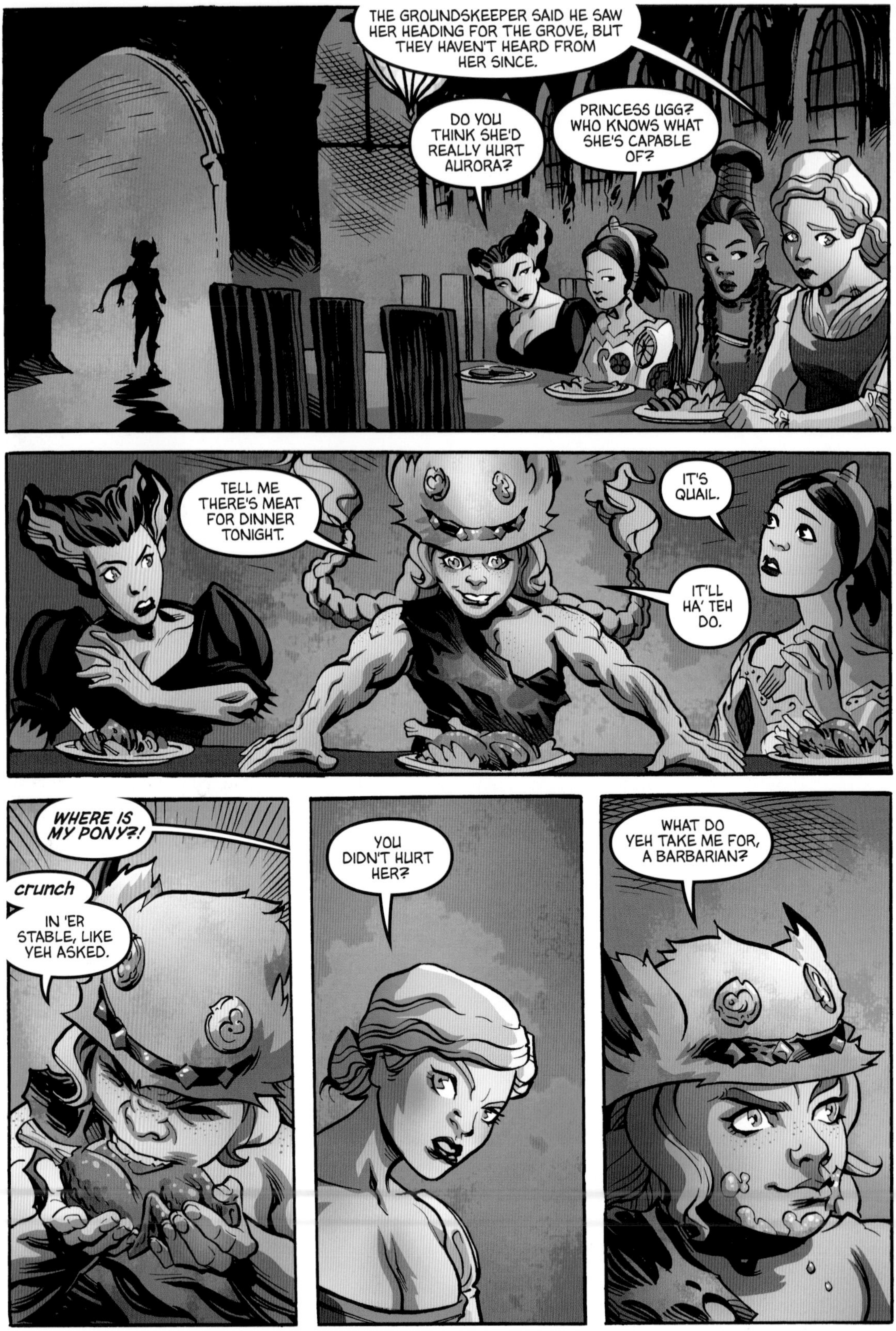
THE GROUNDSKEEPER SAID HE SAW HER HEADING FOR THE GROVE, BUT THEY HAVEN'T HEARD FROM HER SINCE.
DO YOU THINK SHE'D REALLY HURT AURORA?
PRINCESS UGG? WHO KNOWS WHAT SHE'S CAPABLE OF?
TELL ME THERE'S MEAT FOR DINNER TONIGHT.
IT'S QUAIL.
IT'LL HA' TEH DO.
WHERE IS MY PONY?!
crunch
IN 'ER STABLE, LIKE YEH ASKED.
YOU DIDN'T HURT HER?
WHAT DO YEH TAKE ME FOR, A BARBARIAN?

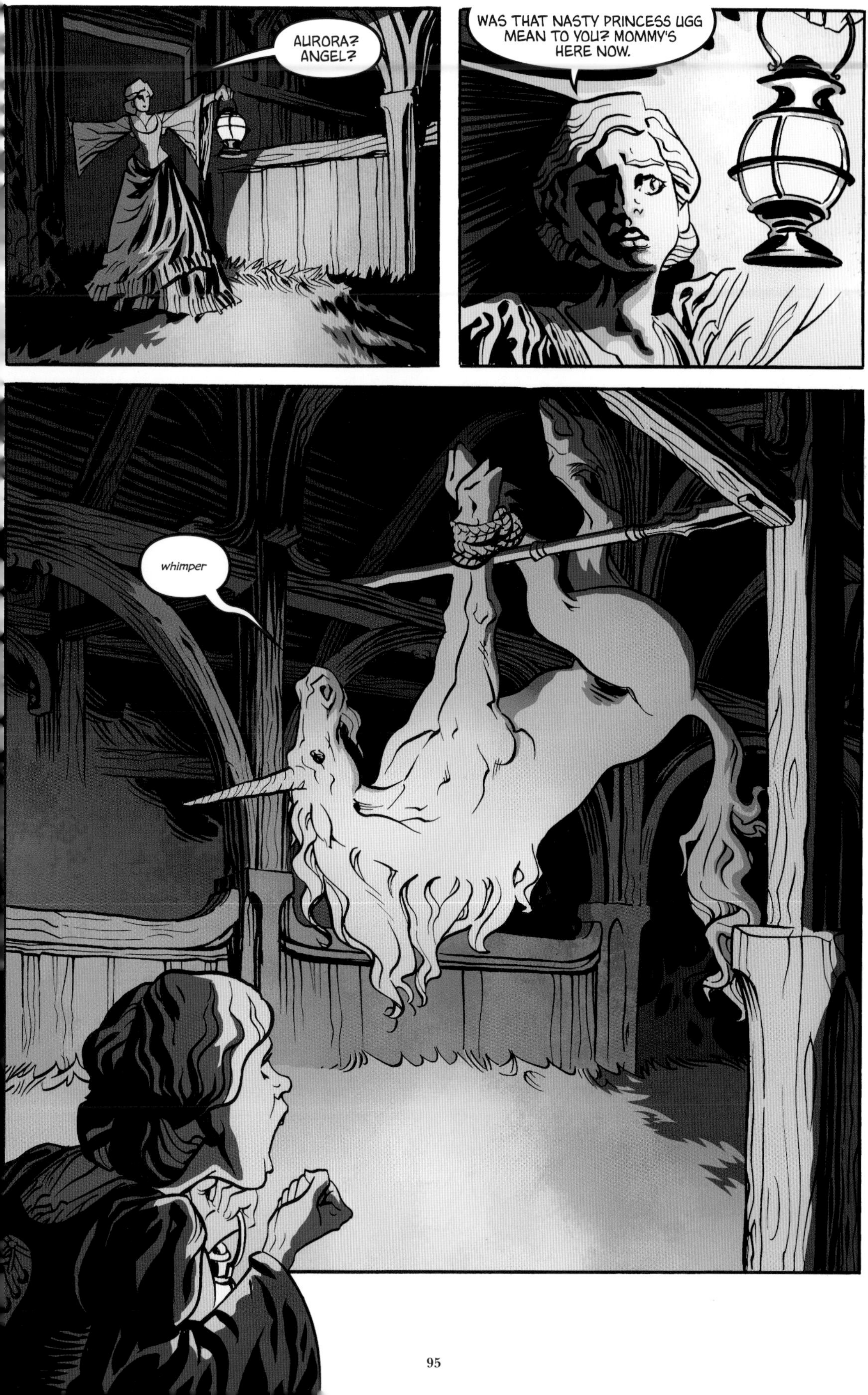
AURORA?
ANGEL?
WAS THAT NASTY PRINCESS UGG MEAN TO YOU? MOMMY'S HERE NOW.
whimper

AND YOU'LL ALL BE PLEASED TO HEAR THAT, IN THIS CASE, THE PRINCESS GOT HER HANDSOME PRINCE.

HER PAST INDISCRETIONS WERE HUSHED UP, AS WAS HIS ILLEGITIMATE SON, AND THEY LIVED HAPPILY EVER AFTER.

AND SO DID THE MERCHANT COMMUNITY, NOW THAT TRADE BETWEEN THE KINGDOMS WAS REESTABLISHED.

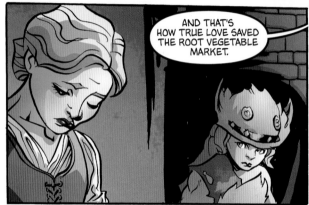

AND THAT'S HOW TRUE LOVE SAVED THE ROOT VEGETABLE MARKET.

LOOK, HONEY, A SHINY SWEET APPLE.

PLEASE, ANGEL, COME TO MOMMA. PLEASE!

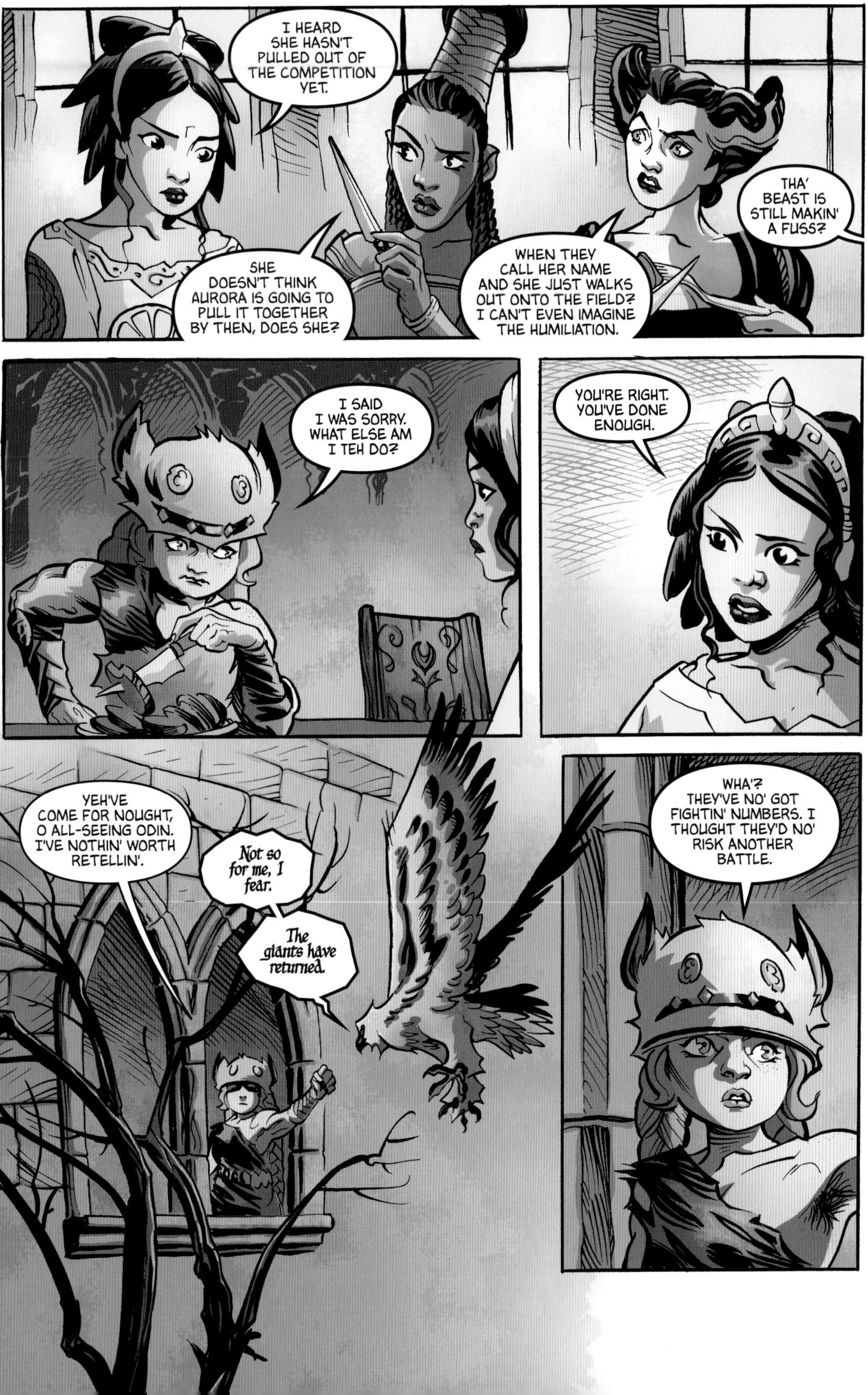
I HEARD SHE HASN'T PULLED OUT OF THE COMPETITION YET.
SHE DOESN'T THINK AURORA IS GOING TO PULL IT TOGETHER BY THEN, DOES SHE?
WHEN THEY CALL HER NAME AND SHE JUST WALKS OUT ONTO THE FIELD? I CAN'T EVEN IMAGINE THE HUMILIATION.
THA' BEAST IS STILL MAKIN' A FUSS?
I SAID I WAS SORRY. WHAT ELSE AM I TEH DO?
YOU'RE RIGHT. YOU'VE DONE ENOUGH.
YEH'VE COME FOR NOUGHT, O ALL-SEEING ODIN. I'VE NOTHIN' WORTH RETELLIN'.
Not so for me, I fear.
The giants have returned.
WHA'? THEY'VE NO' GOT FIGHTIN' NUMBERS. I THOUGHT THEY'D NO' RISK ANOTHER BATTLE.

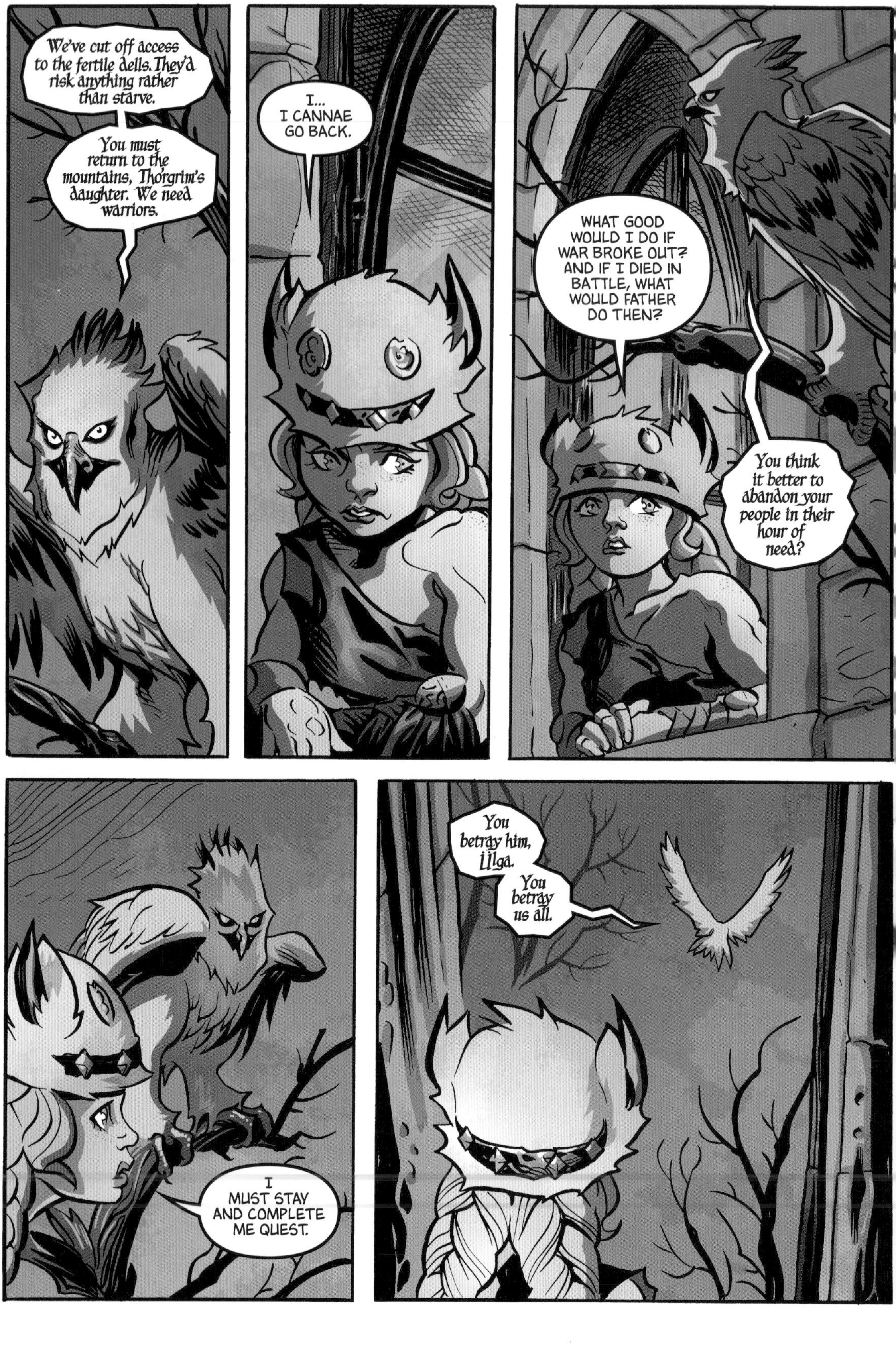
We've cut off access to the fertile dells. They'd risk anything rather than starve.
You must return to the mountains, Thorgrim's daughter. We need warriors.
I... I CANNAE GO BACK.
WHAT GOOD WOULD I DO IF WAR BROKE OUT? AND IF I DIED IN BATTLE, WHAT WOULD FATHER DO THEN?
You think it better to abandon your people in their hour of need?
I MUST STAY AND COMPLETE ME QUEST.
You betray him, Lilga.
You betray us all.

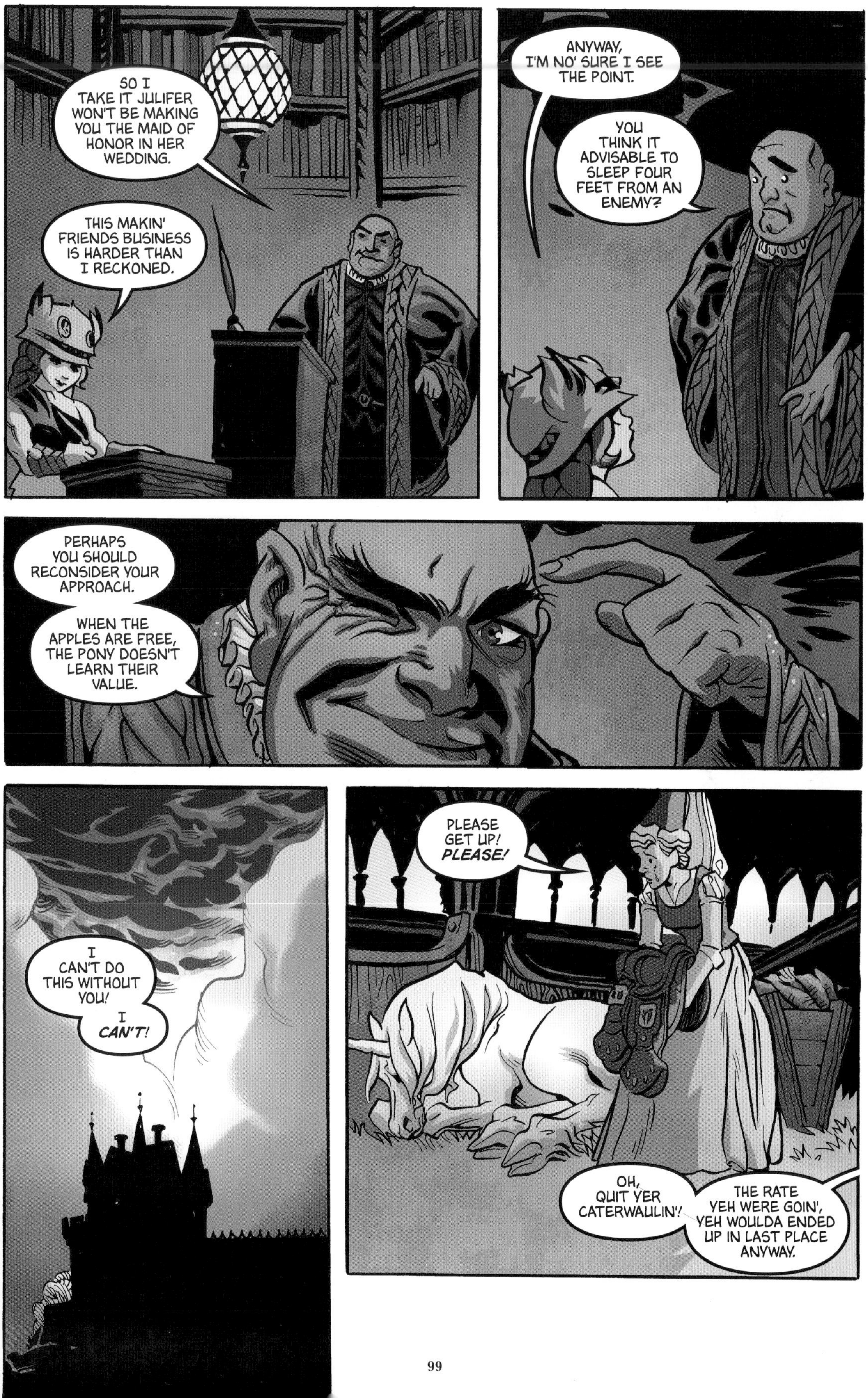
SO I TAKE IT JULIFER WON'T BE MAKING YOU THE MAID OF HONOR IN HER WEDDING.
THIS MAKIN' FRIENDS BUSINESS IS HARDER THAN I RECKONED.
ANYWAY, I'M NO' SURE I SEE THE POINT.
YOU THINK IT ADVISABLE TO SLEEP FOUR FEET FROM AN ENEMY?
PERHAPS YOU SHOULD RECONSIDER YOUR APPROACH.
WHEN THE APPLES ARE FREE, THE PONY DOESN'T LEARN THEIR VALUE.
I CAN'T DO THIS WITHOUT YOU!
I *CAN'T*!
PLEASE GET UP! ***PLEASE!***
OH, QUIT YER CATERWAULIN'!
THE RATE YEH WERE GOIN', YEH WOULDA ENDED UP IN LAST PLACE ANYWAY.

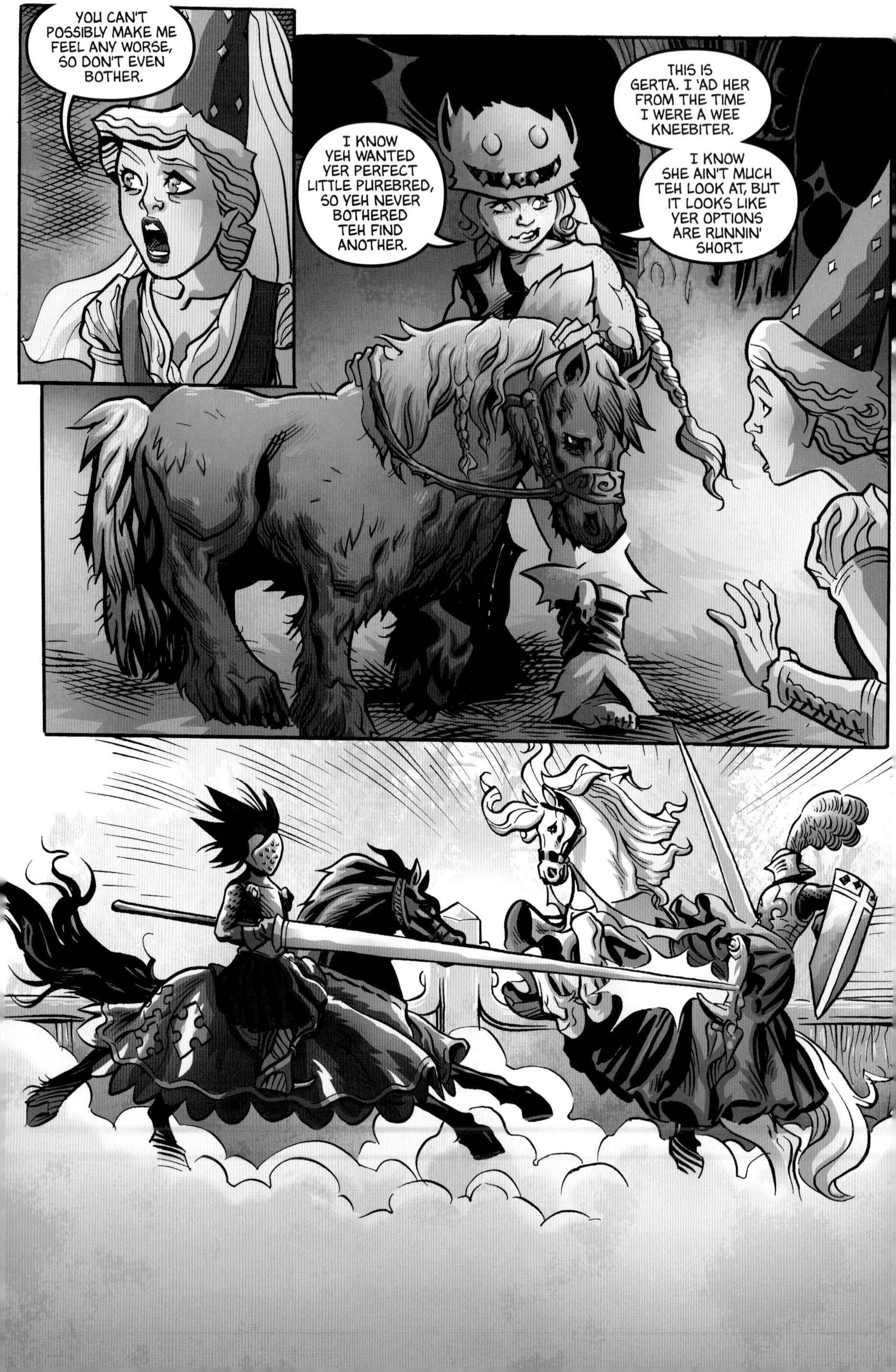
YOU CAN'T POSSIBLY MAKE ME FEEL ANY WORSE, SO DON'T EVEN BOTHER.
I KNOW YEH WANTED YER PERFECT LITTLE PUREBRED, SO YEH NEVER BOTHERED TEH FIND ANOTHER.
THIS IS GERTA. I 'AD HER FROM THE TIME I WERE A WEE KNEEBITER.
I KNOW SHE AIN'T MUCH TEH LOOK AT, BUT IT LOOKS LIKE YER OPTIONS ARE RUNNIN' SHORT.

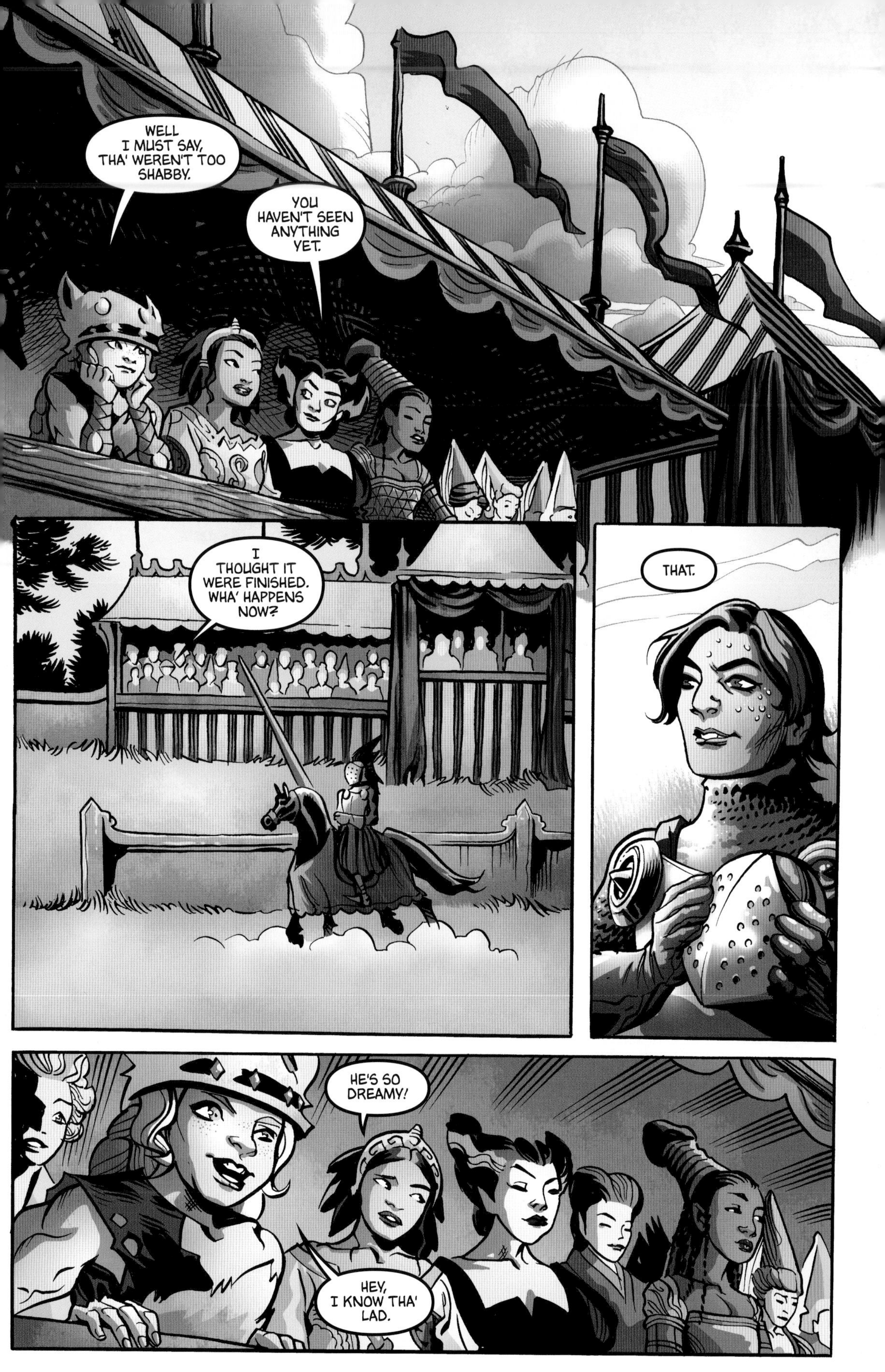
WELL I MUST SAY, THA' WEREN'T TOO SHABBY.
YOU HAVEN'T SEEN ANYTHING YET.
I THOUGHT IT WERE FINISHED. WHA' HAPPENS NOW?
THAT.
HE'S SO DREAMY!
HEY, I KNOW THA' LAD.

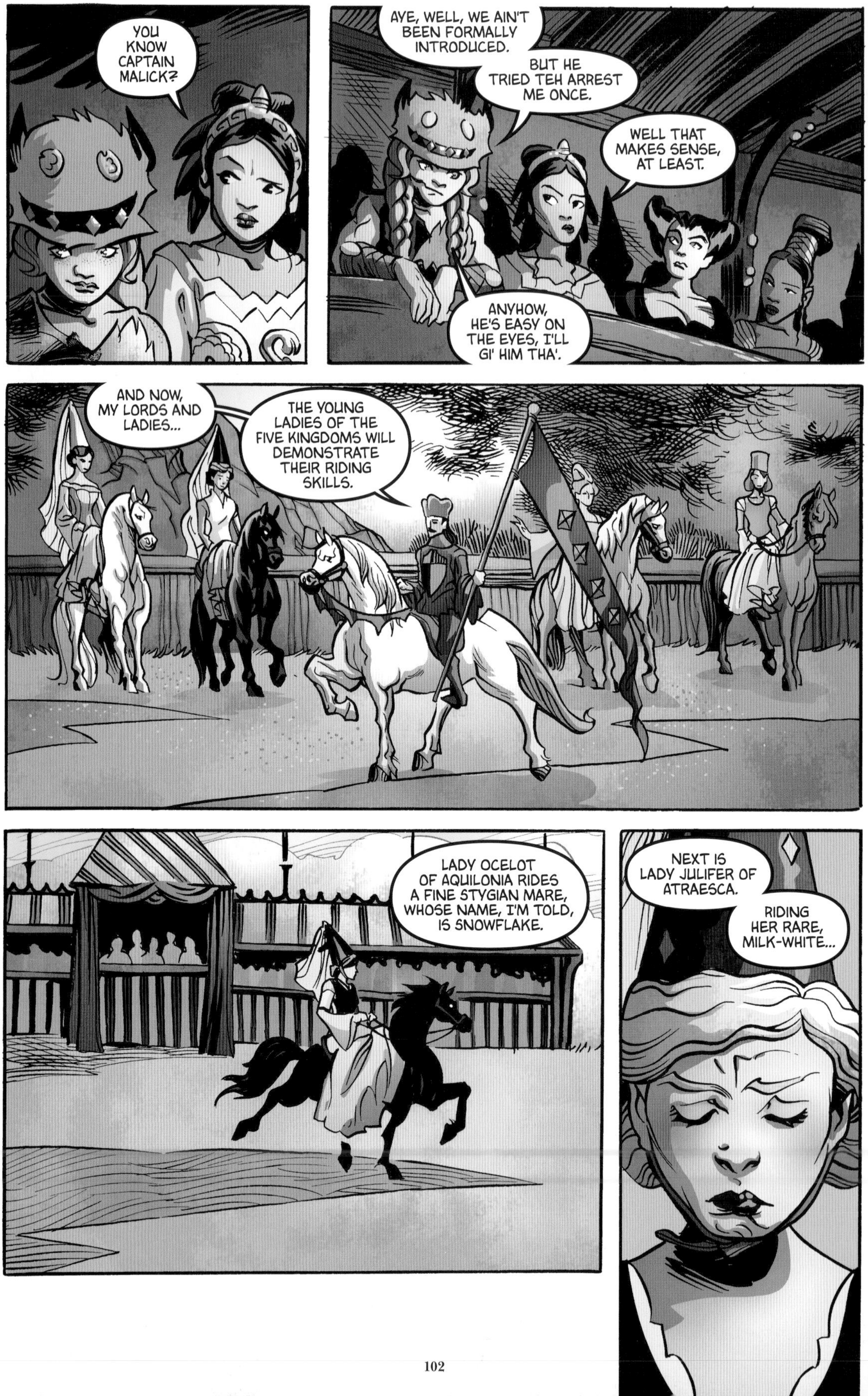
YOU KNOW CAPTAIN MALICK?
AYE, WELL, WE AIN'T BEEN FORMALLY INTRODUCED.
BUT HE TRIED TEH ARREST ME ONCE.
WELL THAT MAKES SENSE, AT LEAST.
ANYHOW, HE'S EASY ON THE EYES, I'LL GI' HIM THA'.
AND NOW, MY LORDS AND LADIES...
THE YOUNG LADIES OF THE FIVE KINGDOMS WILL DEMONSTRATE THEIR RIDING SKILLS.
LADY OCELOT OF AQUILONIA RIDES A FINE STYGIAN MARE, WHOSE NAME, I'M TOLD, IS SNOWFLAKE.
NEXT IS LADY JULIFER OF ATRAESCA.
RIDING HER RARE, MILK-WHITE...

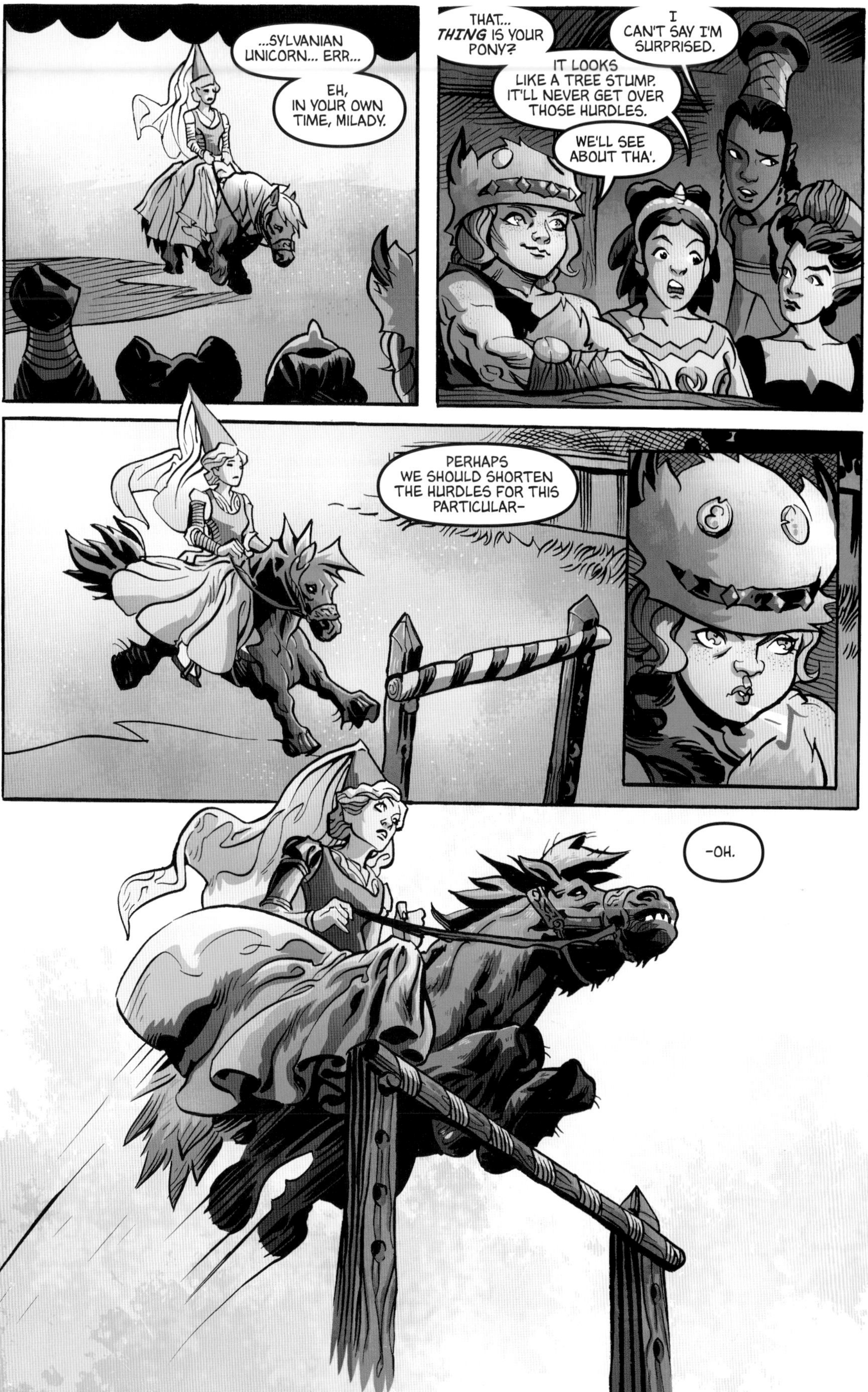
...SYLVANIAN UNICORN... ERR...
EH, IN YOUR OWN TIME, MILADY.
THAT... THING IS YOUR PONY?
I CAN'T SAY I'M SURPRISED.
IT LOOKS LIKE A TREE STUMP. IT'LL NEVER GET OVER THOSE HURDLES.
WE'LL SEE ABOUT THA'.
PERHAPS WE SHOULD SHORTEN THE HURDLES FOR THIS PARTICULAR-
-OH.

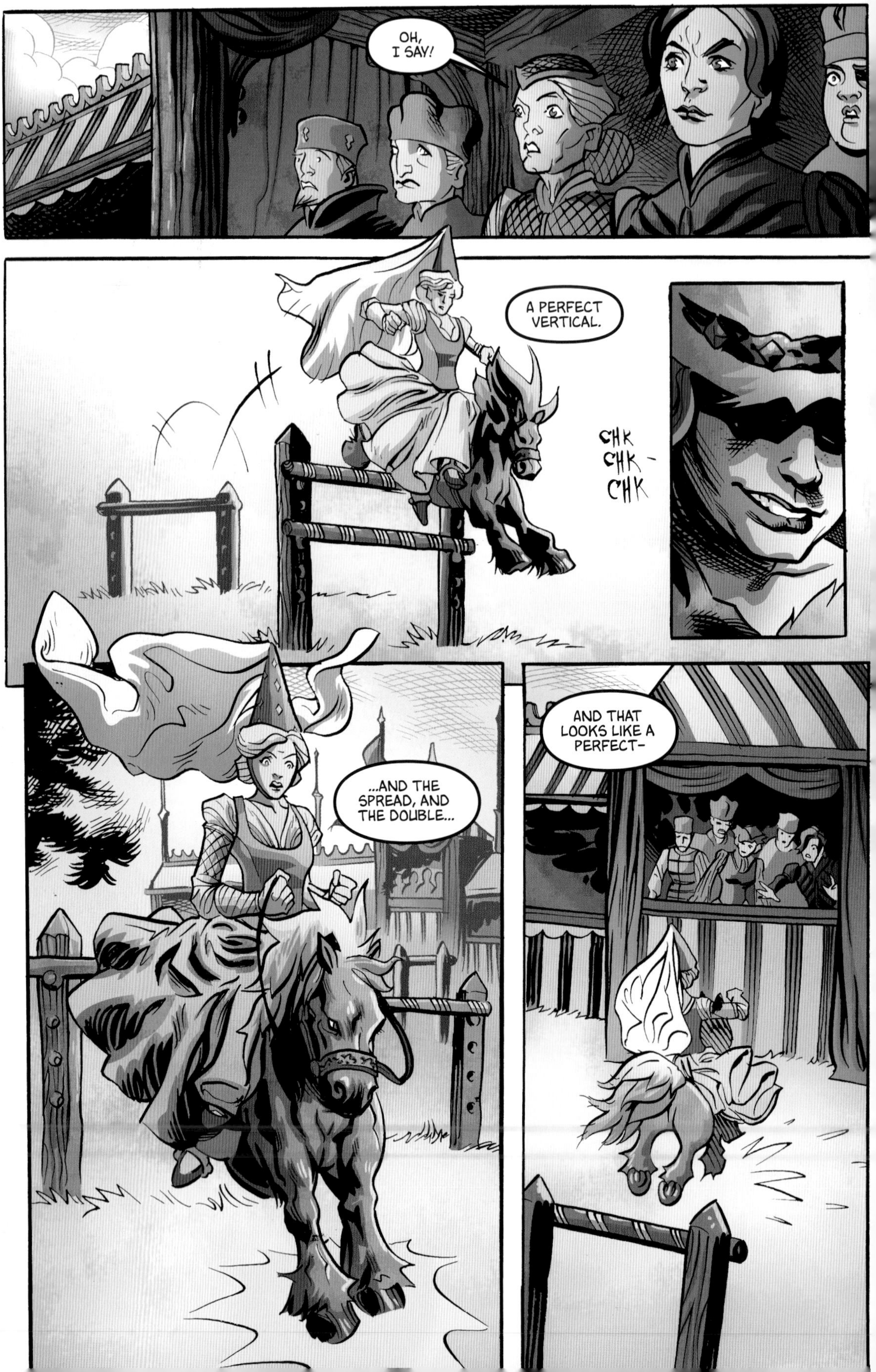
OH, I SAY!
A PERFECT VERTICAL.
CHK CHK- CHK
...AND THE SPREAD, AND THE DOUBLE...
AND THAT LOOKS LIKE A PERFECT-

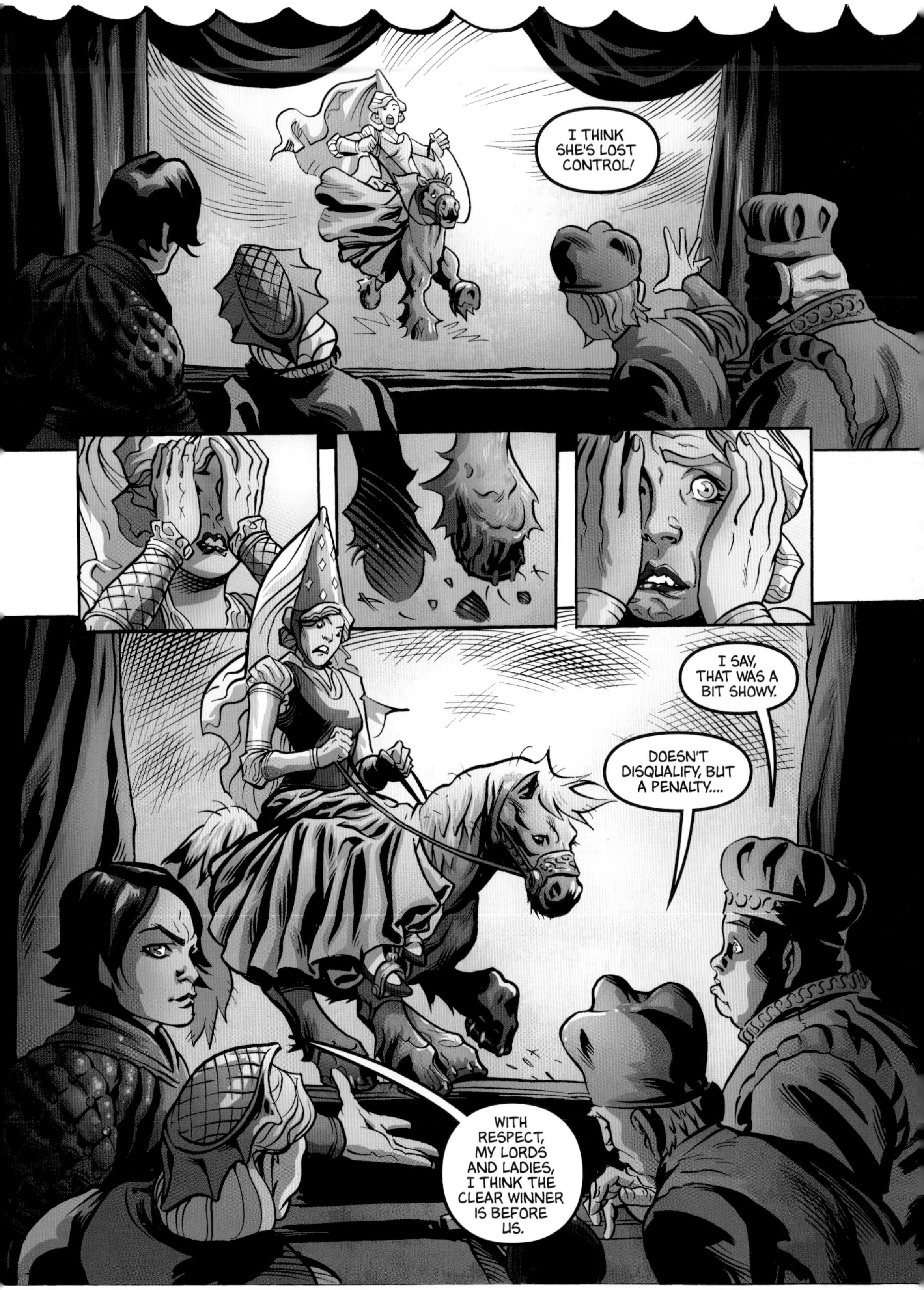
I THINK SHE'S LOST CONTROL!
I SAY, THAT WAS A BIT SHOWY.
DOESN'T DISQUALIFY, BUT A PENALTY....
WITH RESPECT, MY LORDS AND LADIES, I THINK THE CLEAR WINNER IS BEFORE US.

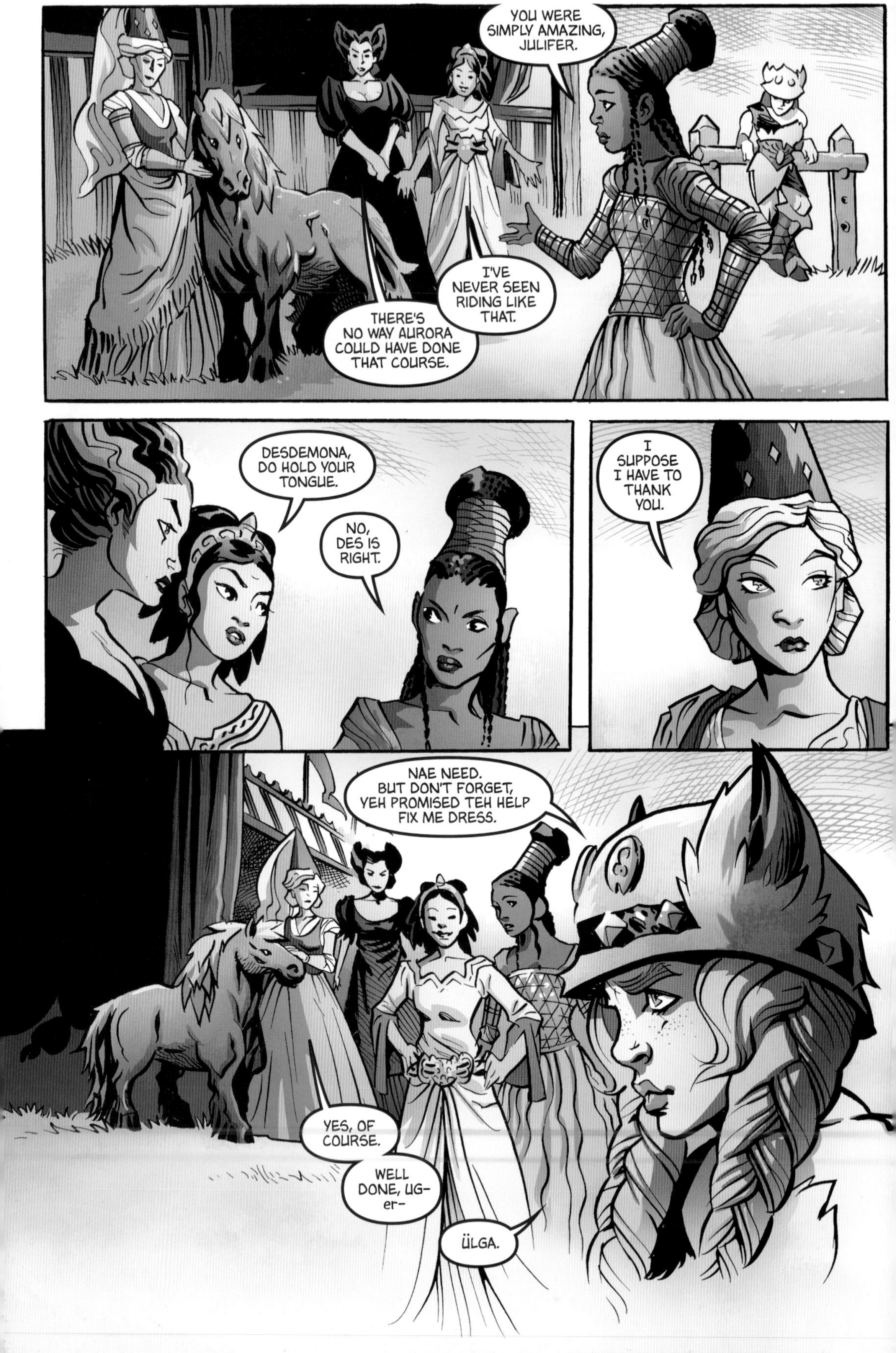
YOU WERE SIMPLY AMAZING, JULIFER.
I'VE NEVER SEEN RIDING LIKE THAT.
THERE'S NO WAY AURORA COULD HAVE DONE THAT COURSE.
DESDEMONA, DO HOLD YOUR TONGUE.
NO, DES IS RIGHT.
I SUPPOSE I HAVE TO THANK YOU.
NAE NEED. BUT DON'T FORGET, YEH PROMISED TEH HELP FIX ME DRESS.
YES, OF COURSE.
WELL DONE, UG- er-
ÜLGA.

Ted Naifeh's

PRINCESS UGG

COVER
&
PINUP
GALLERY

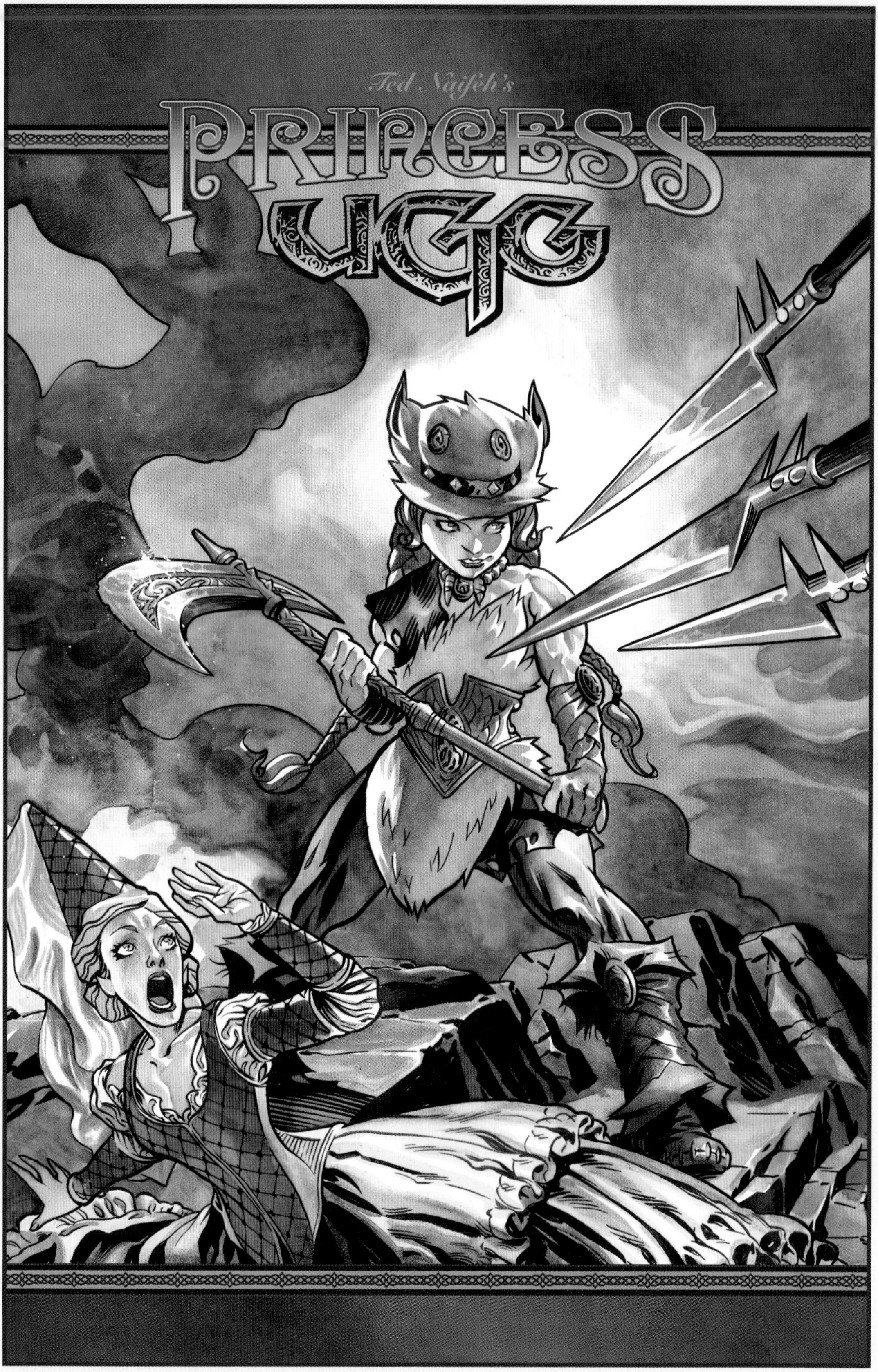
Ted Naifeh's
PRINCESS
UGG

Issue #1: Retail Edition

Cover for Princess Ugg #1 illustrated and colored by Ted Naifeh

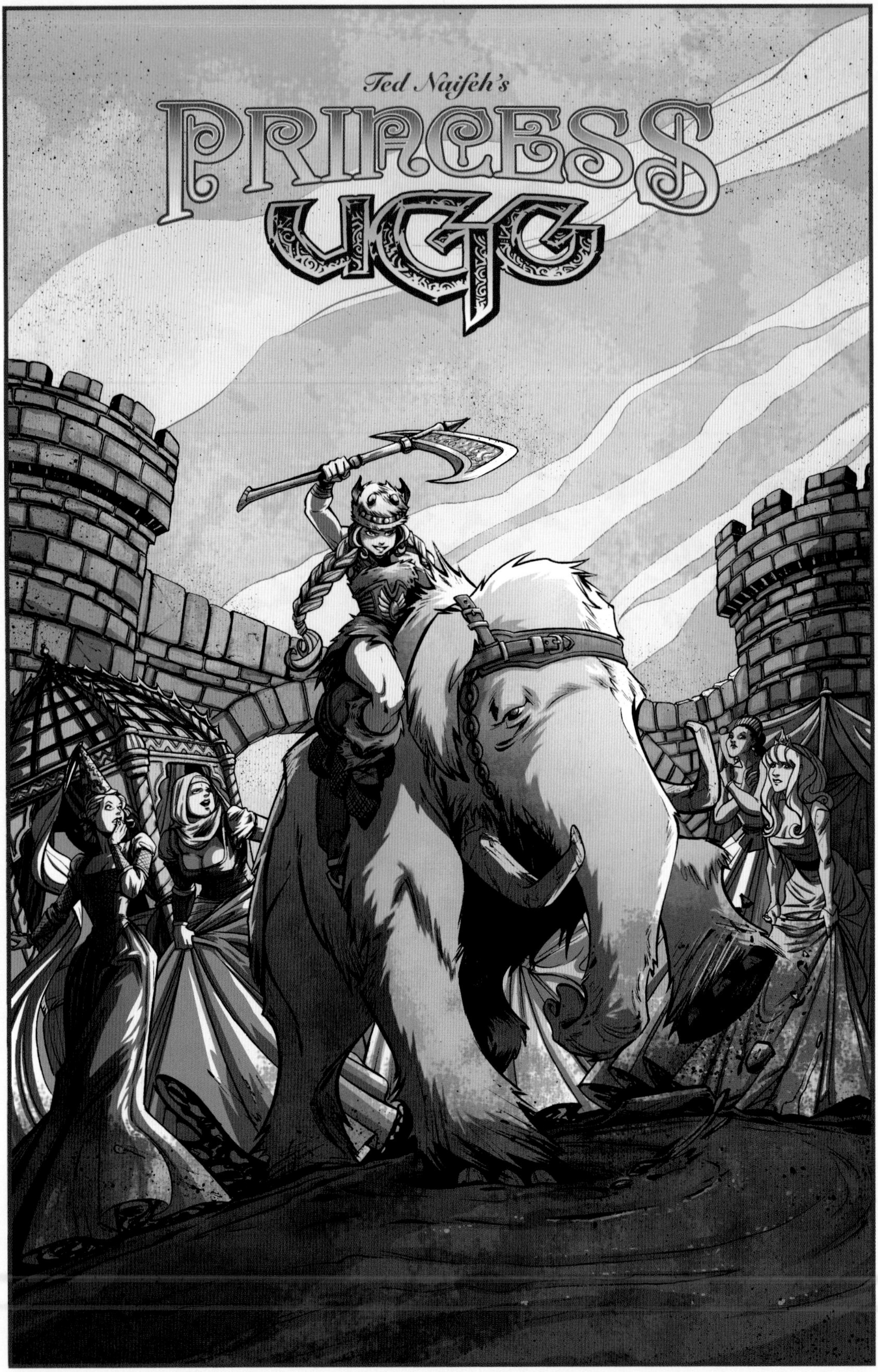
Ted Naifeh's
PRINCESS
UGG

Issue #1: Joëlle Jones Variant

Variant Cover for Princess Ugg #1 illustrated by Joëlle Jones and colored by Warren Wucinich

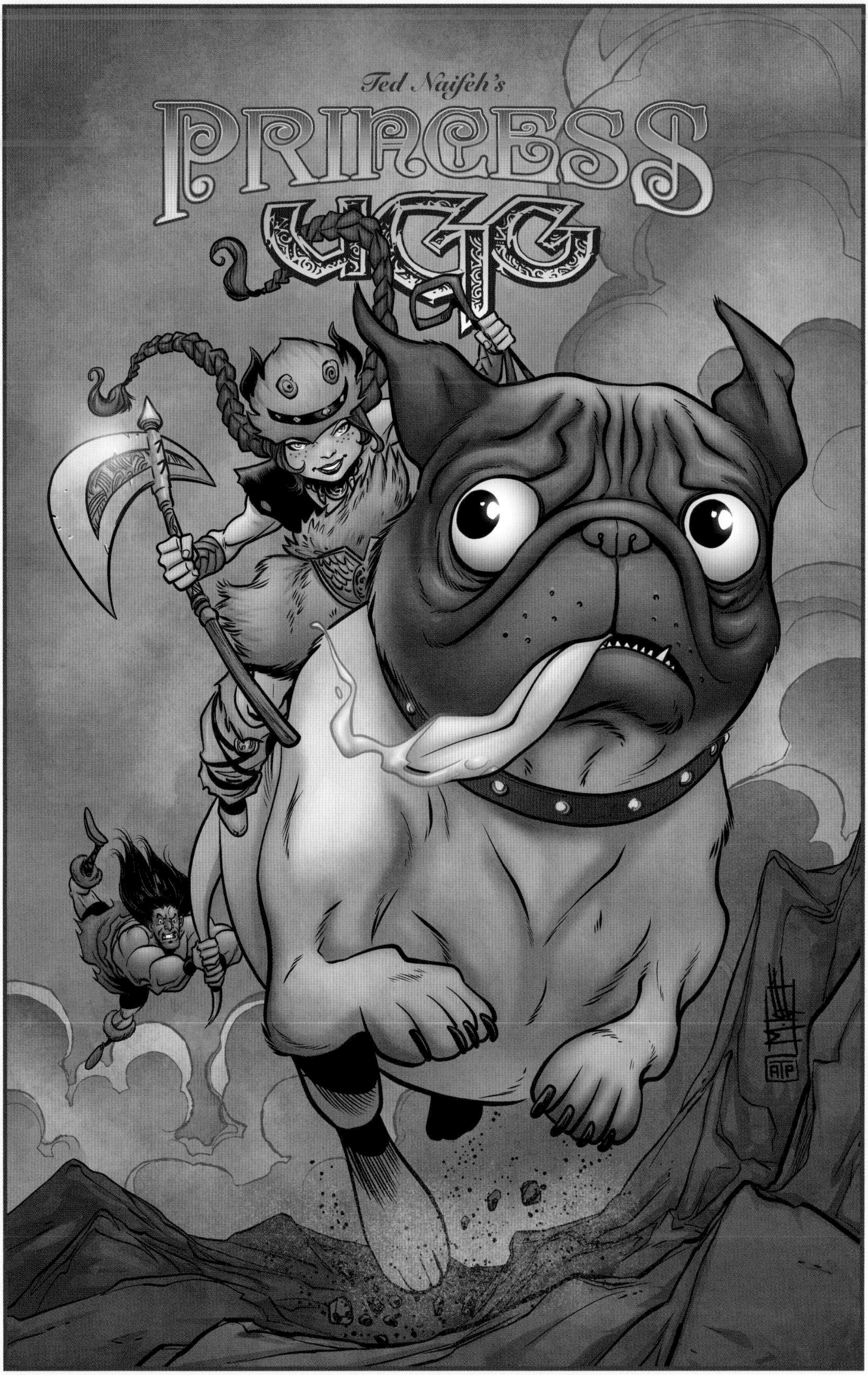
Ted Naifeh's
PRINCESS
UGG

Issue #1: Mike Norton's BattlePug™ Variant

Comic-Con International: San Diego 2014 Exclusive Variant Cover for Princess Ugg #1 illustrated by Mike Norton and colored by Allen Passalaqua

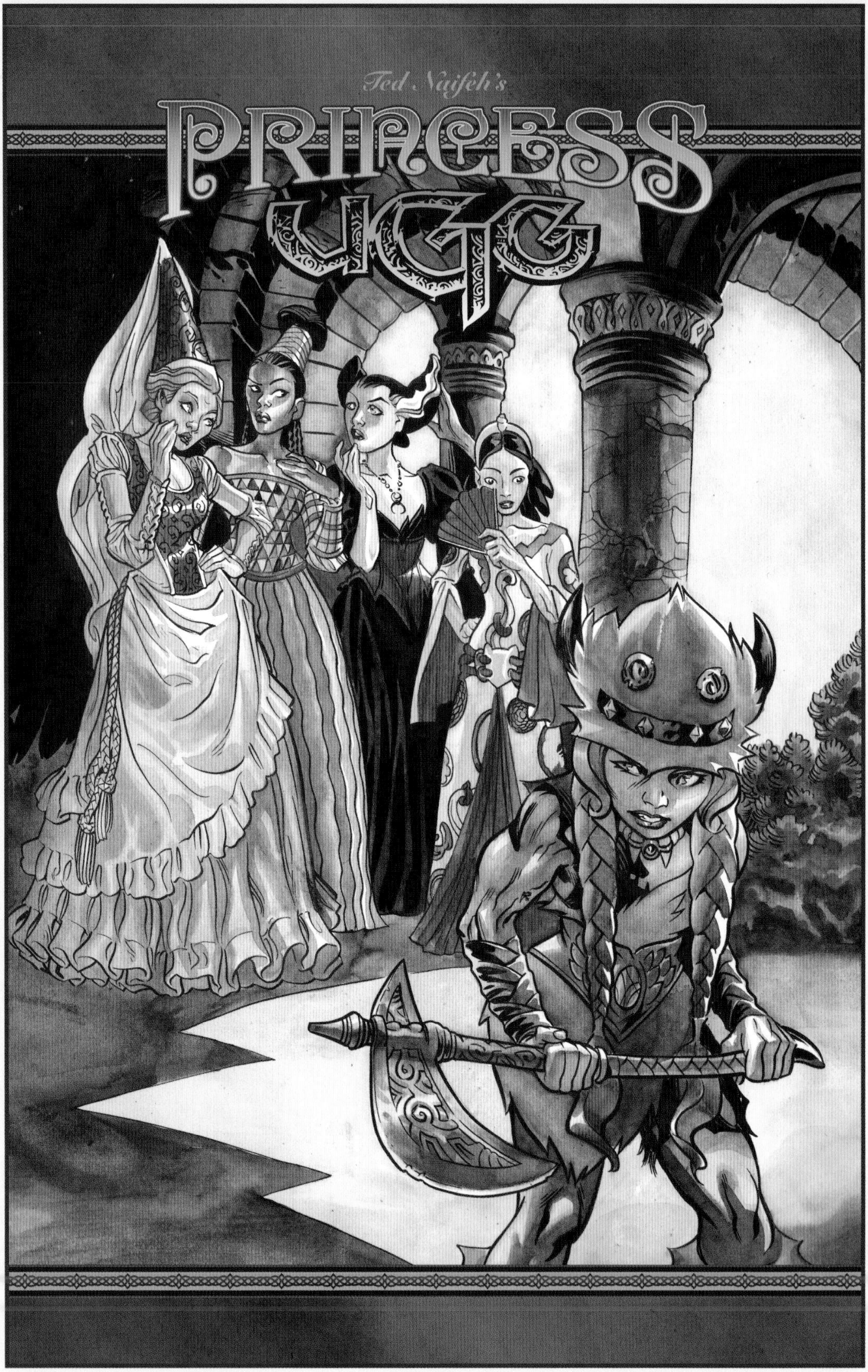
Ted Naifeh's
PRINCESS
UGG

Issue #2: Retail Edition

Cover for Princess Ugg #2 illustrated and colored by Ted Naifeh

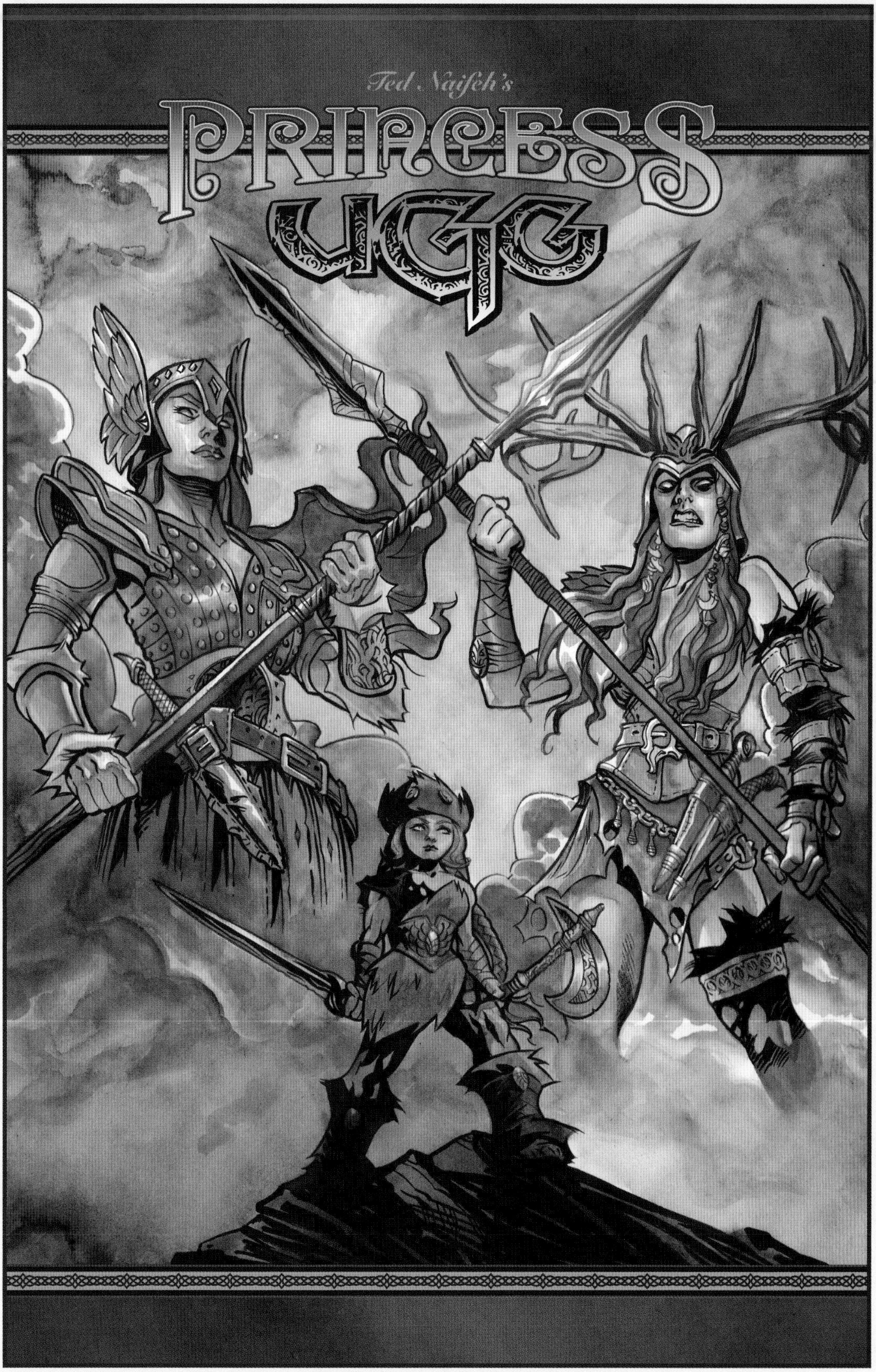
Ted Naifeh's
PRINCESS
UGG

Issue #3: Retail Edition

Cover for Princess Ugg #3 illustrated and colored by Ted Naifeh

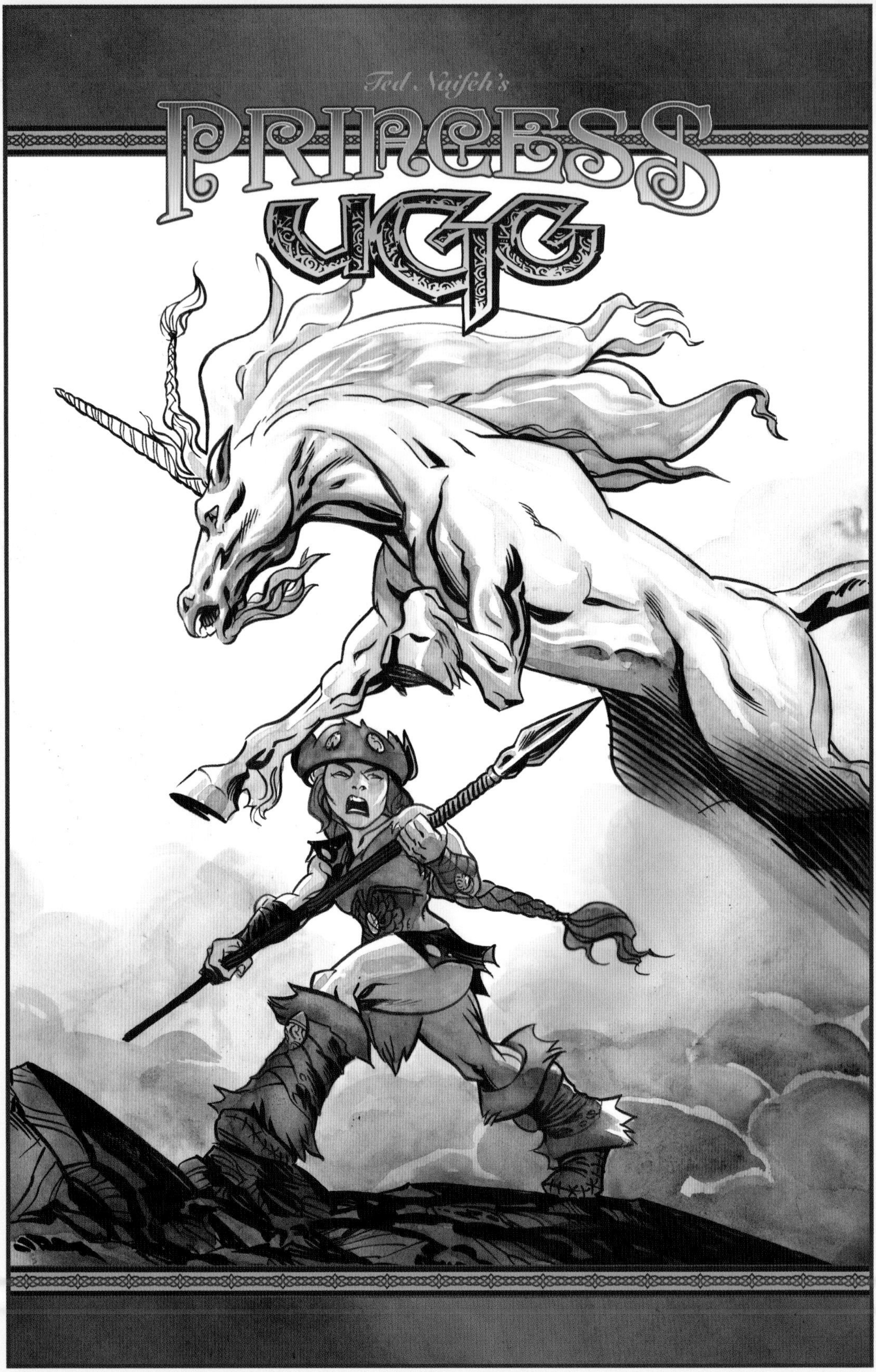
Ted Naifeh's
PRINCESS
UGG

Issue #4: Retail Edition

Cover for Princess Ugg #4 illustrated and colored by Ted Naifeh

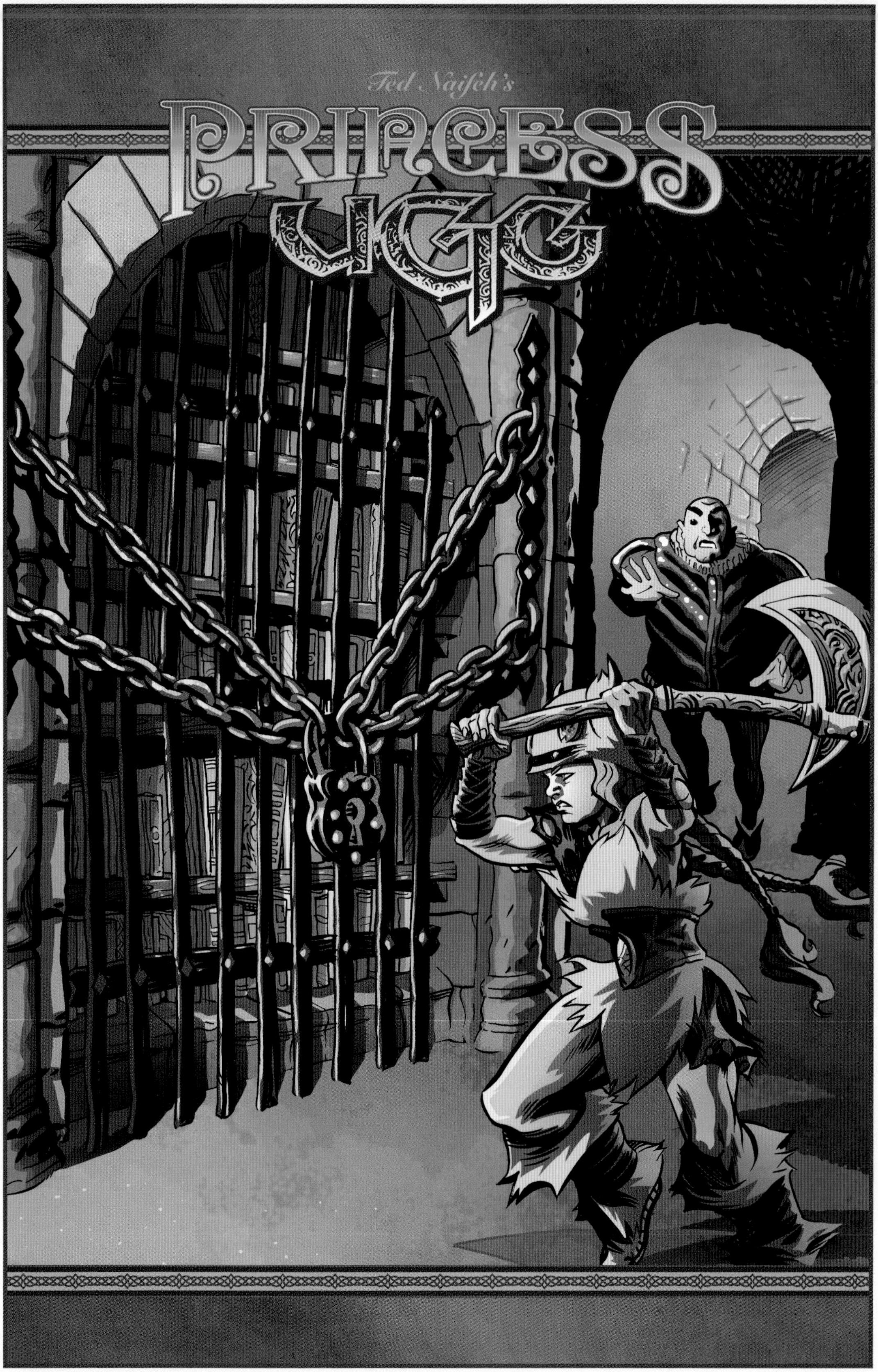
Ted Naifeh's
PRINCESS
UGG

Issue #4: CBLDF Variant

CBLDF Variant Cover for Princess Ugg #4
illustrated by Ted Naifeh and colored by Warren Wucinich

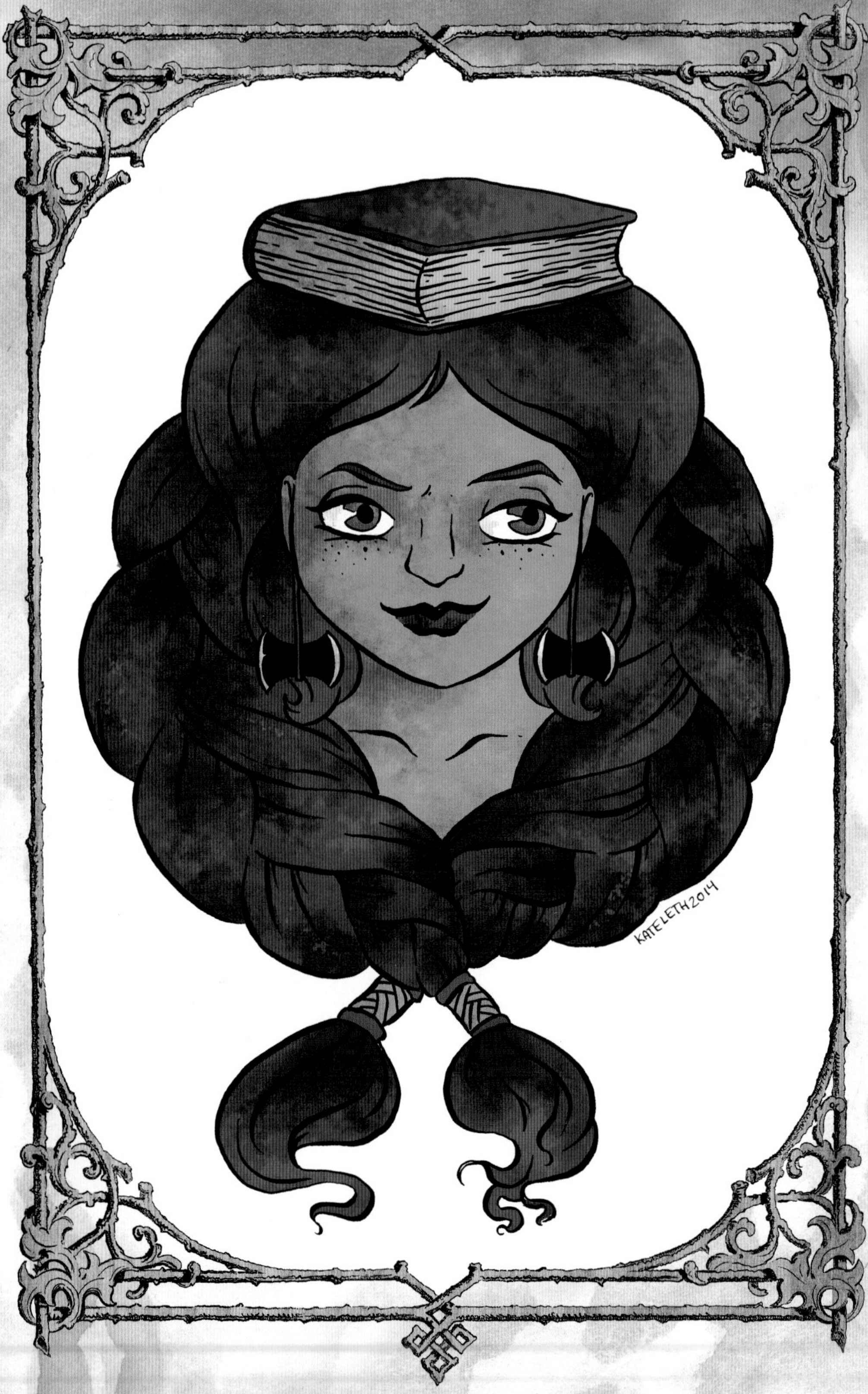
KATELETH2014

Pinup by

kate leth

‡

@kateleth · kateordiecomics.com

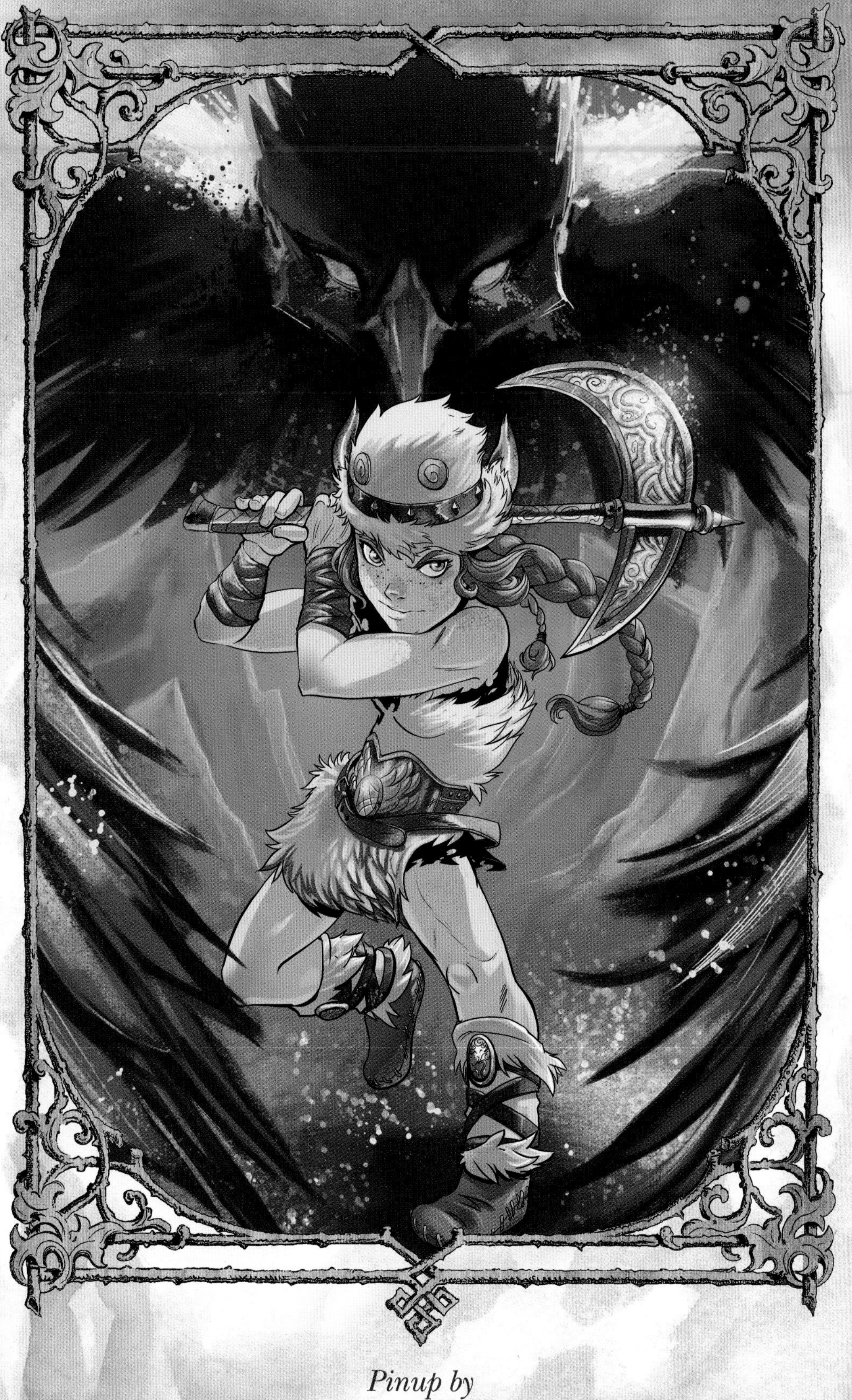

Pinup by

JAKE MYLER

‡

@lazesummerstone · jakemyler.com · jakemyler.tumblr.com

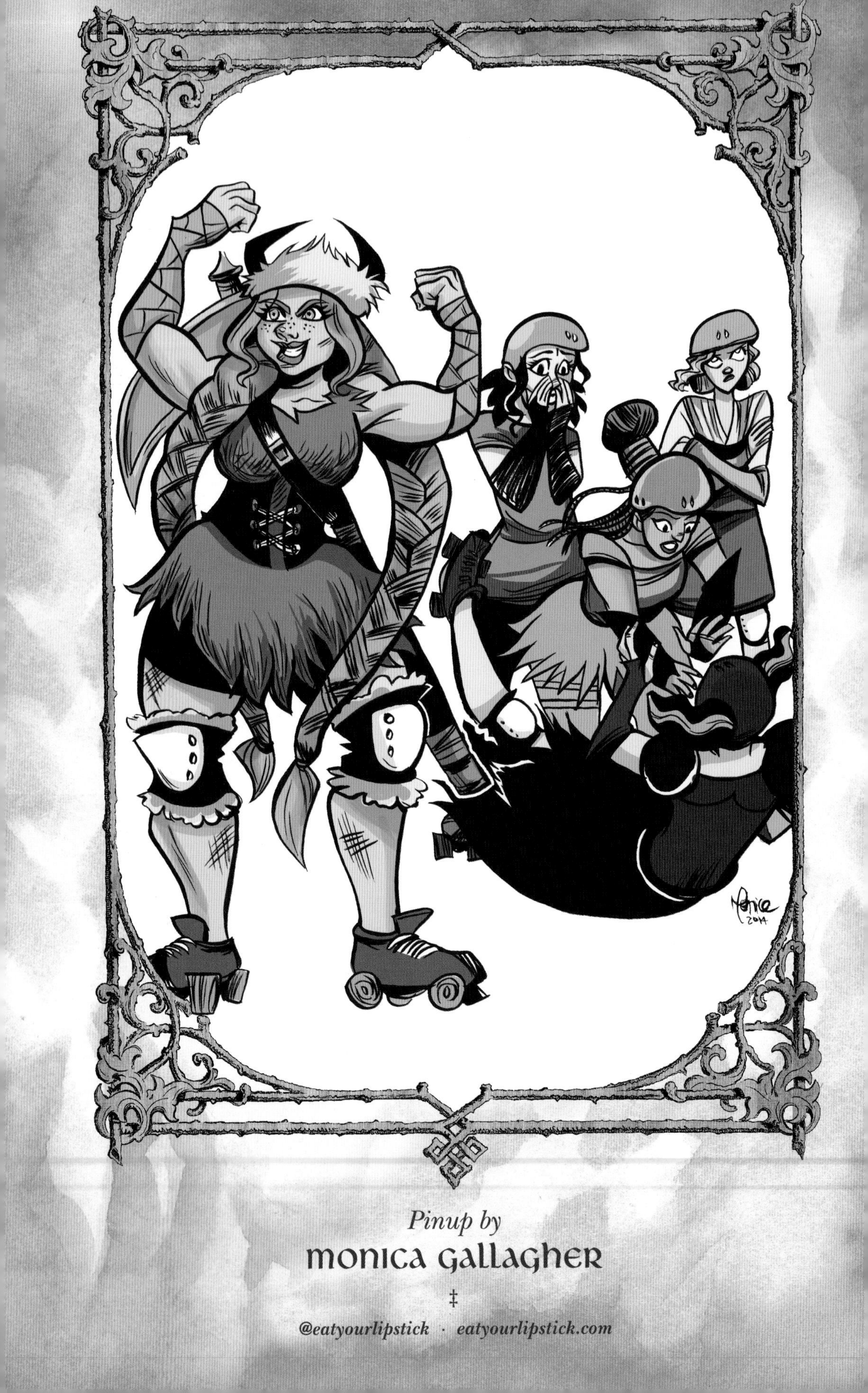
Monica
2014

Pinup by

MONICA GALLAGHER

‡

@eatyourlipstick · eatyourlipstick.com

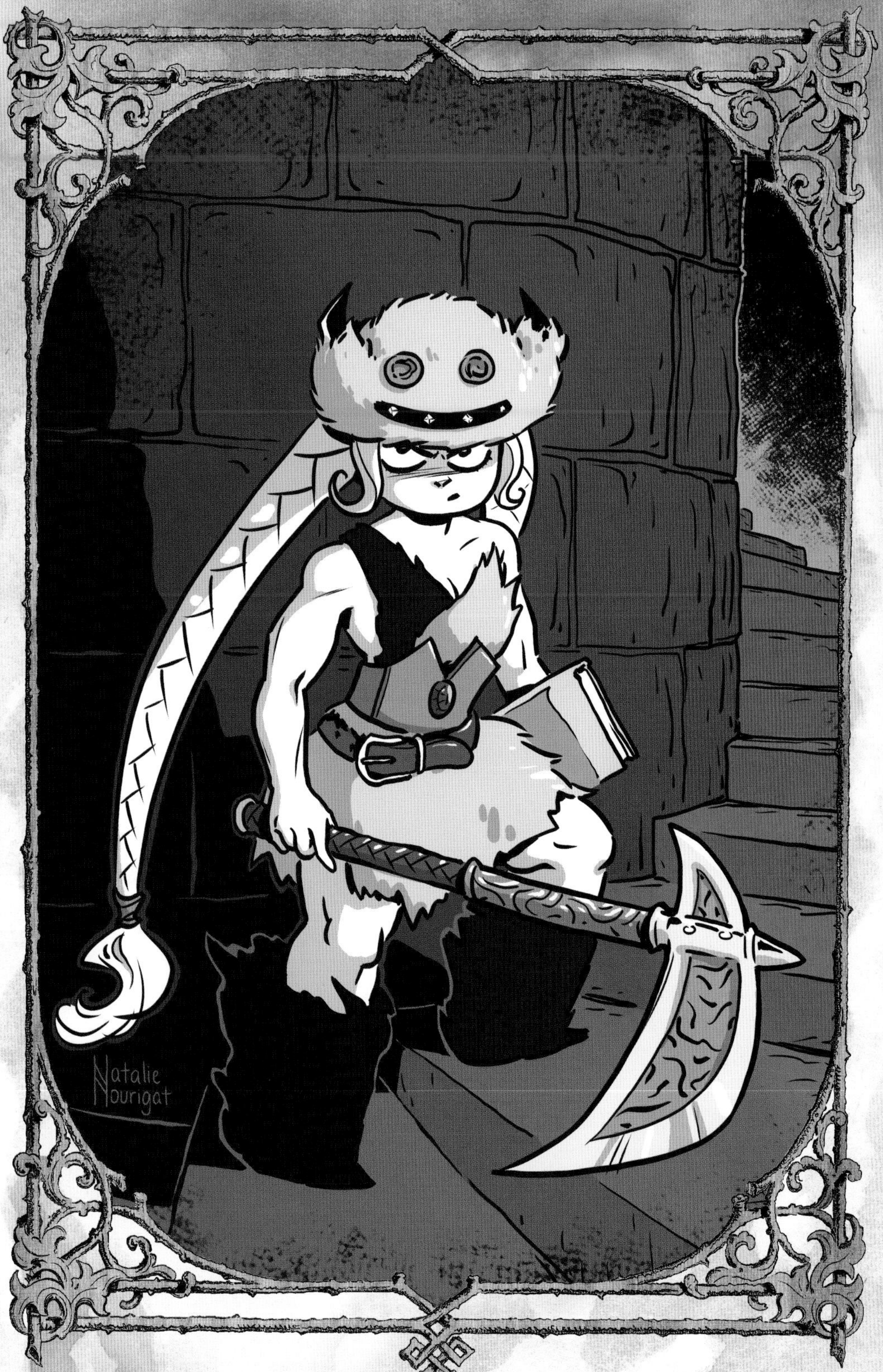
Natalie
Nourigat

Pinup by

natalie nourigat

‡

@tallychyck · natalienourigat.com

ted naifeh

Ted Naifeh has been creating successful independent comics since the late 90s. He co-created *Gloomcookie*, the goth romance comic, with author Serena Valentino, and soon after began writing and drawing *Courtney Crumrin and the Night Things*, a spooky children's fantasy series about a grumpy little girl and her adventures with her Warlock uncle.

Nominated for an Eisner Award for best limited series, *Courtney Crumrin's* success paved the way for *Polly and the Pirates*, this time about a prim and proper girl kidnapped by pirates who believe her to be the daughter of their long-lost queen. *Courtney Crumrin* now has six volumes, plus a spin-off book, and *Polly and the Pirates* has two.

Ted also co-created *How Loathsome* with Tristan Crane, and illustrated two volumes of *Death Junior* with screenwriter Gary Whitta. More recently, he illustrated *The Good Neighbors*, a three-volume graphic novel series written by New York Times best-selling author Holly Black, published by Scholastic.

Recently, Ted has contributed work to many major comics companies, including *Batman* comics for DC, and the horror anthology *Creepy* for Dark Horse.

---

warren wucinich

Warren Wucinich has worked as a professional illustrator and cartoonist since 1999. Serving as either illustrator, colorist or letterer, Warren has worked on several Oni Press titles including *Courtney Crumrin, Jam! Tales From the World of Roller Derby, Rascal Raccoon's Raging Revenge!, Resurrection* and *Spell Checkers* among others.

Warren has also published works through Image, Pop! Goes the Icon and Poseur Ink. He currently resides in Durham, NC where he spends most of his time making comics, watching *Star Trek* reruns and complaining about mosquitoes.